NONFICTION

NONFICTION FOR CHILDREN
How to Write It • How to Sell It

FOR CHILDREN
How to Write It · How to Sell It

By Ellen E. M. Roberts

Writer's Digest Books

Cincinnati, Ohio

In memory of John Blackmore and Paul E. Johnson
and
In tribute to Peter C. Grenquist and Elliott P. Roberts
—Scholars and fathers

Nonfiction for Children: How to Write It, How to Sell It. Copyright © 1986 by Ellen E. M. Roberts. Printed and bound in the United States of America. All rights reserved. No part of this book may be reproduced in any form or by any electronic or mechanical means including information storage and retrieval systems without permission in writing from the publisher, except by a reviewer, who may quote brief passages in a review. Published by Writer's Digest Books, 9933 Alliance Road, Cincinnati, Ohio 45242. First edition.

Library of Congress Cataloging-in-Publication Data

Roberts, Ellen E. M., 1946-
  Nonfiction for children.

  Bibliography: p.
  Includes index.
  1. Children's literature—Authorship. I. Title.
PN147.5.R64 1986   808.06'8   86-19120
ISBN 0-89879-238-X

Design by The Antler & Baldwin Design Group

Acknowledgments

Twice a year at least, sometimes six times, yet another New York writer will shake his head in wonder at me. "Why would anyone who lives in New York City write for a publisher in Ohio?" The answer is simple, though not exactly short: Because of Howard I. Wells III, the managing editor of Writer's Digest Books, who stood by this project for the five years it took to publish it. Because of Beth Franks, an editor who understands books, writing, and books about writing. Because of Chris Dodd, who is devoted to the cause of consistency in her work as a copy editor; because of Linda Sanders, meticulous in her organization and aesthetics, as she steered the project through production; because of Sallie Baldwin, the designer, and Carole Winters, of the WDB Art Department, who know when a picture is worth a thousand words and also when it's not. And because of Johanna Hoff, the marketing manager, and Mert Ransdell, the business manager, who can be heard asking "why not?" when the rest of us are still wondering "why?"

Since this is a book about books, the contributions of the Writer's Digest Books staff have been crucial. To say that it was a pleasure working with them is to gloss over the best part of the story. While the mistakes that eluded us are solely my responsibility, the book that you are holding now is the result of an exciting team effort.

Permissions

Contents

Introduction:

The Why and How of Children's Nonfiction

"When I am introduced as a nonfiction writer," popular science writer Seymour Simon remarks with a grin, "I feel as though I am being called a non-American, or a nonentity. I write real books for children. Maybe fiction should be called nonreal writing." Simon is successful enough that he can laugh at the second-class status nonfiction writers have to endure from their audience, from the editor who first buys the manuscript, to the adults—teachers, librarians, and parents—who purchase the copies, to the kids who head for the nonfiction shelf to pad out homework assignments on the space shuttle or weather forecasting.

But nonfiction books can be beautifully written, wonderfully illustrated, eye-opening in subject matter, and happily read for pleasure. Textbooks have given nonfiction a bad reputation, but think about what *you* read for pleasure: Don't you get a kick out of a biography of Gloria Vanderbilt, or a week of fascinating afternoons reading about the history of your town, or finding something to dazzle your friends with at parties from a chronicle of the last election campaign? Sure you do. Because truth is stranger than fiction, and you learned that when you were too young to read by yourself. An adult's appreciation of fiction, poetry, even painting and music, comes from an early exposure to the excitement of the world around us, particularly through books.

What would be the point of a historical romance without history? What's the charm of science fiction without science? What good is a war story without humankind's long experience of war? Nonfiction is the basis of

1

reading pleasure, and it enhances the beauties of fiction. Nonfiction for children provides that base, and the more enthralling the informational book in a child's formative years, the more curious a reader he becomes throughout his life.

Editors, serving a large market of schools and libraries, are scrupulous about the nonfiction they buy from writers and sell to these experts. Many great editors, like Elizabeth Riley, who founded the Crowell juvenile list fifty years ago, to Frank Sloan, who is editing the Franklin Watts juvenile list today, prefer to work on nonfiction, for both professional and personal reasons. "When I started publishing books for children," Riley recalls, "I thought about my own reading habits. I especially enjoyed nonfiction as leisure reading, and I thought I'd share my enjoyment with children by publishing good nonfiction books for them." Sloan takes a slightly different tack: "Nonfiction writing is tough, because you have to suspend your readers' disbelief, and really convince them that what you are telling them is true. It's the hardest kind of writing, not only from the research point of view, but from the writing point of view. It's a challenge for everyone, from the author to the editor to the artist."

This is a book about nonfiction for children written from what may seem a peculiarly passionate point of view. I think the eighties have been a rough period for nonfiction books for children because, on the one hand, computers have threatened to usurp this domain of reading, and, on the other, the dreary offerings of the sixties and seventies have conspired to drag the genre down. But if you look carefully, you'll see that some of the finest practitioners of the art of writing for children have launched a strong creative campaign to save this precious medium. That's what this book is about—the best of children's nonfiction, what makes these books the best, and why nonfiction will be the children's book of the future. We will explore what's been done, what is being done now in the words of the people who are doing it, and what is left for you, the writer, to do.

The line between fiction and nonfiction has become increasingly blurred in the last decade. The stunningly successful best sellers by such leading authors as Arthur Hailey, Judith Krantz, and James Michener are so loaded with information that they could almost be reference books. And I have to wonder when I peruse titles like *How to Make $10 Million in Real Estate with No Cash* or *Jane Fonda's Workout Book*, how "realistic" these nonfiction best sellers can be. Of course, I've never completed a Fonda workout or made $10 million in real estate, so I could be missing something.

To further complicate the question of nonfiction for children is the problem of gearing the book to a particular age group. Since the inception of children's literature publishing in this country after World War I, publishers have tried to make it easier for their adult customers to purchase appropriate books by designating the interest and ability levels of each new title. If you look at the bottom of the front flap of a children's book jacket, you will see a mysterious combination of numbers—for example, K-3/4-7. In trans-

Lilies, Rabbits, and Painted Eggs

are more and more and more. And most people believe that the hare or rabbit of Easter is
a symbol of new life, as it probably was in
religions far older than Christianity.

The Easter Lamb

The little lambs on Easter cards, toy
lambs, and lambs made of candy or
pastry go back far beyond Easter to the first
Passover of the Jewish people.

It was at the time their ancestors were
slaves in Egypt. Before the angel of God took
the firstborn in all Egyptian homes, the Hebrew leader Moses ordered a sacrifice. Every
Hebrew family was to sprinkle the blood of a
young lamb over its doorframe. The lamb had
to be roasted and eaten, together with bread
baked without yeast, and bitter herbs. If this
was done, Moses said, the angel would pass
over their homes, and bring them no harm.

Hebrew people who joined the Christian

35

For Edna Barth's Lilies, Rabbits, & Painted Eggs *(Clarion, 1970), Ursula
Arndt illustrated the Easter symbols by picturing holiday themes in a cheerful, light-hearted style, inspiring awareness of continuing and varied customs.*

lation, this tells you that the publisher deems it appropriate for children from kindergarten to third grade, from ages four, the youngest kindergartner, to seven, the youngest third grader. But if you know kids, you know that these standardized designations are ballpark estimates, not perfect formulas. Eight-year-old Matthew, stumped by a book of simple magic tricks aimed at six-year-olds, may breeze through a book of football biographies. Or ten-year-old Amy may have no trouble with a book on making animated films, designed for teenagers, but that same book of football biographies could just as well be written in Urdu.

Nonetheless, the age/interest recommendations are the only clues the publisher can give the general reader about the appropriateness of the material to the majority of children. The buyer has to exercise his instincts, because he best knows the book's ultimate consumer: the child. Amy's teacher knows how much Amy loves movies, Matthew's father knows how much Matt loves football, so they can exercise their judgment accordingly. The publisher has to operate within standard norms, because a little information that will help a reader choose a book is a whole lot better than none. Since I have spent my adult life as an editor, I've come to believe in these standard designations and have used them as an essential support in the structure of this book. Shortcomings aside, they are helpful to the writer who wants his work published, because they are so ingrained in publishers' ways of choosing and marketing manuscripts.

These large issues—the validity of nonfiction for children and the importance of tailoring your manuscript to a specific age group—underlie all I have to say in the following pages. The history, the present publishing practices, and the future of nonfiction publishing for children will all be related to these two premises. The aim of this book is to help you understand what is available in the way of markets for your work, and why; how to write for those markets; and how to enjoy the eminently exciting (though not always comfortable!) life of a nonfiction writer for children, either as a sideline or as a primary occupation.

PART ONE

Everything You Need to Know About Writing for Different Age Groups

My son Andy has been a great influence on my writing both through the force of his own personality and through his actions constantly reminding me of something in my own childhood. My books have grown up with Andy, beginning with the simple idea and treatment of Big Pig when Andy was seven years old. As Andy grew the story line became more complex, there were more words to the page and the illustrations were filled with more details, characters, and backgrounds.
—Dennis Nolan

Mommy and Sally and Harry washed the dishes —and the kitchen floor.

They made the beds.

They cleaned the house.

They drove to the grocery store to buy food and other things that they needed at home.

Fanciful illustrations are mines of real information in Richard Scarry's What Do People Do All Day? *(Random House, 1968).*

CHAPTER 1

All About Age Groups

During the Middle Ages, children were treated as small and inexperienced adults. A quick look at a Renaissance painting will show you that this attitude permeated European thought well into the eighteenth century. Children in nineteenth-century America were accorded some of the considerations of childhood, such as education and toys, but they were expected to work at an early age.

The concept of childhood, then, is a new idea. The analysis of child development, breaking down the childhood span into individual years, is an even newer one. It was a remarkable thing when psychologists figured out what six-year-olds could do, how tall eight-year-old boys are, what to expect in the way of social and emotional responses from a thirteen-year-old. Like many good ideas, this one, first introduced in the 1920s, was accepted wholeheartedly by American adults working with children in any capacity. Fifty years after this careful quantification captivated the country, programs for children who didn't fit the mold began to spring up like mushrooms: There's more than likely a Head Start program in your area for socially disadvantaged children, a Talented and Gifted program for children who are functioning beyond age and grade level, a program for learning disabled children, still another program for the handicapped, et cetera. We are beginning to see the differences clearly, but the standard norms still hold for most children. The special-interest educational programs are crying for material, and certainly their needs shouldn't be overlooked, but the general audience still fits into the cubbyholes designed and adopted decades ago.

Cynics like to say that book publishers are the least innovative of the media. I'll dispute that until I'm blue in the face—for example, the age group concept is one area in which publishers are preserving a tradition that makes good sense. It may not be elegant, but it's efficient. Three-year-olds have a vocabulary of 560 words, 90 percent of which are nouns. How do I know that? Because someone did a study that proved it. Children don't like to read about children who are younger than they are, but they do enjoy reading about children who are older—but not much—than they are. How can I say that? Because somebody did a study that proved it. Developmental psychologists have given us an age for teething, an age for reading, an age for puberty, an age for leaving home. All of these are "norms," statistical averages, ballpark figures.

Publishers, in turn, have become more sophisticated about assigning age groups to the books they publish. The Frye Readability Graph, for instance, correlates reading ability to grade level. The Dale-Chall Test measures vocabulary according to grade level. I am not suggesting that you embrace the concepts of controlled vocabulary wholeheartedly, but I do think it's important to consider the child's reading ability, interests, and attention span in writing nonfiction. Any bookstore clerk can tell you of the hundreds of times a parent has asked him, "What's good for a six-year-old?" or an aunt has wondered, "What are thirteen-year-olds reading these days?" or the eager father who has asked for a book to interest his preschool child in football.

For classroom teachers or school librarians, the age distinctions are even more important. Textbooks are geared to given age groups both in terms of format and vocabulary. Librarians arrange their books according to age and ability levels, and the twelve-year-old who wouldn't be caught dead in the children's room is proud to be seen in the "young adult" corner of the adult section of the library. Trade books—supplementary reading—are also geared to the curricula of certain grades and the leisure interests of certain ages. Thus, however vague and imprecise this assignment of age to each stage of development, to every interest, to each ability, it is a useful index which serves the juvenile reading public far better than the pre-standard era when books were just tossed on the market with no guide for selection.

What Are the Age Groups?

The standard age groups established by book publishers are roughly: ages 2-5, the prereading group; ages 6-9, the group mastering basic reading skills; ages 8-12, the group for whom reading is a new and exciting skill utilized more enthusiastically than at any other time in their lives; ages 10-14, the young teenage group, whose reading competes with diversions such as records, video games, movies, parties, and group activities; and the 12-to-16 group, the young adults who are outgrowing children's books but find some nonfiction designed especially for them appealing.

Picture Books: Ages 2-5 for youngest readers who are learning the physical skills involved in reading (holding a book right side up, turning pages in sequence, sitting still to hear the entire story) and are learning letters through pictures of familiar objects, such as home and neighborhood scenes, parent/child relationships, baby animals, vehicles, and favorite toy and television characters. Because the production costs for these books—often in color, with the use of licensed characters or elaborate formats—leave little room for a royalty for the writer, they are often staff-written, or commissioned for a flat fee ("work for hire"). Occasionally written by a writer who receives an advance and royalty, picture books can be a good way for the beginner to get credits for future sales.

Easy Readers: Ages 6-9 for children beginning school and mastering basic reading skills. Because these books are geared for children to read by themselves, the format is carefully designed (with variations from publisher to publisher) to provide large type with only a certain number of characters per line and a small picture on each page or two-page spread. This, too, is a good area for the beginning writer to reach first publication, and a careful study of the tone and length of text will clue you—and the child reader—into the "magic formula" of the series.

Middle Grades: Ages 8-12 for children in the upper elementary grades who are achieving real fluency in reading. These books range from 48 to 128 pages, usually contain some illustrations, and are best suited to the writer with a discursive style. Kids this age skip from subject to subject, but they love series books and show great loyalty to favorite authors.

Young Teenagers: Ages 10-14 for children of middle school or junior high school age. The format for these books does not vary markedly from that of middle-grade books, but the design is somewhat snazzier, and the subject matter begins to break down into boy interest (field sports, electronics) and girl interest (biographies, art subjects). Both boys and girls are drawn to contemporary subjects, such as popular music, politics, movies, and psychology.

Young Adults: Ages 12-16 for teenagers who generally prefer adult books in the nonfiction area to the carefully tailored "YA" as it's called, because they want to seem sophisticated. The young adult book is usually between 128-256 pages long, contains an index and a bibliography, and is usually more fully illustrated than its adult counterpart. Except for books that address themselves specifically to teen interests—sports, sex, grooming, dramatic histories, and biographies of current celebrities—a writer is better off reaching this age group through adult trade publishing than through a children's book department, although this may change.

Targeting Various Age Groups

As I mentioned in the Introduction, one of the services that publishers provide their customers—the parent, the teacher, the librarian, the child—is an indication of the age level that reflects the interest and ability required to enjoy a book or article. The vast majority of children's books carry an age/grade code on the cover or jacket. This code may be in disguise, such as *0407 PreS-2*. This means the book is aimed at four- to seven-year-olds, in nursery school through grade 2. Similarly, a code might read *0812 4-6*, indicating the book is appropriate for eight- to twelve-year-olds, in grades 4-6. Many teenage books leave off the age/grade code, though sometimes you will see the designation *12 up* or *YA* (for young adult). In Francine Klagsbrun's *Psychiatry: What It Is, What It Does*, the subtitle "A book for young people" indicates with dignity and directness the age group intended.

Why is targeting an age group so important? Because when you have an idea for a book, knowing the age group it's aimed for is just as important as knowing the subject area. Let's say you want to write a book about George Washington. You go to the library and discover a picture book about George Washington, an easy reader about George Washington, and a teenage biography about George Washington, all sitting on the shelves, smirking at you for being so dumb as to think the world needs another book about George Washington. But if you have listened to my comments about age groups, you'll discover something else: *There's no book for ten-to-fourteen-year-olds about George Washington!*

So your book might be a good idea after all. What is it that the young teenage group might want to know about George that the other books don't cover? What do they know about American history that their younger counterparts don't? What do they want to find out that their teenage brothers and sisters already know? Keeping these questions in the back of your mind as you do your research will enable you to write a book that has an *angle*, a term you will learn, that fits the subject and suits the reader. Your editor will applaud your professionalism when you write a query announcing that you not only have a subject matter in mind but also an audience. And that is the juggling act any writer of nonfiction for children has to keep going without a slip—interest/ability/subject, interest/ability/subject, interest/ability/subject—for the long hours of research and writing it takes to create a successful children's book.

Friends and Enemies

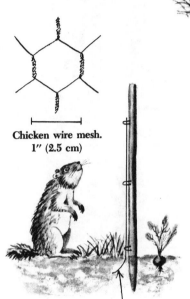

**Chicken wire mesh.
1″ (2.5 cm)**

**Chicken wire, buried underground,
curving away from garden**

34

GARDEN ENEMIES

Rabbits and Woodchucks

A fence around your garden may prevent nibbling by these animals. A 3-foot (100 cm) chicken wire fence with 3 inches (7.5 cm) underground and fastened to stout posts will help. It will be low enough for you to climb over. It looks like this:

Cut Worms

These worms eat the stems of the newly-planted tomato and pepper plants and also the roots of all garden plants. They are greyish-brown in color and a little less than an inch (2.5 cm) long, and as fat as a pencil. To prevent damage, place a collar of heavy paper around the stem.

Black and white illustration with softening wash from Easy to Grow Vegetables *by Robert Gambino, illustrated by Anne Marie Jauss (Harvey House, 1975) emphasizes beauty as well as instruction.*

11. Building a Cord Cradle

When the lumberjack judged he had enough logs for a cord,
or several cords, he set about building a cord cradle.
A cord is 4 feet high, 4 feet wide, and 8 feet long. Thin or
useless logs were used to make a framework to hold
that quantity of wood alongside the strip road. I made this
lithograph to show how it was done. Two upright poles
were stuck into the ground at either end and braced against an
under-frame. A notched crossbar held the vertical poles
together at the top. The logs were then piled in. The saw was
used as a rough measure because it was approximately
4 feet long, from tip to tip.

In William Kurelek's Lumberjack *(Houghton-Mifflin, 1974), the compact text
is offset by primitive pictures.*

WHICH AGE GROUP WILL YOU WRITE FOR?

Sometimes your choice of age group will be determined by other
books already available on your chosen subject, as in the George Washington example. Other times you may need to consider the appropriateness of
certain ideas for different ages—no books about the death of a parent for
two-year-olds, or no books for nine-year-olds on anti-Semitism, for instance. Or you may discover that your subject has special appeal to one particular age group—seven-year-olds are interested in dinosaurs, while nine-
year-olds are more likely to be interested in snakes.

Curriculum guides, available through your local school board, can
provide helpful information about the subjects being covered on each grade
level. The guides, usually in booklet form, provide information on the ob-
jectives and areas to be covered in a specific subject area—for example,
English or social studies. The guides are updated periodically.

Various theories of educational psychology will give you detailed information on the child's psychological and cognitive development at any
given stage; studying Piaget and Montessori can be particularly helpful.
But, theories and studies aside, probably the best approach is to get to
know children of different ages, and to read books written for them.

Whatever you do, don't fall into the trap of thinking you can write a book that will appeal to all ages. Gene Perme, marketing director at Prentice-Hall, maintains that an "all ages" designation on a book is actually code for "no interest to any age." And Joe Ann Daly of Dodd, Mead, confirms this: "Gone are the days of the 'all ages' book. We often publish books geared to only one or two grades, with the ability needed to master the material carefully correlated to a single age." But also remember that age-group distinctions are meant as general guidelines; editors agree that a well-written manuscript can be edited up or down to suit the age group for whom it holds the most interest.

One of the great discoveries of the twentieth century is that of the child's capacity to learn. And to learn at *any* age. We have seen the emphasis shift from books for teenagers to books for beginning readers, and, most recently, to books for children just old enough to hold a book open, with a little help from Mom or Dad. You can write for whatever age child you are comfortable with, without fear that writing for the "wrong" age group is going to minimize your chances for publication.

Choosing an age group is the essential first step. It will affect the approach you take to research and the style of the finished manuscript. In the following chapters you'll get an overview of each age group, including basic interests and abilities, trends and taboos. Although you may want to break the rules laid down here, it won't hurt you to know them. And on page 68 is a self-test to help you find out which age group is best for you.

THE HORNS ON THE GOAT'S HEAD GIVE THE IDEA
OF THE CHARACTER
YANG: GOAT OR SHEEP.

You Can Write Chinese *by Kurt Weise (Viking/Penguin Junior Books, 1942, renewed 1970) shows that with simple layout, difficult concepts are not "babyish" despite large format and two-color art in this classic instructional book.*

pile
crowd
group
bundle
bunch
herd
flock
row
team

stack

Using photographic realism to illustrate collective nouns, Tana Hoban's More
Than One *(Greenwillow Books, 1981) is a combination counting book, word
book, and shape book for beginning readers.*

CHAPTER 2

The Picture Book: Ages 2 to 5

I write and I draw, but what I really do is learn. I learn about something that interests me, something I can find wonder in, and I try to explain it clearly—without losing the wonder." This is Jan Adkins speaking, author of *The Art and Industry of Sand Castles*. He understands, as the success of his many books attests, that the most ordinary objects and events make for a successful picture book, so long as the author doesn't lose that essential sense of wonder.

A picture book is a child's first introduction to reading. Usually oversize in format, illustrated on every page, it presents a story concisely and evocatively. It used to be that publishers aimed their picture books at ages 4-7 or 5-8. This has changed; publishers have discovered the early age groups as an untapped market. Editors are now looking for picture books for the two- to five-year-old: *The younger the offering, the more successful the book*, was my rule of thumb as an editor of 150 picture books.

The reason for this downward shift in age groups is that there is a new and still growing market for preschool materials. The day care center attracts very young children who want books for their story hours. Parents, better educated and more affluent than at any time in the past, are eager for their children to get the reading habit early, and encourage looking at books long before the child is able to read by himself. "Sesame Street" has introduced literacy and curiosity about the outside world at earlier and earlier ages. For children of two and three, the wonders of the world around them are ten times as fascinating as any fantasy. Nonfiction gives young children the mind-stretching relaxation that older children get from fiction. The picture books with the broadest appeal are in the nonfiction category, and that's where the biggest acquisition search among editors is going on.

But mention "picture book" to a parent, librarian, or teacher, and you will undoubtedly hear a list of fiction: *Curious George, Make Way for Ducklings, The Runaway Bunny, Where the Wild Things Are*, and even *Little Black Sambo*. (This is a phenomenon I understand well, since any child who comes to me for reading matter is presented with *Blueberries for Sal, Stone Soup*, and the Provensens' *Mother Goose*, because these were books I enjoyed myself.)

The things that make a picture book successful are embodied in these old favorites. They combine excitement with a cozy resolution, they tell a story in a short space, with pictures doing more than half the work, and they reflect the concerns of early childhood. But although the old favorites are largely fiction, times are changing and bringing with them something new for this book form—nonfiction.

THE WAVE OF THE FUTURE

The most important trend in children's picture books is the emergence of more nonfiction titles. There are several reasons for this, the most important of which is the essential conservative nature of the picture book selection process. Children are growing up faster now: Kids are going to school at two, start playing electronic games at six, and want to start dating and smoking cigarettes when they're ten.

Teachers, librarians, and especially parents would like to slow down the progress of childhood. They want picture book offerings to reflect the interests of early childhood in an appealing way. The new conservatism is responsible in part for the recent success of picture books on nonfiction subjects; plain facts tend to be a lot less controversial than a personal interpretation. Byron Barton's *Airplane*, Douglas Florian's *The City*, and Donald Crews's *Harbor* work as picture books without a traditional story. The experiences they represent are real-life sequences: a trip on a plane, a shopping trip to an art show, and a tanker's arrival in the harbor.

What's new in nonfiction picture books is information that isn't "fictionalized" with characters. These books present nonfiction in a reportorial way, without the benefit—if it is a benefit—of a leading character. Events speak for themselves. The books being published now present a reality on its own.

Nonfiction picture books fall into three categories: identification books, informational books, and awareness or observation books. Each type has its own demands which the writer will do well to keep in mind.

The Identification Book

Since the picture book is for young children, it has to be simple, and the simplest form—one that's perennially popular—is the identification book. In a book of this kind, objects familiar to childhood are presented and named. This may seem like an idiotically simple concept with little need for an author's genius behind it, yet some identification books are downright inspired. Take *What's in Mommy's Pocketbook?*, a study of the contents of Mother's handbag. Or Harlow Rockwell's *Toolbox*, which explores Father's tool chest item by item, the names clearly spelled out in large type.

Selection of objects that will fit most children's frame of reference and pique their interest is the key to a successful identification book. In C. B. Fall's *ABC*, published fifty years ago and still selling, the author features animals all the way through the alphabet, from the familiar, like the swan, to the more exotic, like the ibis. For the child just learning the alphabet and the joys of the zoo, this book is a perennial favorite.

The counting book is another popular identification subject for the youngest age group. In *One More and One Less*, Betsy and Giulio Maestro present addition and subtraction concepts using animal characters with a special appeal to young children.

The Informational Book

The informational book, such as Bernice Kohn's *Raccoons*, covers one subject area with the depth of an encyclopedia article, but the text is written with the picture book format in mind. Each sentence or two should lend itself to a picture and a discrete idea.

In her popular group of informational books, Gail Gibbons has explored places and objects familiar to the young person—a department store, trucks, and, for older readers, clocks and locks and keys.

The informational book appears to be the simplest to write for very young children, yet here again, the author's contribution begins with the problem of selection. "The younger the age group," says veteran editor Norma Jean Sawicki, "the more research is necessary because the author has to know what can be left out. There's not enough room to include everything, and a thorough mastery of the subject is required to highlight some points and leave others out." In *A Little Schubert* by M. B. Goffstein, the author does not fuss with dates and influences. Instead, in gem-like pictures, she shows the impoverished and inspired musician dancing to keep warm. At the end of the book, she includes a little record of Schubert waltzes so the child can also dance to the music. This kind of biography is well suited to the youngest readers, as it gives a feeling for the great musician without bogging them down with meaningless dates and events.

The Awareness or Observation Book

For writers who are comfortable with a looser structure than the informational or identification forms offer, there is the awareness or observation book. This kind of book is developed by following a simple observation through many different situations. In *One Way: A Trip With Traffic Signs*, author/illustrator Leonard Shortall follows a family in a convertible, completely packed with mother, father, kids, dog, and picnic lunch, through all kinds of traffic situations. The book serves a nonfiction purpose by focusing consistently on traffic signs, despite the changing landscape.

In the awareness book category, Margaret Wise Brown created the Noisy books—seven books about a little dog named Muffin and the sounds he hears in the city, the country, and indoors. These are ideal for sharing with preschoolers, since with the help of pictures, children can imitate sounds—the swish of a broom, the click of a light—and heighten awareness of their surroundings. In the Brown tradition is Charlotte Zolotow's *The Park Book* which shows the activities in a park from sunup to sundown. H. A. Rey's pictures show telling details—like the trash baskets filling up as the day progresses—which add a dimension to the whole.

The nonfiction awareness book for the picture book age is the exploration of an idea, the development of a thought structure aimed at the youngest child. Donald Crews introduces the sights and sounds of a train in *Freight Train*, an observation book that is accessible to the young child with dramatic graphics that appeal to the adult reader. Unlike Kohn's *Raccoons*, which packs a lot of information into the text, the concept book introduces an idea and gives children a sense of the world around them. For instance, in *Freight Train*, the text reads "across a trestle," with a dramatic, full double-page spread of a trestle, *showing*, rather than *telling*, what a trestle is. Most concept books are aimed at the very youngest readers. As Gertie Geck of The Tree House Book Store notes, "With the current interest in parenting and in the preschool group, we see an upsurge in the number of concept board books, especially the small hand-sized books."

ANATOMY OF A PICTURE BOOK

Young children are interested in the same things their older brothers and sisters are, but the size of the book—and the idea behind it—must necessarily be smaller for preschool children. It takes a keen sense of observation, attention to detail, and a child-sized perspective to take small ideas and approaches and turn them into book-sized ideas.

In all kinds of nonfiction picture books, there are five rules of thumb that a successful writer keeps in mind:

1. *Read-aloud quality.* Children this age can't read. They are read *to*. Is your manuscript rhythmic, dramatic, and exciting? Does it lend itself

to different nuances of voice and delivery? Monotonous rhyme, choppy sentences, and poor organization can drive an adult reading aloud stark raving mad. As Linda Zuckerman of Intervisual Publications points out, writing for children is a special art, even though there still exists the mistaken notion that it's an "easier" one. "It's a little like assuming it's easier to write poetry than a novel, and it's not," she says.

2. *Appeal to adults.* Preschoolers don't buy their own books. After they have become acquainted with a book, they may request it again and again, but adult appeal will determine whether your book gets read to the child in the first place. Is your subject matter one that adults want children to be interested in? A book about candy, for instance, might grab a child's attention, but it's unlikely to find favor with adults. Is your description of the subject well written enough to appeal to adults who face the prospect of reading the book over and over again?

3. *Illustrate-ability.* Children of the picture book age expect their books to have lots of pictures in them. Do your ideas lend themselves to illustration? Are your images graphic enough to reinforce the visuals an artist will provide? "Illustrate-ability" is an elusive quality, but it can be summed up in two major points: concrete images and careful sequence. The book, once it's illustrated, should have artistic unity and easy-to-follow structure.

4. *Simplicity without superficiality.* Many authors find subjects that interest them, and figure all they have to do is simplify the idea for the youngest child. But unless a subject is truly child-sized, your picture book will not work. A simple treatment with the interest level exactly at the two-to-five range will necessarily leave out important facets of the subject, resulting in a simplistic treatment. Your young audience wants to know *everything* about the subject your book discusses, so it's important to choose an idea with small enough dimensions so that it can be explored fully in a short picture book.

5. *Child-level continuity.* Continuity is very important in writing nonfiction for the youngest age group. Children want suspense and surprise, but their powers of comprehension are not so well developed that they can jump from subject to subject. The concept for your picture book should be simple and small enough so that you can explore its ramifications logically and carefully, bringing your audience along with you as you go.

These rules of thumb are essential to writing for young children; every manuscript you write should take them into consideration.

The picture book for preschoolers is traditionally thirty-two pages long, with three of those pages going for the title page, dedication page, and copyright page. This allows you only twenty-nine pages—twenty-nine sentences or short paragraphs—to pursue your ideas. This is a difficult task, demanding the economy of poetry, the adventurousness of a novel, and the word/picture synchronism of a movie. But don't despair. There are tricks to help you.

FINDING A FOCUS

The first trick, and probably the best one, is to structure your idea carefully. This enhances the illustrate-ability, the read-aloud quality, and the continuity of your text.

For very young children, some ready-made structures exist that you can borrow—or even steal—for your nonfiction telling. You need a focus of interest. One such focus is the alphabet. An excellent example of this kind of writing for the youngest children is Anne Alexander's *ABC of Cars and Trucks*. Using the alphabet for a skeletal structure, the book explores the many different kinds of cars and trucks children see as they walk around the city, the country, and the suburbs. Recognition is part of the pleasure the young child gets from reading this kind of book.

Another such focus is counting. Children this age are struggling to master numbers beyond one, two, three, and a book can help them. In *Where's the Fire?* author Rodger Wilson traces the numbers in sequence through the number of wheels on various vehicles. For one wheel, a unicycle is pictured. For two, a bicycle. For three, a tricycle, for four a car, up to ten which shows a big rig with extra wheels to carry its heavy load. By identifying the number of wheels on each vehicle, the child can exercise newly acquired counting skills while learning to name the vehicle he's seen on car trips and walks.

Children from two to five enjoy nonfiction so long as it is simply presented. Children this age are involved in the naming game—over 90 percent of their vocabulary is nouns. Thus, alphabet and counting books focus on objects. An alphabet of unrelated objects, or a counting book featuring illustrations of uninteresting colored dots, will not catch and hold a young reader's attention. Children want the continuity that alphabets and counting books offer. The ideas can take off from there.

For older children with a more sophisticated sense of numbers, Haris Petie has created a book of large number concepts, entitled *Billions of Bugs*. In this book, she shows natural groupings of insects, from thirty no-see-ums to a thousand Monarch butterflies, to acquaint children with the idea of counting by hundreds. Bugs are the perfect vehicle for this lesson, because they can be pictured on the page in life-size scale to create a sense of reality. Accuracy is very important in a book of this kind, and not only did the editorial staff drive itself to distraction checking and rechecking to see that the counts were accurate, but so did conscientious reviewers. The

Count the bunnies on a walk.
Bunny parents fondly talk.
While the baby bunnies snore.
All show 2 x 2 is 4.

Bunches & Bunnies of Bunnies *by Louise Matthews, illustrated by Jeni Basset (Dodd, Mead, 1978), shows the rare instance in which a child's drawings really do enhance a book.*

adults involved in this project figured that kids themselves would be doing the counting, and judging from the letters the author received, they did. This is one example of how you can't be too careful in the preparation of non-fiction!

The Illustrations

Some surprising topics lend themselves to illustrate-ability. When Harriet Gore, a mother and nurse, saw the need for a book on first aid for very young children, she took a seminonfiction tack. She created characters but did not concern herself with a setting or a plot, as a traditional storybook author might. Instead, she concentrated on the how-tos of first aid, carefully outlining the procedures that a young child should follow when confronted with a snake bite, a bad case of sunburn, or the puncture from an ill-placed nail.

In *Animal Fact and Animal Fable,* author Seymour Simon and illustrator Dianne De Groat decided to feature whimsical illustrations in their treatment of animal myths. This didn't take away from the serious fact-checking that Simon, best known for his science books for older children, had to do. The fairly sophisticated concept underlying this book—debunking such animal myths as bulls getting angry when they see red—brings forth facts that are news to some adult readers and well within the grasp of young children. The book is carefully structured. The myth is presented on a right-hand page with the question "Fact or fancy?" leading in to the answer on the following left-hand page.

Once you develop a structure for your book, you can be very playful. In her ABC book, author/artist Dorothy Schmiderer shows the evolution of letters in four frames. She draws the letter "a," for example, with two transitional drawings following, before she finally evolves the letter into a picture of an anteater. Kids find this book, which shows the concept of transformation, fascinating far beyond the picture book years.

GOOD IDEAS IN SMALL PACKAGES

Beyond a careful structure, it's important to find ideas that lend themselves to the picture book format and age group interests. Adults selecting books for children of this age are likely to pick a book that deals with a subject kids are already interested in. Since a small child's world is so circumscribed, his interests are bound to be obvious to an adult. The picture book writer is a person who understands the magic behind these seemingly pedestrian interests. Rare is the writer who can look at a commonplace object or experience and see possibilities for exploring it in a book-length manuscript. Putting yourself in a small child's shoes may seem ridiculously simple—until you try it.

To a toddler a leaf is an object of awe, a visit to the doctor is a main event. Harlow Rockwell follows this logic in creating his reassuring introduction to the routine checkup in *My Doctor*. Here every injection, every ritual from being weighed to saying "Ah" is carefully delineated in illustrations. The genius the author offers is not so much in the writing as in the observation. The genuine respect for a child's interests, and the accompanying detail to which they are attended, is the basis for this successful exploration of an ordinary event.

Herbert Zim is one of the masters of capturing a small child's enthusiasm and turning it into something wonderful between hard covers. Zim knows the magic of thunder and lightning, of telephones and octopi, and he explores his subjects with dignity and simplicity.

Child-Sized Ideas

Everyday interests can take on exotic dressing. In *People*, author/ artist Peter Spier shows the variety of people of all colors and costumes throughout the world. When Spier prepared the book, he studied costumes very carefully, so you can imagine his surprise when he noticed two of his Japanese friends giggling over the cover. "What's wrong?" Spier asked them. "You have a couple in wedding outfits, and the woman is carrying a baby," his friends said. Spier removed the baby, leaving a little white space on the cover of the book that is noticeable only to the most discerning eye.

Ordinary life in an unusual setting is one way of livening up a topic for a book-length treatment. Tom Allen developed his *Where Children Live* from a feature in *Sesame Street Magazine*. Each month he drew another child in another culture. He approached publishers with the idea, making a book from these single paintings. He picks a representative child from each culture and country, first showing them outside, then with a close-up view of what their houses look like inside.

Finding unusual situations in everyday life is another way of catching your readers' interest. Many children this age are interested in how things are made. With very few words and colorful cartoon-like pictures, Byron Barton shows the steps involved in *Building a House*. Tom Morgan shows action verbs in another how-to house book, *The Building Book*. In this one, a moose and a frog collaborate in a series of comic strip-like sequences showing the meanings of such words as "pull," "pour," and "dig."

Places. Children this age don't take places for granted. What we adults call a "farm" a child perceives as a cacophony of noises, an array of sights. In Alvin Tresselt's *Wake Up, Farm*, the sights and sounds of country life are carefully explored, one by one, page by page, to guide the reader into the synthesis of animals, buildings, strange noises, and odd smells that adults call "farm." Margaret Wise Brown contrasts sounds alone in two books for very young children, *The City Noisy Book* and *The Country Noisy Book*. These are, again, careful observations of the sounds associated with the city and the country, and give the young child a handle on which to hang his personal observations.

Food is another favorite with preschoolers. Nature writer Berniece Freschet capitalizes on this interest to introduce young readers to raccoons in her book, *Five Fat Raccoons*. Through the summer, a family of raccoons hunts, fishes, and swims, with only one thing in mind—food.

Their own bodies are objects of continuing wonder to young children. P. D. Eastman recognizes this important aspect of being small in his series of books, *The Eye Book*, *The Foot Book*, and *The Hand Book*. The child's body is an important part of his life, because it is continually there for him to observe.

Weather is another subject that adults take for granted and children find fascinating. But instead of considering barometric pressure, temperature, and precipitation as they're featured on TV news, that approach to weather that works with very young children is one of direct sensory appeal. *Rain Drop Splash*, by Alvin Tresselt, explores the ordinary events of a rainfall, from the first drop to puddles. In *Rain Rain Rivers*, Uri Shulevitz shows the effects of rain from a little girl listening to the rain in her attic room to outside scenes to a final picture of the little girl's plant growing.

Opposites are concepts that young children can master at an early age. In *Push, Pull, Empty, Full*, photographer Tana Hoban shows contrasting pictures to demonstrate her ideas. A gumball machine, full of balls, shows the concept of "many," while on the facing page, a photo shot from the same angle but with only a few balls in the machine shows the contrasting concept of "few."

Prepositions also express important new ideas to children this age. In *Bear Hunt*, Margaret Siewart and Kathleen Savage utilize the popular game, "Do you want to go on a bear hunt?" to show the concepts of "over," "under," "through," and "above." The fact that the little bear makes it—as shown by Leonard Shortall's little girl heroine clutching her favorite teddy bear—is reassuring to the young reader.

Imagination, in writing nonfiction, takes the form of seeing sharply the things that interest someone else—in this case, a someone who is small. If you look around you, you'll see that there are myriad opportunities for exploring the world in minute detail. Although this may seem redundant or even tiresome, it's important for the picture book author to imagine the world from eyes just two feet from the ground.

Because the picture book is so simple—deceptively so—many new writers start out with this form. And because it represents such a distillation of ideas, and since behind each word may be hours of selection and rewriting, experienced writers find it a challenge.

PICTURE BOOK PUBLISHING

"Never has it been so easy for new writers to break into publishing," Norma Jean Sawicki at Crown maintains. "Librarians and book buyers are tired of the same old stuff." Connie Epstein of William Morrow disagrees. "It's never been so difficult for a new writer to enter the children's publishing field," she maintains. "Authors' reputations are very important in children's books today. The librarian and parent customer want a name they can trust."

The basic problem that has publishers deviating from the sure and steady publishing programs of the last thirty years is the cutback in library funding. Librarians have always been an educated audience, with children's literature courses under their belts, knowledge of circulation realities within the libraries' children's rooms, and regular exposure to what publishers were publishing each new season. Librarians knew what books would "sell" to their young patrons, and their support of popular authors enabled publishers to keep classic picture books in print, and successful authors and illustrators producing for new lists.

The cutback in library funding has had a deep effect on what editors and publishers are up to. It used to be that the average life of a children's book was twenty years. After the cutbacks of the seventies, this figure came closer to ten years. And these days, children's books aren't so different from their adult counterparts which stay in print for three to five years.

Without the library market to depend on, publishers are counting increasingly on bookstore sales. As Dorothy Briley at Lothrop, Lee and Shepard points out, it's the nonbook that is winning the bookstore's attention. Pop-ups, folding scrolls, block books, and other "manufactured" toy books are winning the limited space on bookstore shelves. Plain picture book offerings are increasingly limited to paperbacks, and therein lies another problem.

No publisher is going to print twenty thousand paperbacks of an untried title. The standard publishing procedure is to print an expensive hardcover edition of a new picture book and pray it gets review attention, library acceptance, and enough publicity to establish the book for a larger audience.

But not all is grim. True, the standard picture book story is having a hard time finding a home. The arrival of a new baby, the adventures of a mischievous animal, or the "good night" book are not as readily accepted as they have traditionally been. But editors are facing the realities of the marketplace and trying something new. Some of their solutions are actually old as the hills: the gimmicky pop-ups that are proliferating now are often reprints of books that were published seventy-five years ago. But the situation can present an exciting challenge to the nonfiction author. Television, day care, and other influences have made little ones more aware of the world than ever. Writers who can "picture" it interestingly and informatively will always be in demand.

More than any other age group, the picture book crowd is discerning and enthusiastic once they've picked a favorite. Your book, once it is published, may be read over and over, with the young reader never tiring of hearing it, long after the adult doing the reading is sick and tired of the same old story.

Adrienne Adams, excellent and prolific author/illustrator, puts it in a nutshell: "I love children's books, and I feel very lucky to be involved in them. As I became involved, I discovered the satisfactions of a field which can be sweetly innocent of the rank business-and-profit taint as any I can hope for, simply because a book cannot succeed unless little children love it and wear out its cover and pages so thoroughly that librarians must reorder it for the library shelves; you cannot tell a child what to like."

CHAPTER 3

The Primary Grades:
Ages 6 to 9

The early school years are a time of astonishing progress in children's lives. They have mastered speech skills, and are attacking reading with enthusiasm and determination. They are learning to tell time. And for the first time, they are encountering a world outside of family life. Their interests are broadening and their skills progressing beyond the intuitive learning that characterized them as picture book readers to processing information through concrete operations. They are learning how to learn.

One of the biggest things children of this age must confront is their own decision making—what to wear to school, whether to have apple juice or orange juice at break time, whether to play on the jungle gym or swings, and what book to check out of the library. Because they're inexperienced at making decisions, the time it takes them to weigh alternatives may drive parents and teachers mad, but this process is essential to growing up. Making decisions and living with the consequences of those decisions is central to a child's development.

As experience in decision making increases, children in primary grades are better able to classify and recognize likenesses and differences. These logical skills enable them to understand history, basic mathematics, crafts operations, and science projects from beginning to end. The primary grade child loves books and eagerly searches out those that say, "You can read me."

The 6 to 9 age group is targeted by publishers as the "easy reader" group; these children are beginning to find books to read by themselves. They are developing their own special interests and are beginning to experience their first homework assignments. But they are still uncertain about their reading ability. The easy reader is designed to reinforce a child's curiosity and confidence. Unlike the picture book, which originally developed as an art form with little regard for its audience, the easy reader is the product of the fifties and sixties wherein a scientific approach to education helped publishers target the right balance of words and pictures.

EASY TO READ, HARD TO WRITE

The easy reader, as a category, sells very well. This is partly because it is a relatively new form and partly because it is an outgrowth of the interests television has fostered, interests the child wants to know more about. But mostly it sells because it is so difficult to write.

The easy reader, of all books for children, demands the sharpest angle, the approach that isolates a subject for study that is substantial enough for a book, but is not so overwhelming that a child who is still mastering reading will be put off by it. These books follow a standard format whether they are aimed at first or third graders. The format is designed to give the child a sense of reading alone, and contains generous spacing to create the illusion that he has mastered a "real" book.

One of the masters of writing for this age group is Louise Armstrong, author of *How to Turn Lemons into Money*, *How to Turn War into Peace*, and *How to Turn Down into Up*. In these three volumes, she addresses

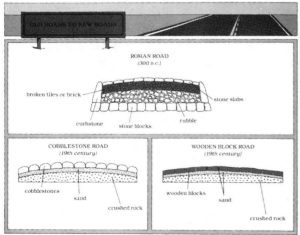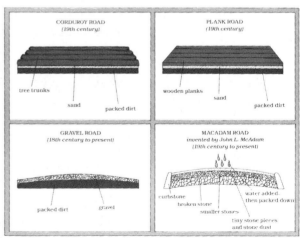

These simple four-color illustrations from New Road! *by Gail Gibbons (Thomas Y. Crowell, 1983) trace the process of road building for 5- to 9-year-olds.*

questions that reflect adult interests which filter down to the 6 to 9 age group through the television news. In *How to Turn Lemons into Money*, she explores the basics of a lemonade stand economy. In *How to Turn Down into Up*, she creates a sequel addressing questions of wage and price hikes, cost of living increases, and unemployment. Her writing is direct, and scaled down to child-sized interests. In *How to Turn War into Peace*, using a seaside setting and two sandcastle builders, the author introduces terms: *You will mobilize your troops* (organize the other kids). *Decide on your goal* (to defeat Susie). *Plan your strategy* (to drive her off the beach). *Outline your tactics* (to throw stuff at her castle). When everybody gets hungry and you break for lunch, this is a *temporary cease fire*.

Humor is evident to adults reading this, but for kids, the cuteness is more of a bridge to understanding. We see this same approach in *Looking at Maps* by Erick Fuchs. In this highly illustrated book, the author starts with a boy, then moves to his room, next to his house, on to his block, and into his town. By steps, Fuchs shows the components of an address on an envelope and points out that the envelope *could* read "Ben's Room, 38 Garden Street, Redford, Millstone, Peacedom, Middleland, Earth, Solar System, Milky Way Galaxy, Universe." This introduces young children to the idea of maps by starting at a point they can identify with.

Robert Froman, the author of *Hot and Cold and In Between* and *Less Than Nothing Is Really Something*, says of his writing for this age group: "Some of my science books for young readers have grown out of articles I wrote for magazines, and in the books I was able to go much deeper into the subjects. I'm always trying to make certain aspects of science and math as exciting for young readers as they are for me."

Fuchs, Armstrong, and Froman understand that beginning readers are curious and eager to exercise their independent reading skills. Books for this age group must be simple enough to keep readers interested without frustrating them. There is no magic age when children begin to read independently. A recent study of a typical group of first graders showed reading levels ranging from that expected of a three-year-old (the ability to recognize letters alone), to fourth grade (the ability to read a substantial book without help). For most children, however, reading is a skill that is introduced in the first grade curriculum. Reading readiness, including the study of phonics and identification of the alphabet's letters, begins for most children at the ages of two or three, often through television shows like "Sesame Street."

EASY READER REQUIREMENTS

Research studies show that the average first grader recognizes about twenty thousand words by ear. A text read by a first grader contains far fewer words than this, usually only a couple of hundred, because a book utilizing a large vocabulary is tiresome for early graders to tackle. Yet television has created interest in subjects for children that can be treated in books, if the writer is mindful of three important criteria: the importance of pictures, vocabulary controls, and the correlation of interests and abilities.

The Importance of Pictures

Reading on their own in the first through the fourth grades, children want to be grown up. They are not interested in "baby books" with large formats, colorful pictures, and a minimum of words. An early elementary school student is looking for information in books, and wants to appear as sophisticated as the big kids. Thus the format for easy readers—usually no larger than 6" x 9"—is carefully designed to give children the help they need from pictures without being precisely a picture book. There are several approaches illustration can take.

The illustrations can be diagrammatic. In *Circles*, author Mandel Sitomar shows how to use a compass to find the radius and diameter of a circle. This may sound old hat, but to young readers, it's brand-new. They're fascinated by the ways one can construct a triangle and a square from the radii of circles. The illustrations in *Circles* are diagrammatic and very simple. The text explains the pictures, but the straightforward, uncute illustrations add dignity to the book. And although this book introduces a school subject that is considered a bore by second and third graders, its tricks and activities keep the reader interested.

The illustrations can be graphic. Graphic illustrations, besides being instructive, can be beautiful to behold. In Raymond Sacks's *Magnets*, the attraction and repulsion of the two poles are shown in simple wood engravings by noted artist Stefan Martin. The uncluttered illustrations help readers master the subject matter without making the text look babyish.

The illustrations can be realistic drawings. When Julian May set out to explain why people are different colors in the book by that name, he chose Symeon Shimin as illustrator. Shimin's illustrations show people of different skin colors, but because they look realistic, the drawings come to life as portraits. The book stresses the moral question of how superficial skin color and head shape differences are, and the realistic illustrations reinforce the point.

The illustrations can be photographic. Millicent Selsam has written many successful books for young children on the dullest subject of all—

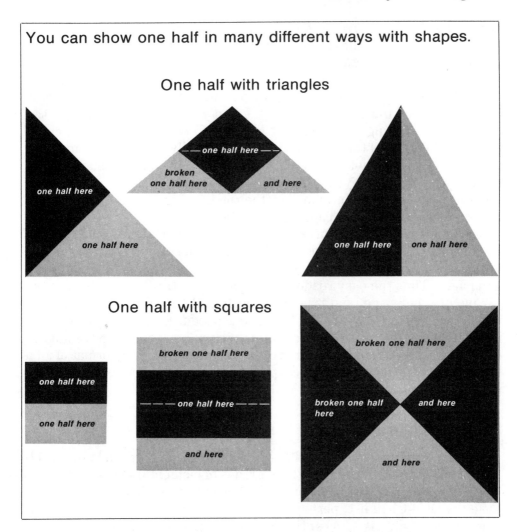

In Fractions are Parts of Things *by J. Richard Dennis (Thomas Y. Crowell, 1971), pictures by Donald Crews graphically illustrate simple math principles for young children.*

vegetables. In *The Carrot and Other Root Vegetables*, she shows the wonders of plants such as the carrot with enlarged photographs of the changes that occur as the vegetables grow.

Whatever illustration approach you and your editor choose for your easy reader, you must be mindful of the importance of the pictures in the book you are writing. Children just learning to read have been watching television for most of their lives, so they are visually sophisticated in a way that most adults are not, and can never be. Illustration is second nature to the TV generation. They know how to read a picture for information. They count on pictures to help them over the rough spots in reading, to clarify concepts that would take pages to describe.

As important as pictures are to the easy reader, the book's format still needs to be as grown up as possible. Children reading their own books like to have chapters, good stopping places, complete ideas covered in several pages. Thus the easy reader is designed with three or four sentences per picture, per page, and type generously laid out with lots of space between the lines (called "leading," pronounced *ledding*) to make reading easier. The easy reader is emphatically *not* a picture book, in which the illustrations take center stage, but is above all a *reading* book. The format of an illustration on every page, short chapters, and a length of generally 48 or 64 pages, is intended to serve the child's *reading* needs.

Vocabulary Controls

What can you expect a child to be able to read? This is a knotty problem for the author. In the first three grades of elementary school, reading levels vary so greatly that no one list is going to provide a magic formula. Take the Dale-Chall list, perhaps the best-known list of words for controlling vocabulary. It lists 769 of the 20,000 words first graders recognize by ear. This list includes "nose" but not "chin," "finger" but not "toe," "second" but not "third," "breakfast," but not "lunch." The arbitrary character of these lists can confuse the writer who follows them religiously, and worse, confuse the reader as well.

Define your terms. Young children love big vocabulary words. You can stick to controlled vocabulary lists and describe a moon crater as a "big dish," both of which words are on the list, but you are sure to lose something in the translation. And if you are writing about electronics, computers, spaceships, and other high-tech subjects, it's almost impossible to describe them without lapsing into highly specialized jargon. Don't hesitate to use the jargon, which your young reader will welcome (as another way to feel grown up), but do take the time to define each word you introduce in simple terms.

Use reader identification to get ideas across. Sometimes the most elementary concepts are difficult to describe. In *Big Is So Big*, author Bertha Dodge introduces a character named Tom. Young Tom, helping his father measure a room, first measures it in "toms." Then Dodge introduces the standard measurements of feet and yards. By beginning with a specific experience (measuring the room) and point of identification (having Tom measure in terms of his own body) she is able to convey a difficult though elementary concept. The author comments: "Paradoxically, I came to perceive the need for such a book some years ago when I was a humble assistant in a college freshman mathematics course and found my class rather hazy on the subject of units of measurement. So when an editor of a science series approached me about a book for the quite young, this was the book I wanted to write. Having tested it on two eight-year-old grandchildren, I believe it may serve its end."

In Byrd Baylor's *When Clay Sings*, she introduces a new concept to six- and seven-year-olds: archaeology. Rather than approach it as an encyclopedia might, admonishing children to respect the tiny shards of pottery found throughout the Southwest, she tells her readers that Indian parents tell their children that pottery should not be thrown away because each piece "has its own small voice and its own song." Baylor brings each piece to life and builds up to the history that artifacts tell. By beginning with a specific vocabulary and point of identification, she introduces a complex concept to young readers without relying on complexity.

Allow only one new idea per sentence. Simple terminology means more than controlling vocabulary. It means controlling the flow of ideas, introducing one concept per sentence, and taking nothing for granted. Metaphors are one useful way to describe something totally new. If you were describing hibernation, for instance, you could use the metaphor of a long nap after lunch; to describe a satellite's movement, the metaphors of a jogger circling the track or a bicycle rider going around the block.

The child's eye angle is the secret of writing nonfiction that doesn't require a sophisticated reading level. The important thing is to write in bite-sized pieces, using short and simple sentences, compact units, and clearly delineated chapters.

Interest/Ability Level Correlation

Television has acquainted young readers with subject matter that was relegated to an older age group a generation ago. Three-year-olds watch the news, six-year-olds watch the space shots in the classroom, and wildlife footage on TV makes sophisticated naturalists of third graders who have had a chance to watch a number of exotic animals close up. This has

Somebody on the block was playing a Beatle record.

42

"That's good bug-hunting music," Annie said.

43

Harold Krieger's photographs for The Bug That Laid the Golden Eggs *by Millicent E. Selsam (Harper I CAN READ, 1967) emphasize the spontaneity of a real-life situation.*

provided wonderful opportunities for the nonfiction writer because a project can no longer be dismissed with the editor's saying: "Oh, no, children in the early elementary years are only interested in family stories." Children this age are interested in subjects that are difficult to explain—animal behavior, space travel, computers, and medical breakthroughs. The problem is no longer a paucity of subject matter of interest to young children but the difficulty of honing it down to book-sized ideas.

Relate to children's concerns. When Paul Showers took on the subject of digestion—which can fill an eight-hundred-page medical book—he starts off with "I like hamburgers." This text, *What Happens to a Hamburger*, is geared to the young reader's interests, his likes and dislikes, so that the subject matter is easy to swallow. From this cheerful beginning, author Showers proceeds to show how the digestive system turns a favorite meal into energy, new tissue, and byproducts.

In writing about the life and times of Theodore Roosevelt, Ferdinand

Monjo uses the same approach. He doesn't try to evoke the spirit of the times as a writer for an older age group might. Instead, he makes young Quentin Roosevelt the narrator of the book, entitled *The One Bad Thing about Father*. It is through Quentin's eyes that the reader experiences Roosevelt's political and military feats. The "one bad thing" about him is that he is rarely home to play with Quentin and his brother.

Borrow techniques from fiction. Writers for early independent readers are resourceful at finding ways to hook their audience. Unlike the picture book, which is shared with an adult, the easy reader must be simple enough to master on a child's own. Yet children this age are looking for empathy, not sympathy, and usually need a gimmick to catch and keep their attention. The main character as the focus of the telling is one important fictional technique borrowed by nonfiction for this age group. For instance, in Jean George's *All Upon a Stone*, she describes life in a small-scale ecosystem. She focuses on the mole cricket, so that the reader can follow this small "hero" from beginning to end. It gives readers a frame of reference for the information and concept of the book.

In *Eric Plants a Garden*, author Jean Hudlow uses a fictionalized situation and characters to make her point. In watching Eric plant a garden, the reader sees the components of gardening: measuring, planting, cultivating, watering, and finally harvesting. A garden without a protagonist would scarcely engage a young child's attention, which is usually focused on himself and other children his age.

Find a dramatic focus. Once you have captured it, holding the attention of 6- to 9-year-olds is also difficult. Many writers find that a slow and steady survey of a field is not enough. Some aspects have to be explored at length, while others have to be treated quickly or bypassed entirely. Sensational facts can save a book for this age group. In *You're a Good Dog, Joe*, dog expert Kurt Unkelbach explains the basics of dog care for young readers. He then introduces two aspects of the subject usually left out of introductory books: what to do when your dog is blind, and what to do if your dog has a poor sense of direction. These problems are not standard, but they are both common enough and interesting enough to justify inclusion in the book, and give readers some interesting magpie information to tell their friends.

In *The Flight of the Snow Goose*, Berniece Freschet discusses the life pattern and ecological environment of this lovely bird. She also introduces exciting encounters with a hunter, an oil slick, and fire. Not only are these possible dangers to the geese she describes, they add dramatic excitement and flair to her story. She avoids melodramatizing, but keeps the action fast paced, exploiting every angle to keep her readers' interest, long jaded by the constant action of television.

How to Tie a Not Knot

You show a piece of rope or string.
You tie a knot right in the middle.
Everyone sees the knot.
Everyone is sure it is there.
But wait a moment.
You flick the rope.
There is no knot.
It was a not knot!

How Is It Done?

Hold the rope by one end tightly.
Do not let go of this end at all.
Wrap the other end over your wrist.
Tie a knot with the end of the rope
    using your other hand.
Keep holding the first end tightly.
Let the rope slip off your wrist.
The knot will vanish.

54

Layout for instructional material is illustrated with light-hearted cartoons in
Now You See It—Easy Magic for Beginners *by Ray Broekel and Laurence B.*
White, Jr., illustrated by Bill Morrison (Little, Brown, 1979).

Franklyn Branley uses the same technique in *Oxygen Keeps You Alive*. Rather then sing the praises of this element he focuses on what happens to people in places without enough oxygen—divers, astronauts, mountain climbers. Not only does this add drama, it also reinforces his point that oxygen is necessary for life.

Have a point of view. Just as young readers want a strong central character and lots of dramatic action to sweep them along, so they like to know where the author stands. They aren't yet old enough to understand a thoroughly balanced treatment, as one might find in an encyclopedia, and want the author to have a voice, a point of view, an opinion. In *Scaly Wings*, Ross Hutchins talks about dangerous moths. To an older reader, this kind of polarization might not be necessary. But to seven-year-olds, it helps clarify the central point. After the author discusses the "bad" moths who eat our clothes, he discusses the "good" moths who participate helpfully in the pollination process. A strict scientist might take exception to this grouping of good guys and bad guys, but to a child the division makes the comprehension easier.

Write about what interests you. The personal interest that spurs you to write about a subject for children is part of the spark that will make your writing succeed. Children come to the easy reader because the format is clear without being babyish. Children finish the easy reader and recommend it to their friends because the writing, while concise, has enthusiasm and personality. Remember that primary grade children need an emotional leg-up into the world of ideas. Macmillan's Lauren Wohl comments: "Subject, format, illustration, and above all, writing with the reader's limited capabilities and unlimited interests in mind—these are the secrets of writing the easy reader."

6

Vertebrates are the most important animals on earth. They are the fishes, amphibians (frogs and their kin), reptiles (snakes, turtles, and lizards), birds, and mammals. This last great group ranges from shrews that weigh less than a dime to great whales weighing well over 100 tons. All of these vertebrates have skeletons of bone, and all are built pretty much on the same plan.

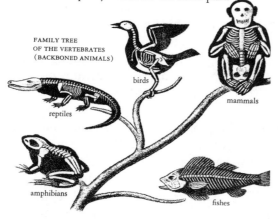

FAMILY TREE
OF THE VERTEBRATES
(BACKBONED ANIMALS)

birds

reptiles

mammals

amphibians

fishes

MICROSCOPIC VIEWS OF THREE CONNECTIVE TISSUES

 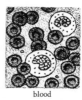

cartilage   blood   bone

Bone is one of the tissues of the vertebrate body. Tissues are groups of similar cells (and materials between the cells) that do the same work in the body. Bone is one kind of connective tissue. Other kinds include blood, fat, fibrous tissue (as tendons), and cartilage.

Your growth, inch by inch, is mainly the result of your bones growing longer. This

23

...l, the bones of the body fall into ...groups. Long bones have a slight ...ch helps them support a load ... if they were perfectly straight. The ends of the shafts are swollen and made of softer, spongier bone with a thin, hard cover. Here muscles, which move arms and legs, are attached. Most of the movements that are fun—the running, jumping, and throwing—make use of your long bones.

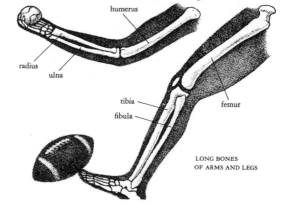

humerus

radius

ulna

tibia

fibula

femur

LONG BONES
OF ARMS AND LEGS

These illustrations by Rene Martin in Herbert Zim's Bones *(William Morrow and Company, 1969) help provide a thorough introduction to a complex subject for 8- to 12-year-olds.*

CHAPTER 4

The Middle Grades:
Ages 8 to 12

The upper elementary school grades are a wonderful time for children. School has become second nature, and a new independence drives children in the third through the sixth grades to seek friends, usually of the same sex, for deep alliances that include the sharing of books. This is a time of enormous reading: one study shows that fourth graders spend more time reading for pleasure than any other age group—including adults. It is not unusual for a fourth or fifth grader to read two hundred books outside of school work each year.

THE BOOKS KIDS LOVE

Books for children this age fall into two distinct categories—books that help with homework assignments, which publishers call "curriculum-oriented texts," and true leisure-time books that kids read because they want to read them, not because they are assigned in school. As Jean Karl, longtime editor at Atheneum Publishers points out, "A leisure book can be used in the curriculum, but it's far less likely that a curriculum-oriented book will find its way into a child's leisure reading." If you are interested in writing nonfiction that will really catch on with this age group, make yours a book that kids will pick up on their own. This means focusing on their interests, sharing their addiction to television and sports, judging their abilities in arts and crafts, and helping them understand the world.

An interesting characteristic of this age group is the way children segregate themselves according to sex. Whatever the feminists say or wish to be so, the interests of boys and girls diverge at this age. Boys tend to be interested in machinery, electronics, and sports; girls tend to seek out biographies, art books, and craft how-tos, as well as books that give them information about clothes and appearance. But this doesn't mean that interests don't overlap, as Manfred Riedel's books on the economy and statistics show. Using child protagonists, he explains basic questions about the economy in *A Kid's Guide to the Economy*, with appeal to both boys and girls. In *Winning With Numbers*, his introduction to statistics, he features examples of both boys and girls in his stories that introduce elementary statistical concepts, so that the appeal is broad-based. (His fan mail is about equally divided between girls and boys.)

Both sexes in this age group are interested in natural history. For boys, the Cub Scouts begin; girls join the Brownies and Campfire Girls. Scouting fosters interest in the outdoors, and often in the course of earning achievement badges, children find they want to learn about a natural history subject in depth. Nan Hayden Agle captures children's interests in a nonsexist way in her memoir, *My Animals and Me*. The book is simply a collection of anecdotes about the pets that Ms. Agle kept as a young girl before the First World War. In addition to its historical interest, the book covers her involvement with the standard pets and strikes a chord of familiarity with boys and girls who love animals.

The Facts, Please

Children this age are fact freaks, and they like their books to be packed with facts they can memorize and quote, whether batting averages or animal speed records. The writer for this age group is competing with the encyclopedia, which these readers have just learned to use. A book has to offer more than the encyclopedia does in the way of depth and point of view. Little touches, like the pronouncing glossary in Alvin and Virginia B. Silverstein's *Metamorphosis*, make the difference. In this collection of encyclopedic information, the authors cover the changes that take place in butterflies and moths, but also in honeybees, toads, salamanders, sea squirts, and starfish. They offer a more comprehensive structure than the encyclopedia because they consider the advantage metamorphosis offers for many animals in the struggle for survival. The introduction of a central idea, supported by many examples, sets this book apart from the encyclopedia, even though the information in it can be found in separate encyclopedia entries.

Allow for Inductive Reasoning

Herbert Zim pioneered the "species" book with such titles as *Lions*, *Pandas*, and *Chimpanzees*. As a teacher at the Ethical Culture School in New York City, he discovered that children this age are interested in specifics, not generalities. Whereas an adult book, or even a book for young adults, might start from a general premise and proceed to specific facts, Zim, a science educator as well as a writer, discovered that children in the 8 to 12 age group want specific facts first, and slowly assimilate the facts to build up to generalities. Thirty years ago, Zim, working for his doctorate in science education, submitted a questionnaire to his students, asking them to list the subjects they were interested in reading about. Sixty books later, he still has not exhausted the list.

The Eight- to Twelve-Year-Old Collector

Children this age collect more than facts: they find great comfort in amassing comic books, insects, sea shells, rocks, autographs, or stickers. The average ten-year-old in one study had eight collections going. One of the things children like to collect is books. Even if they don't get to own the book, and simply take it out of the library, they like to be able to say, "I've read every book by this author,"or, "I've read every book in that series."

Publishers for this age group have had great success with series books. The Landmark series, published by Random House, features many different authors, all experts on their subjects. The result is a hodge-podge of writing styles, but children are devoted to this series on history because they know they can count on a standard length, type size, illustration approach, and subject interest. The "First Books" published by Franklin Watts for this age group also feature a standard format on a variety of subjects. Writers find they can explore abstruse subjects once they are working for an established series, because kids find it irresistible to read every book in a collection. A series can offer a good way for new writers to get a specialized subject published.

Youthful Enthusiasms

Interests flare up with a real passion at this age. The baseball bug strikes many children, boys, especially. Teachers and parents often find that the only way to keep their children reading is to feed the youngsters' consuming interests and hobbies. This is good news for the writer, because it means there is always room for one more book on popular subjects. There is an undying demand, for instance, for new, up-to-the-minute hockey and football books.

Other topical subjects are fed by television. When Walt Disney popularized Davy Crockett on the tube, nine million books on the subject of this southern pioneer were sold. Every time a child sees a television program, he is interested in a new topic. A smart writer for this age group counts on television for his research, and not just on children's programming: a documentary on Nazi Germany shown at ten o'clock at night is just as likely to create interest as a feature on "The Electric Company."

KEEPING UP AND DROPPING OUT

The highly socialized environment of the upper grades in elementary school makes children this age subject to peer pressure for the first time. Age and reading levels can vary up to five or six grades, so that one fourth grader can barely master reading skills, while another can read on the high school level. This means that children are competitive, wanting to read what their friends are reading—and more. But it also has a sad side: A fourth grader who is still reading easy readers can be the butt of painful jokes. Many children in the upper elementary grades stop reading altogether because they find they can't read the same books their friends are reading.

☆ Fountain Pens

The inconvenience of interrupting one's thoughts while writing in order to renew your supply of ink presented an irresistible challenge. A number of inventors thought up solutions to the problem of supplying a nib with a large reservoir of ink.

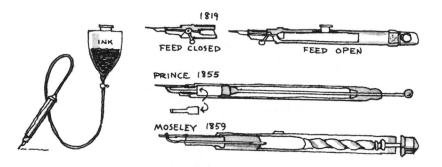

There is still room for creativity. Try your hand at building a better fountain pen!

In The Secret Life of School Supplies, *the stylized drawings convey both information and illumination of Vicki Cobb's thorough text.*

Thus there is an enormous need for dignified but easy reading treatments for the 8 to 12 age group. One way to achieve this without having the book look babyish is to include small chapters of information, sometimes only two or three pages long. In *ABCs of the Ocean* and *ABCs of the Earth*, Isaac Asimov explains everything from aquaculture to zoo plankton with two entries per letter. His format is easy to follow, but his information is substantial enough to give the good reader something to think about.

Magpie information, presented in small units, is particularly appealing to this age group. In *Sports Star: Pele*, S. H. Burchard brings in some general information to tone down the adulatory tone that characterizes many sports biographies. She says, "Many kings invited him [Pele] to dinner," and then goes on to point out "During the war that took place between Biafra and Nigeria, the war stopped for a day so that Pele could cross into Biafra to play in a soccer game." This current affairs touch is memorable and adds spice to her biography.

Diametrically opposed, but just as effective, is the long book written in a spontaneous and even loquacious style. In his biographies for young people, Ronald Syme, author of *Bolivar the Liberator*, goes on for almost two hundred pages. The young reader has the illusion that he is carrying around a "real book" because it has the bulk of an adult book. The type is large, however, and the margins are generous: the book is also livened up with an illustration here and there. Syme covers Bolivar's life—a good choice of subject because it's inherently exciting—by describing his evolution from hotheaded young gambler to committed revolutionary.

An enterprising author can create books for this child that are accessible without seeming juvenile. As a science teacher, Seymour Simon saw kids throwing paper airplanes in class. In *The Paper Airplane Book,* he uses demonstration projects to show how the various parts of the airplane contribute to the demands of flight. It is a particularly good example of a book for this age group because its how-to aspect disguises its more abstract lessons about the construction of actual airplanes. It appeals to good readers and poor readers alike.

Even good readers, children capable of reading *Alive!* or *The Thorn Birds*, like to slip back to easier reading between these demanding tomes. Sandy Peele, a bookseller at The Corner Bookshop in Manhattan, points out that older elementary school children often stop by on their way home from school and curl up with a Richard Scarry book, or *The Story of Babar*. "The way these kids regress is amazing," he says with a smile.

Nonfiction Storytelling Techniques

Another way around the gap between interest and ability is a lightly fictionalized touch. Richard Armour covers the animals of the Cenozoic period, cramming in lots of information between two covers, by means of poems. On the megatherium, poet Armour says:

> The strangest thing was how he walked—
> A queer side-footed roll.
> When asked "Why do you walk like this?"
> He said, "To save my sole."

Humor is just one way of adding a fictional touch. Creating a typical situation, based on many case histories, is another way of fictionalizing fact for a more effective nonfiction telling. In her *Children of Appalachia*, author Margaret Shull invents two typical families so her readers have someone to identify with. This way, she is able to cover the large issues facing Appalachian families today—the impact of mining, the isolation of families—without losing her readers' interest.

Nature writing has a long tradition of light fictionalization. *Save that Raccoon*, by Gloria Miklowitz, tells the story of a raccoon who flees to the suburbs when his natural habitat is destroyed. He causes great damage as he forages for food and shelter, and is eventually relocated to a woodland area, where he lives happily ever after. Not only does Miklowitz use a story framework for her account, but also fictional techniques to relate nonfiction details.

> During the night, Raccoon left the garage. He moved from house to house. He was looking for food and water. Strange smells and sounds came to him. Bright lights made the night seem like day, and the dogs barked at him wherever he went.
>
> He tasted the sweet buds of roses at one place, and they were good.

Taking this technique one step further in *Chickaree*, St. Tamara gives her animal character a name and a nearly human identity in the course of conveying nonfiction facts to her young reader. In describing the transfer of her character's babies to a new nest, the author describes a dramatic moment:

> Then she transfers her third and fourth babies and returns to the old nest to make sure that none are left behind. Pfe-e-e-e-e-e! Chickaree has never heard this sound before, yet she knows what has happened. A baby has fallen out of the nest!

SUBJECT MATTER—THE SKY'S THE LIMIT

In planning a book for this age group, you have an almost unlimited choice of subjects. Children this age are interested in many things, and a good book can pique their curiosity about new subjects. The problem in choosing one is limited by the gap in interests and abilities. A biography of George Eliot may be above your readers' interest level, whereas a biography of Rusty Staub may be a reflection of their dearest interests. Many writers feel they can't write about a subject because it's been done before, but nothing could be further from the truth for the 8 to 12 group. The interests of childhood focus on the same things generation after generation: animals, arts and crafts, hobbies, sports, and biographies. As long as the approach is new, there is always room for a new book on a given subject.

Who would think that there would be room for another book about animals? Yet Roger Caras's *Mysteries of the Animal World* finds a new angle and pursues it in a way that captivates the 8 to 12 group. He discusses how a cobra defends itself by spitting, and asks the unanswered question of why whales, the most intelligent animals after man, strand themselves. He explains the explainable phenomena in nature—as many books before his have—but then adds the dimension of pondering that which is unexplained. This gives the young nature buff a chance to dream of being the scientist who discovers "why."

The middle grade child is looking for a place in the world. As a writer, you can provide places from which to look as well as places to see, just as a Sherpa guide acquaints the climber with the vistas and dangers of the mountain to be climbed. The author's perspective is just as important as the subject matter because the child expects the author to provide facts in a book he can read all by himself. The writer for this age group will be rewarded by earning the child's trust—and helping the child learn to trust himself.

NEWSPAPER PUBLISHER

Geoffrey Robinson

I became a newspaper publisher totally by accident. I didn't plan on it at all.

During college, I thought I was going to become a doctor. So I took pre-med courses. Then I started applying to medical schools in my senior year. But I started collecting rejection letters.

So there I was—stuck—at the end of college. Everyone else knew what they were going to do. Some of my classmates were going to law school. Others were ready to go to work for some large company. But me—I was totally stuck. I really had no idea what I was going to do.

A friend of mine was moving to Ohio and I decided to go out there too. I had to decide on some job, some job that would be reasonably interesting. Well, one of the first things I thought of was a newspaper job because I was always intrigued by newspapers. I'd always liked reading newspapers.

Fortunately, I happened to get a job on a newspaper out in Ohio. That was my first job.

After that job, I got another job with a much bigger newspaper. I was an editor which meant I read the stories the reporters wrote and then fixed them up a bit.

I worked for a large daily newspaper. It was a morning newspaper and that meant that all the work had to be done at night which was one reason I couldn't stand it. Newspaper jobs

The chapter opener in What to Be *by Steve Berman and Vivian Weiss (Prentice-Hall, 1978) is enlivened by an irreverent drawing by Judy Beim without detracting from the essentially serious text.*

CHAPTER 5

The Young Teenager:
Ages 10 to 14

From the time that children's publishing became established in the United States in the 1920s, publishers broke down the span of childhood into three distinct groups: ages 4-7, 8-12, and 12-16. Experience showed that there were gray areas and some overlap in these categories: Some books offered for the 8 to 12 group seemed too young, while books published for the 12 to 16 group were too difficult. When librarians and teachers pointed this out to publishers, a new category was introduced: the 10 to 14 group.

This age group, often referred to as "pre-teen" or "early teenager," covers grades 5-9 and has much in common with the 8 to 12 age group. Books in this age category are usually illustrated. They reflect the interests that publishers had formerly associated with teenagers. The books publishers are now offering the 10 to 14 age group attempt to bridge the difficult gap between childhood and adolescence.

GROWING UP AND GROWING OUT

Children this age are beginning to experience impatience with their parents, to react to strong peer pressure, to enjoy a sense of independent achievement, and to understand individual responsibility. This is also an age when many children stop reading. Publishers and their customers—the librarian and the teacher—are actively seeking good books for this age group, books that will keep kids reading. It's a wonderful group to write for because the fans you win—once you win them—are devoted. But it's also a difficult group to target because interests are often far ahead of reading abilities.

The Five Characteristics of Young Teens

Rebellion Children this age are striking out, however tentatively, on their own. They are pursuing interests that are different from, and often opposed to, those they have shared with their parents and families up to now. Parents no longer have the last word.

Independence The information base broadens at this age. No longer do parents control what their children are exposed to. Kids may go off to camp, stay up late watching television, depend on friends for insights, and be influenced by teachers, librarians, scouting leaders, and other adults they meet.

Puberty The 8 to 12 group is sexually segregated: this changes as children move into the 10 to 14 group. Now there are parties and dances, and giggles over the opposite sex. Young teens are interested in being pretty or handsome. They are turning to books to answer their most intimate questions about menstruation and acne, birth control and dating, clothes and grooming.

Personal Accomplishment A sense of personal accomplishment enhances ten- to fourteen-year-olds' confidence in studying new fields and trying new activities. They want to know "how" as well as "what about." As their interests become more specialized, they want both specific *and* general information. There is room for more than one title about a given subject.

Peer Pressure School, scouting, and neighborhood groups become more important to children of this age than previously. Influenced by what their peers think, children develop strong feelings about teachers. It's not uncommon for a child to say "I love him" or "I hate her," and these opinions affect dislikes and enthusiasms for the subjects the teachers are teaching. Through reading, young teenagers can be turned on to subjects they've never been exposed to before.

For the ten- to fourteen-year-old who continues to read, books can be an important part of growing up. The early teens are a time when children want to read the books their friends are reading, when they want to enrich their understanding of a classroom subject or increase their expertise in a hobby. It is a solitary time too, when personal concerns about growing up are eased by books written by sympathetic authors on sensitive subjects.

Reading ability in this age group varies widely. Some children this age can master teenage books, while others are still exploring the 8 to 12 category because their reading ability limits them. In general, however, the reading ability of this group is pretty solid. They have been reading books on their own for at least a couple of years. Their other abilities, including skill in sports, mastery of crafts projects, and the responsibility to act independently of their parents, all conspire to encourage them to try new things and expand their horizons.

But these kids are not yet teenagers. They still depend on pictures to help them understand key concepts in nonfiction. Their interests include the interests of childhood: animals, holiday projects, playground sports, and activities shared with friends. The so-called "young adult" book, geared to the twelve- to sixteen-year-old, doesn't offer the background or the step-by-step supervision they expect from a nonfiction book geared to the 10 to 14 age group. When publishers developed the latter, they were mindful that they were addressing an in-between group, with one foot firmly planted in childhood, and the other moving tentatively toward adult interests.

WHO WANTS WHAT

Writers for this age group are gratified by the range of topics which appeal to their readers. The offerings for the 8 to 12 age group are, as we have noted, read omnivorously by third, fourth, fifth, and sixth graders, the upper elementary grades. More advanced readers, especially those in junior high, are ready for the next step. The fifth grader who loved Vicki Cobb's *Science Projects You Can Eat* is now ready to step up to A. Harris Stone's *Have a Ball,* a collection of more advanced science projects. Writers for this age group are not constrained by the extensive need for introductory background material that characterizes the true introduction for the 8 to 12 group. As you write for the 10 to 14s, you can assume that your readers have a basic framework of information and are eager to add to it. They are also interested in more specific subject areas, such as stilts, statistics, and Sioux Indians, rather than overviews of toys, numbers, and Native Americans.

If you want to write for the 10 to 14 group, you are freer to explore new subjects than any other writer of children's nonfiction. The subjects can be very specific, even advanced, and the audience will most likely be receptive. Young teenagers are capable of trying new subjects and undertaking new projects; they aren't turned off, as teenagers often are, by the formats of children's books. A teenager with a special interest usually turns to an adult book for further information.

Yet there are guidelines for success in writing for this age group that the writer should be aware of. The constraints are far fewer than they are for other age groups, but the formula that emerges from a study of hundreds of books gives the author some rules that are worth considering. Note that I say *consider.* You can break all the rules you want as long as you understand what your audience—from editor, to teacher, to librarian, to the child—is looking for.

Crafts

Craft books are very popular with this age group because they not only call on a child's reading ability, but also cater to the development of other skills that children pick up outside of books.

Elyse Sommer wrote a book on decoupage that is carefully geared in reading ability and art expertise to the 10 to 14 age group. Her directions, liberally illustrated, reflect a keen understanding of her audience. The projects are shorter than they would be for an adult book on the same subject, but they reflect the full diversity of this specialized craft. Like most craft books, Sommer's *Decoupage* finds its biggest audience among girls. A Girl Scout troop may find that a decoupage project is just the thing for a fundraiser or Christmas project. Other craft books, like Barbara Corrigan's *Sew It!*, are also aimed at girls. Writers for this age group find that even though their readers share social activities, craft activities are often broken down along sex lines. Interests that capture girls' attention are often spurned by boys.

Cars and crafts

Harvey Weiss is one author who writes craft books for both boys and girls. His first series, for Young Scott books, explores the various media at an artist's disposal. *Paint, Brush, and Palette; Paint Brush and Roller;* and *Clay, Wood, and Wire* appeal to both boys and girls. These books did well for Weiss, but he really scored when he moved to Crowell Publishers and developed a craft series appealing to boys. *The Gadget Book, How to Run a Railroad, Model Cars and Trucks and How to Make Them,* and *Motors and Engines and How They Work* are especially geared to boys. Of course, girls read these books and make the models that Weiss describes, but the real appeal of these books is that a teacher or librarian serving a whole community of children can recommend them to boys without taking the chance that the books will be dismissed as "sissy." Parents and adults working with children welcome these books because they give boys a chance to exercise creativity without resorting to such typically feminine pursuits as sewing, embroidery, or crocheting.

Crafts have traditionally been big business for the 10 to 14 age group. Ten years ago any craft book could find a publisher, no matter how sloppily it was put together. But publishing is subject to trends, and editors today look for originality and thoroughness before they offer to publish a crafts book.

Harvey Weiss is one author whose craft books represent the qualities publishers look for in this area. He is known as a "perennial producer," a term publishers use for reliable and creative authors who produce books year after year. These "perennial producers" become known to their read-

Insect Zoo volunteers did the gluing of a cockroach mob caught in the act of scrabbling. The point of the exhibit is that Nature produces in abundance. If the offspring of one roach pair survive for three generations, then a kitchen like this one becomes a disaster area, and the cook copes with 130,000 roaches.

The dead roaches for the glue job came as a gift from the U.S. Department of Agriculture. At the museum they were freeze-dried to keep them from rotting, and then they were sprayed with insecticide. Not, it seems, with enough. For before the gluers began their work, tiny dermestid beetles had invaded the buckets of roaches and done quite a bit of chewing.

It was lucky the damage happened here to these all-alike members of the most common household species, *Blattella germanica,* which are nothing more than props for show. If there'd been nibbling at any of the 117,000 roaches in the study collection upstairs (where each roach is labeled with when it was collected, by whom and where), there'd have been an awful commotion.

As it was, work went ahead. It was slow and meticulous. Some high-school student volunteers carried kitchen panels home and bags of bugs to glue at odd moments. They'd spell out "Hi, Mom!" and "Tina" and draw a giraffe in bug bodies and then camouflage their jokes with more roaches. Now visitors photograph each other in front of the roach kitchen. No one has complained that the total number is not 130,000. Work stopped 50,000 short.

This double page spread from Auks, Rocks and the Odd Dinosaur *(Crowell, 1985) reflects author Peggy Thompson's understanding of the middle-graders' appetite for wacky information.*

ers, and librarians and teachers look forward to their new offerings.

"I always have a book in the pipeline," Weiss admits. His Connecticut farmhouse is surrounded by sculpture that he has created, and he is busy with university teaching. But Weiss makes time for writing books for young people, about one every year or so. First, in tandem with his editor, Marilyn Kriney at T. Y. Crowell, he develops an idea for a book. He tries to find subjects that lend themselves to the tinkering mentality but go beyond the simple how-to. In *Motors and Engines and How They Work,* he begins with a paragraph that is a model of effortless prose:

> Late one afternoon, I sat down and tried to think of how many motors and engines I had seen or used in the course of the day. There were so many, I finally lost count. First was the alarm clock that woke me up in the morning. That has two engines inside: a spring engine that turns the hands on the face of the clock and another that makes the alarm sound . . .

This charming opening paragraph sounds as if the author just sat down at the typewriter and wrote what came into his head. Weiss is the first to admit that this seemingly effortless style is difficult to establish. He works hard to set a tone that engages his readers' interest while he covers the specifics of the subject.

After the manuscript has been typeset, Weiss creates a dummy book, filling in illustrations to complement the text. Since he not only explains the engines in the book but also explains, painstakingly, how to build a model of each type discussed, the diagrams he draws are an important part of the book. Weiss fleshes out the illustration material by obtaining photographs of engines and motors at work.

A hallmark of the books is Weiss's use of the caption. "I know a lot of my readers pay attention to captions," he says. "Captions serve to capture the attention of a kid who might want to take my book out of the library. They also give the browser a good idea of the points that I make in the text." The captions for each illustration take hours to compose, since they are a distillation of Weiss's conversational style of writing in the text. "The captions come last," he says. "Sometimes they are as long as the text."

Sports for Boys and Girls

The writer of the sports book for this age group faces the same problems as the writer of the craft book. The author depends not only on the reading skill of the audience, but on athletic skill as well. The need for careful how-to instructions, reinforced with illustrative diagrams and photographs of athletes in action, is just as great. George Sullivan, who has written sports books for both boys and girls, knows that his work hasn't ended when his manuscript is complete. Sullivan combs photo archives and sometimes takes his own photographs to get the illustrations that will complement his text. But illustrations can create problems, too: feminists sometimes protest that there are no pictures of girls making touchdowns or boys practicing dance aerobics in the books. His editor at Dodd, Mead recognizes the problem but takes it with a grain of salt. "I have never heard of a boy interested in synchronized swimming," she says. Yet when Sullivan wrote a book called *Synchronized Swimming for Girls*, the letters came pouring in: "Why don't you have any pictures of boys?"

Whether for girls, or boys, or both, sports books are usually good sellers. While craft book writers must sometimes adjust to wild fluctuations in the market, writers of sports books always know they have an audience. The problem with writing about sports is how to approach the subject in a new way. "Baseball books were a glut on the market," says Barbara Francis, the editor at Prentice-Hall. "But when I was offered what I thought was just another baseball book, I discovered that with the recent rule changes there was room—even demand—for a new introductory baseball book."

Old Favorites

Some topics for the 10 to 14 age group don't change. When editor Clare Costello at Scribner's was presented with a book by Kathleen Lasky called *Dollmaker*, she knew immediately that the book was suited to that age group. Why? "The subject matter was right . . ." she said, revealing an editor's instinct. But there is a lot behind this instinct: if you consider the subject matter—how beautiful dolls are made and restored—you can see that it is a little beyond the 8 to 12 group. Yet slightly older girls (and note that the audience is pretty much limited to girls) still have the dolls they loved when they were younger. They are interested in dolls as art objects, not as toys and companions as their younger siblings still are. They can appreciate the beauty of dolls that are collectors' items and understand the process of restoration that is required to bring dolls, abused by years of little-girl love, back to their original beauty. A teenager in the 12 to 16 age group is less interested in the accoutrements of childhood—dolls have less appeal—but the idea is perfect for the 10 to 14 age group. Illustrated with photographs, *Dollmaker* has done very well, because the subject matter, the illustrated format, and the age group interest were coordinated by a concerned author and an experienced editor.

"When I grow up . . ."

Not many children will grow up to be doll restorers, but *Dollmaker* reflects a recent trend that is popular in publishing. Children are interested in hobbies that lead to careers. The career objective of a young teenager may be realistic, but more often "dream careers" have a special appeal. Yvonne Anderson capitalizes on young teens' interest in movie making in her book *Make Your Own Animated Movies*. The author gets the dreamy director-to-be off to a good start by explaining the rudiments of filmmaking. She discusses positioning, filming, simulating motion, synchronizing, and splicing in a carefully illustrated book that gets star-struck kids into making movies of their own.

Girls of this age can become fascinated with ballet as a career. Walter Terry exploits this interest in his book *Ballet: A Pictorial History*. He uses a biographical approach to capture his readers' attention and to teach them to enjoy ballet. Though this demanding career is not for most boys and girls, it does lead them to an appreciation of an entertainment that can be a lifelong pleasure.

Sports heroes offer the same glamour for young teenagers. Sports biographies require a special skill, combining biographical information—always an effective hook with young readers—with sports statistics. "Two things from my childhood reading strongly influenced my writing today," says Robert B. Jackson, the biographer of such sports heroes as Earl the

Pearl Monroe, Joe Namath, and Bobby Orr. "They were the importance of action and the need to explain some factors that adults take for granted but which children question." A working librarian, Jackson is in touch both with what kids ask for and what adults wish kids would read. He writes on popular subjects to satisfy the demands of his young library patrons, but he tries to hone his writing to the highest standards of teachers and librarians. "I'm always spotting possible improvements," he admits, "even in published things."

Heroes and Histories

The biographical approach works for leisure-time interests, and it is also effective for school assignments. The 10 to 14 reader is looking for identification as well as information. You can look upon this approach as sugar-coating the pill, but it works well for this age group. In his biography of Anwar Sadat, George Sullivan caters to this group's special needs by tracing Sadat's life from his childhood on. Since the reader wants to identify with the subject, a concentration on childhood is one of the characteristics of good biographical writing for children. The 10 to 14 age group doesn't need as much emphasis as do younger children, but they are still vitally interested in what heroes were like when they were the reader's age. A careful balance between the subject's childhood and his adult accomplishments is reflected in Sullivan's clear account of the complicated character of both Sadat and the Middle East. This emphasis proved appealing not only to young teenagers, but also to adults. Thousands of adult readers, stunned by the senseless assassination that occurred the very week this book was first published, found Sullivan's approach readable and pertinent.

Children of this age group have a taste for the contemporary hero, whether in sports, politics, or entertainment. Historical biography, so popular with the eight- to twelve-year-old group, is not as likely to catch on with the 10 to 14s, who are influenced by newspapers, television, and movies in their choice of heroes—*unless you can develop a special angle*. John Ernst, who has written for several age levels, wrote a biography of Jesse James for the 10 to 14 age group. Here the historical biography succeeded because the author, the former juvenile editor at Doubleday, recognized that kids are breaking away from parental values and looking for their own heroes and anti-heroes at this age. Jesse James has quite a reputation as a swaggering outlaw, and this appeals to kids. Ernst, as a historian, wanted to debunk the myth of James as a champion of the poor, a sort of latter-day Robin Hood. Rather than propagandizing, he sticks closely to the facts, letting the bloody murders that James perpetrated speak for themselves. At the end of this grisly but fascinating book, James emerges as anything but a hero.

The writer who is interested in history for children needs to find a way to engage the reader, and an emphasis on a hero's childhood is a good way of interesting the reader in his adult accomplishments. In turn, a biographical approach can acquaint children with concepts of civics and history that you would normally expect to find only in textbooks. Douglas Liversidge, the author of biographies of Lenin, Stalin, and Prince Charles, included in his biography of Elizabeth II some background information that one wouldn't expect to find in a children's book. "In *A Picture Biography of Queen Elizabeth*, I gave not only biographical material but explained in simple terms what the British constitutional monarchy really means," he comments. "Many adults, as well as young people, would gain information by reading this book." Adults can pretend that they know all they need to know, but children are still frank about their curiosity.

A more indirect way of approaching history is through the group biography. Janet Stevenson, in *The First Book of Women's Rights*, includes short biographies of suffragettes to help young girls get a handle on questions of equality and womanhood. By using a biographical approach, the author keeps the subject down to a manageable size, and increases the reader's interest in the historical subject matter. Stevenson is aware of history, and she says of her varied books, which also include *Spokesmen for Freedom*: "In the field of writing for young readers, I seem to have ridden two horses only: stories that concern the long American struggle for equal rights—black and white, men and women; and stories about women in roles where they're not usually expected to appear. Maybe after all, it's the same horse." Like Stevenson, the writer can find a field of history that is of interest, and using the same research and subject area, create a body of work. In Stevenson's case, the ability to combine history with biography has made her a favorite with the ten- to fourteen-year-olds.

Science and Nature

School assignments play a big part in getting kids to study history. History for this age group requires an understanding of the upper elementary and junior high curriculum. This doesn't mean that you have to go out and get a Ph.D. in education, but it does mean that you should talk to teachers and librarians to acquaint yourself with the subjects being studied in school. For the writer who doesn't cotton to this kind of research but wants to write nonfiction anyway, there is the subject of nature, always a favorite with this age group as the kids discover the great outdoors. "I prefer to write nature and conservation books for young people," says veteran author J. J. McCoy, who has written seventeen books for children. "I firmly believe that young people are more interested in these areas—and that they have the task of undoing the damage to the environment which was done by past generations. For instance, I wrote *The Hunt for the Whooping Cranes* because the plight of the cranes was desperate and needed to be brought before more people. Few people knew—at least at the time I wrote my book—that there were fewer than fifty big cranes in the world, or that it took ten years to locate their secret nesting grounds in Northwest Canada. Today, thanks to the publicity given the cranes through my book and other media, there are more than seventy of the cranes." In nature writing, the author can make a difference by pointing out the threat of extinction or mistreatment of animals. The approach to nature writing can be downright propagandistic in a way that history or biography can't. Animals can't stand up for themselves, so the author stands up for them.

When Dorcas McClintock discusses giraffes in her book *A Natural History of Giraffes*, she points out, "The future of giraffes depends upon the efforts of the African governments to conserve at least a remnant animal population within the parks and to increase man's understanding and appreciation of these ambling creatures, full of grace." Like McCoy, McClintock expresses ideas that cannot be found in an encyclopedia. In both style and content, she is personal, selecting the facts that support her case and expressing these facts in a more poetic, less concise way. The reader feels that a person is talking, and the message becomes all the more effective.

This approach is especially appealing to ten- to fourteen-year-olds because they have moved beyond the stage where they want only facts. They are learning to synthesize, to form information into opinion and opinion into action. They admire the expert, and in them the writer finds good listeners. Helen Ross Russell, the author of field guides for Little, Brown, such as *Soil: A Field Trip Guide*, and *Winter: A Field Trip Guide* recalls her own initiation into the world of nature, which led her to create a career of writing about nature for children: "As a teenager, I started leading groups of young people on exploring trips and I learned with them. And I'm still doing it—exploring, learning, teaching. I have had some wonderful teachers who took us outside the classroom and challenged us to observe and to think, as well as the youngsters who asked questions that were best answered with 'Let's find out together.' "

In the phrase "Let's find out together" lies the secret of writing nature books for this age group. The author's exploration of the subject is a fresh look, imbued with curiosity, that is contagious to the reader. Often involved in scouting, camping, and hiking, young teens welcome books that expand their horizons. Although careful research is important in writing for this age group, it's not the starting point. The place for the writer to begin is to find a point of view that is his own, that he can write about with passion.

Dorothy Shuttlesworth is that rare kind of author who writes about nature as well as history. She offers a new way of looking at the woods in her book *Natural Partnerships*, where she explores the symbiotic relationships between birds and beasts, plants and animals, plants and plants. This kind of background book creates a context for a hiking expedition and encourages children to look at nature with an educated eye.

Sometimes the subject covered in a book is surprisingly small; in *Insect Masquerades*, author Hilda Simon presents a garden in terms of the common insect camouflages found there. She divides her subjects into those that use "traps and trickery" to frighten their prey and those whose "nightmarish" appearance is a survival asset. The result is a natural science lesson with the thrill of a science fiction story.

The same sense of accomplishment which leads a youngster to become a more informed naturalist works in other areas of science. In *Have a Ball*, scientist and teacher A. Harris Stone shows experiments about such properties as force, penetrability, spin, and elasticity. These projects are useful for either a dull Saturday afternoon or a full-fledged science project. Since interests aren't always lasting at this age, the author recognized that the young reader is not going to be able to talk his parents into buying him a lot of equipment: he limits his materials to simple objects found around the house.

History, crafts, science, and biography are all topics that the ten- to fourteen-year-old is getting to feel more confident about. School and scouting groups enhance his sense of achievement. The enthusiasm about new-found knowledge at this age is unique. As children become accustomed to school and organized leisure projects, they become more adventurous about what they want to try, and books often serve as introductions to new hobbies and interests. But look at the fiction children this age are reading: problem novels, escapist science fiction, romances. The ten- to fourteen-year-olds are growing up, and they are looking for books that will help them master that process.

Health and Grooming

In *Pretty Girl*, author Bruce Curtis addresses the grooming and hygiene questions young teenage girls have. He keeps the book from being a textbook by featuring a pair of young teen models who are twins. The emphasis of the book is on exercise, natural food, good health habits, and careful attention to grooming, precisely the lessons that home economics teachers teach their students in personal hygiene classes. But the glamorous treatment that Curtis offers sets his book aside. It's a book that teenage girls want to read, not one they *have* to read.

In *So You're Getting Braces*, Alvin and Virginia Silverstein describe the hows, whys and wherefores of this common teen experience by using their own three children as examples.

FACTS AND RESEARCH

By now you should be asking yourself whether the 10 to 14 age group is the one you want to write for. Successful writers for this age group often come from journalism, science writing, and nature writing for adults, because children at this age are interested in becoming adults and seeing the adult way of looking at things. Consider the success of *The Guinness Book of Records*. Although this is not strictly a children's book, it is popular with 10 to 14s because it contains facts, facts, facts—not the kind of facts that you would find in an encyclopedia, but facts with a special twist. The approach to information in a book for the ten- to fourteen-year-old is as important as the information itself.

No "Old News"

Information must be new in a book for this age group. As adults, we are willing to accept information that is five years old, but to kids, it's out of date. After all, they were only in kindergarten when the information was news.

Editor Connie Epstein explains how up-to-dateness in both the subject chosen to write about and in the research for the book is essential for this age group. As a case in point, she holds up a book called *Sex Hormones: Why Males and Females Are Different* by Caroline Arnold. "We're looking for people who can write," Epstein maintains. "But there are so many good writers around that we have to look beyond that, to find people who do research well, too. And to make matters even more complicated, the people who have access to new subject areas, where gound is being broken, have an added advantage. Arnold is not a scientist, but she is married to a scientist who is doing research in this area. Her up-to-date data promises a long life for the book and broad interest in its publication."

If research is your interest, you will find writing for this group very congenial. The more information contained in the book, the better they'll like it.

Writing for 10 to 14s is harder than it looks, because it is difficult to pack information into a structure that is simple enough for the reader to master. It also requires more of a gimmick than writing for the 8 to 12 group: The book has to be more specialized, a little flashier, and even more original than nonfiction books for the younger child. Yet it can't be the short adult book that is appropriate for the older teenager. It has to be carefully planned, with short, intertwined chapters.

Finding the Right Illustrations

Illustrations are also important here. Too many pictures make the book seem babyish; too few make it seem forbidding. The quality of the pictures is important, too: realistic drawings and photographs have the most appeal. As printing technology has improved, making it possible to reproduce photographs cheaply and well, photos have become more common in children's books for all ages. Yet for the 10 to 14s, the photo is especially appealing: photographs appear more modern, and you can count on the camera not to lie.

As noted earlier, captions are a good way of drawing the reader into the book. If it is attractively illustrated, with captions that lead into the text, the young reader will be far more likely to pick up a book and take it home to read.

Illustrations present another kind of research—finding just the right picture for your book. Sometimes you will have to resort to taking your own pictures, or commissioning a professional photographer to provide them. As Daniel Cohen, author of *The Magic of the Little People* and *UFOs*, points out, it can take many months to find the right picture. "On top of that, you may have to write five letters before you find the person who actually can grant you the permission to use it. Movie companies are especially bad that way. In the end, it may cost you only twenty-five dollars to use a still from a movie, but you may have to wait months before you hear anything." If you enjoy research, hunting down pictures can be as much of a challenge as hunting down facts. (Photo research will be covered in greater detail in Chapter 10.)

Should you decide to work for this age group, you will find that your efforts are rewarded. As more and more teenagers turn to adult books for information, the 10 to 14 group is booming. Good writing, up-to-date research, and careful picture handling are the three qualities that most appeal to editors.

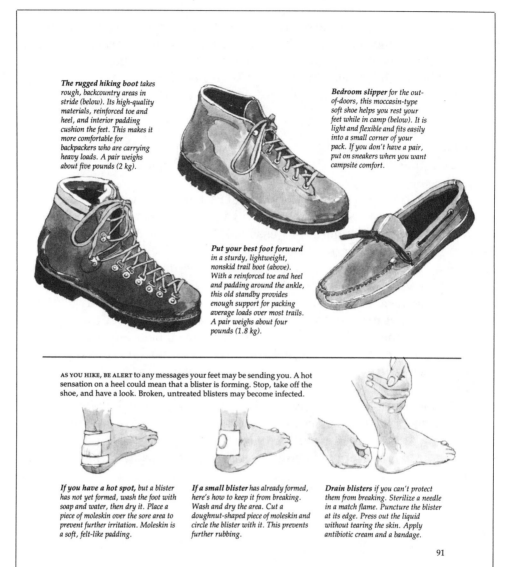

The rugged hiking boot takes rough, backcountry areas in stride (below). Its high-quality materials, reinforced toe and heel, and interior padding cushion the feet. This makes it more comfortable for backpackers who are carrying heavy loads. A pair weighs about five pounds (2 kg).

Bedroom slipper for the out-of-doors, this moccasin-type soft shoe helps you rest your feet while in camp (below). It is light and flexible and fits easily into a small corner of your pack. If you don't have a pair, put on sneakers when you want campsite comfort.

Put your best foot forward in a sturdy, lightweight, nonskid trail boot (above). With a reinforced toe and heel and padding around the ankle, this old standby provides enough support for packing average loads over most trails. A pair weighs about four pounds (1.8 kg).

AS YOU HIKE, BE ALERT to any messages your feet may be sending you. A hot sensation on a heel could mean that a blister is forming. Stop, take off the shoe, and have a look. Broken, untreated blisters may become infected.

If you have a hot spot, but a blister has not yet formed, wash the foot with soap and water, then dry it. Place a piece of moleskin over the sore area to prevent further irritation. Moleskin is a soft, felt-like padding.

If a small blister has already formed, here's how to keep it from breaking. Wash and dry the area. Cut a doughnut-shaped piece of moleskin and circle the blister with it. This prevents further rubbing.

Drain blisters if you can't protect them from breaking. Sterilize a needle in a match flame. Puncture the blister at its edge. Press out the liquid without tearing the skin. Apply antibiotic cream and a bandage.

91

In Wilderness Challenge, *a multi-author book published by the National Geographic Society, the first eight chapters cover such exciting outdoor activities as kayaking, mountain climbing, and winter camping in full-color photographic splendor. The last chapter is filled with practical outdoors information and simple line drawings to help inspired readers get started in camping and backpacking.*

CHAPTER 6

Young Adults:
Ages 12 to 16

Teenagers are not called "teenagers" by publishers. They are called "young adults." A young adult is a student at a junior or senior high school who is between the ages of twelve and sixteen. Young adult reading habits have been thoroughly dissected by reading specialists and marketing experts, only to produce some contradictory and startling conclusions. Yes, teenagers read. No, they don't read much. Teenagers prefer adult books. Wrong. Teenagers need their own books, more simply written, more profusely illustrated.

Teenagers are so various that they elude a single classification, so for the purposes of guiding you through the publisher's perception of this adolescent creature, I am going to break the teenage audience into three categories: the poor reader, the average reader, and the good reader.

1. *The poor reader who does read.* These kids like books written on the second- or third-grade level, illustrated with photographs, in a small enough format so that they aren't razzed by their peers for reading "baby books." This format is no larger than 7-by-10 inches, and usually is more like 5-by-8.
2. *The average reader* who reads only when he or she can't go to the movies or the shopping mall, listen to records or practice driving. These are the teenagers who grow up to be the *aliterates*—they can read well enough to succeed in school, but reading for pleasure is not for them.

They regard reading with the same joy and anticipation as their fathers do their stationary bikes, or their little brothers their vegetables—i.e., good for them, but not something they partake of fun. The good news is that these readers, when they *do* read, usually go for nonfiction on the theory that it will give them something to show for their efforts.

3. *The good reader*, who reads voraciously, eagerly reading and re-reading without regard to whether it's considered cool by his peers. Good readers are not necessarily those who do well in school; in fact, many teenager loners find solace in the autonomy of reading that they can't get in the more authoritative teaching they get from adults at home or at school. The best students are often the best readers, but the best readers are not so frequently the best students.

Two kinds of books are best published by young adult departments, which will promote and sell them to schools and libraries serving teenagers. The first kind features subject matter of interest to teenagers—teenage problems such as acne, alcoholism, and shoplifting; teenage enthusiasms such as motorcycles, horses, clothes, appearance, and dancing; and teen idols such as current TV stars, rock and roll giants, and sports heroes. I once talked to a librarian who bragged she had on her shelves a book about motorcycles that cost $180. Envisioning an elaborate art book, I asked her to describe it. "It's a ten-dollar book," she laughed, "but we've had to re-order it eighteen times because it keeps getting stolen!"

The second kind of book appropriate for young adult publication is the curriculum-oriented book which will supply the public and school library with fodder for homework assignments. Schoolwork in junior and senior high school includes science projects, term papers, and reading lists outside of the usual textbooks. The demand for materials that will pique and satisfy young people's interests is unending. Books about science and technology, historical biographies, and background books are in demand with teenagers who are not quite ready to master adult books on the subject.

The conventional wisdom is that girls are better readers than boys by the time they reach the teen years, and that girls prefer fiction over nonfiction. This is a myth that writers have been shattering by offering books that both boys and girls enjoy—biographies of Duran Duran, Margaret Mead, Adolf Hitler, and Ronald Reagan; advice books on divorce, sex, drugs, and college choices; how-to books on electronics, haircutting, career planning, and manners; histories that might be assigned as schoolwork, but are then further explored because they offer the teenager insight into how he got to be where he is; nature books with an activity attached, such as fishing, skiing, hiking, or rock collecting; science books with exciting ideas that the talking teen (that rare breed!) can discuss with her friends, such as genetics, artificial intelligence, or the laws of thermodynamics.

WHY WRITE FOR TEENAGERS?

Teenagers are open to new ideas, and their insistence that they aren't is a universal cover for curiosity. A fifteen-year-old may tell you that it's just too boring to sit down and read, but if he gets hold of the right book, he may well read it in places you can't watch him, like on the bus, in study hall, in the privacy of his room with the stereo blasting so loud that no adult could believe that he is concentrating. Just as a teenager collects a wardrobe of clothes for all occasions, he also develops a collection of reading styles, whatever his abilities are. Some books will be read for *escape*, others for *information*, others for *pleasure* of the emotional sort, others for *intellectual stimulation*. He will handle the material in front of him in many different ways, depending on his purpose and mood.

Escape reading is popular with even the poorest reader. To think that this kind of reading must be science fiction, romance, horror, or mystery is a mistake. Celebrity biographies, true adventure, war stories, sports records, and exposés along the lines of *All the President's Men* all appeal to the teenager's need to get away from it all.

Get with it . . . . Along with the need to get away from it all comes the desire to participate in the world, and books provide information that teens can check out before they move into the swing of things. A good example of this is *The Woman Doctor's Teenage Diet Book* by Dr. Barbara Edelman. Here the teen can find out what will happen if she goes on a diet, what the rough spots will be, what results she can realistically expect, and how to tell her friends and family that she is dieting without getting teased so hard she quits. The book arms her with information that will help her control a situation that is frightening and exciting as well.

You've got a friend. Pleasures of the emotional sort can be found in books where the author shares an experience with the reader, as Sara Gilbert's *How to Live with a Single Parent*. This is a nonfiction treatment of a subject that has dominated many a teenage novel, and the author's success lies in establishing the same kind of empathy that a novelist does. Yet there's an added dimension here that rivets the teenage reader, and that's the book's black-and-white authenticity. With interviews, she shows how each child and each parent must forge her own solution to a pervasive problem. There is no easy or universal answer, but there is an answer. Here Gilbert capitalizes on the fact that she is a former teenager who has become an adult, and she is adept at keeping both balls in the air without a false move. Nonfiction at its best both prepares the reader for fictional treatments of the same subjects and at the same time reinforces the lessons that teenagers have assimilated through fiction.

Do It Yourself   **53**

lotion. But remember. *After soap!* you have skin problems?
More often than not, soap and good food will fix 'em.

(c) *Sleep:* Not less than eight hours per night for teenagers. Better at nine or ten. (This I like.) More than ten
and someone might call you L——zy. But less than eight,
brother, what it can do to your disposition, looks, and vital-
ity!

(d) *Exercise:* Just because we stop playing tag doesn't
mean we're supposed to sit the rest of our life. As teen-agers
we need to outline a possible program for ourselves based
on our athletic interests and the facilities available, and *keep
at it.* Don't give up that bicycle too soon. I rode mine all
through high school, and my wife's when I was at college in
Texas. With a full work-study-home load it was more than
transportation. It was my daily exercise. And f'r goodness
sakes, watch your posture. I know I sound like Aunt Clara
but I can't help it. I promised to level with you and sometimes teen-agers look as if those extra inches were just too
heavy to hold up, either standing or sitting.

(e) *Teeth:* All together now . . . "brush-teeth-after-
each-meal-and-see-your-dentist-twice-a-year."

(f) *Hair:* Shampoo once a week. Brush for girls (Shirley
says fifty strokes for cleanliness and shine!), massage for boys
(let's keep it with us as long as we can!).

I always used to hate to wash my hair because I looked like
a wind-swept haystack afterward. Then Mama recommended
letting it dry under a stocking cap. Oh, boy—I looked like
a painted egg. The answer was to let the barber cut it properly and *keep it cut.* I definitely recommend haircuts and
washings for boys on the grounds of health and cleanliness,
if nothing else.

(g) *Clean clothes:* Always and often. But Great Cooga-
mooga! I didn't need to tell you that. I will tell you this,
though. A famous tap dancer I know auditioned girls for a

Typographical tricks are reinforced, in Pat Boone's 'Twixt Twelve and Twenty
*(Prentice-Hall, 1958), with celebrity photos addressing a wholesome range of
teenage problems.*

"Blow my mind!" The excitement of an intellectual idea is conveyed through nonfiction that is well written, scrupulously researched, and presented in units that are easy to swallow. In his book for teenagers on anti-Semitism, Charles Patterson explores the development of the Western antipathy towards the Jews from the time of Christ to the present. His account is informed and unemotional. For the teenager who is interested in world history, it provides a thread through the maze of events of the last two thousand years. Like Theseus at the entrance to the labyrinth, the young historian has a way of tracking his way through unconnected events because the author never loses his focus on the single unifying theme: the persecution of the Jews. For the teenager who has been reading formula novels and sensationalized news stories, the absence of opinion in this history gives him room to draw his own conclusions, with lots of facts to support his position.

TALKING TO TEENAGERS

Whatever you write for teenagers, it's imperative that you let the reader know where you're coming from. If you are writing your own adolescence, and bringing values from your childhood, not your reader's, it's fine, as long as you make your vantage point perfectly clear. Robert Curtis, a family practitioner based in San Francisco, felt that a book on alcoholism directed at teenagers was much-needed. As a doctor, he had seen the lives of many children destroyed by an alcoholic parent, and increasingly, the lives of many parents destroyed by their teenager's drinking problems. Even though he had an impressive amount of experience with alcoholics, Curtis was not content to sit down at his typewriter and pontificate. Contract in hand, Curtis and his wife talked to teenagers, went to special meetings for teenage alcoholics and supplemented his medical background with a writer's objective perspective. The book that came out of long experience and fresh research—*Questions and Answers about Alcoholism*—is direct, sympathetic, and helpful. He aimed to write a book that was contemporary, and to do so, he switched roles from doctor to writer and back again to create a book that coheres like a good piece of music in that it has a steady bass (background) and a catchy melody (here and now cases).

The sensitive writer for teenagers can make yards of difference in a teenager's thinking. Say "English history" to most teenagers and you will be greeted with a long yawn. Yet in *Mary I: The History of An Unhappy Queen*, Winifred Roll brought Mary Tudor's trials to life by discussing her competition with her more successful sister, Elizabeth I, with her father, Henry the Eighth, covering one of the more spectacular stories of sibling rivalry around. In her forays into the British Museum, Lady Roll discovered that Mary had terrible problems with her menstrual period, and, having taught high school, the author knew how interesting this information would be to teens. Although it would have been an unseemly inclusion twenty years ago, this health information was welcomed by kids and scholars alike. "Bloody Mary" emerges from Roll's book not as a cold and cruel tyrant but as a troubled young woman who was at the mercy of circumstances.

Teenagers also have a tremendous need to stay up-to-date. Rebellious at this age, any subject that interests their parents and teachers is apt to be dismissed as seriously boring. Thus the mature reader's interest in history and philosophy usually needs a protective cover to appeal to teens. Here graphics are an enormous help to the writer of young adult books, and it's often a good idea to visualize both layout and illustration as you prepare your manuscript, from the earliest outline to the finished product.

It's not always possible, but putting historical ideas in a modern context will help an author win over teen readers. For instance, a parent who grew up during the Kennedy years might find a biography of John F. Kennedy fascinating, whereas her teenage son would be far more interested if Kennedy's life were presented from the perspective of current presidential politics and policy. The author can help clarify parallels and comparisons between the politics of the sixties and the politics of the eighties, for example. Short quotations, anecdotes, and other miscellaneous tidbits can lure a teenager into reading a book on a subject that is apparently too difficult or abstract for the child's experience or abilities.

Attracting the Non-reader

The teenage non-reader is the most difficult kid to reach; books have a place in their lives, a place they don't like particularly, i.e., school. But they can get turned on to reading if the book has more of a magazine format, with graphic tricks borrowed from computer games and television. Line drawings, once considered tasteful and appropriate for the teenager, have fallen out of fashion. Adolescents who see color photos in their daily newspapers, who are used to the dynamic graphics of advice and gossip columns, and who thrive on celebrity photographs in popular magazines want photographs—and they don't have to be good ones. The role of art and design in a teenage book is to make the non-reader comfortable enough to stick with the book long enough to get involved with its text.

The poor reader also needs these visual aids, but for different reasons. For teenagers who read on the second-grade level, and there are a surprising number of them, pictures and graphics act as a guide through the text. Although large type is considered babyish, the leading can be wider than the type itself without putting the semiliterate teen off. The ample spacing, short lines, wide margins, and generous array of photographs all help the teenager master reading skills that he should have learned ten years earlier. You will find a list of publishers who specialize in "hi-lo" books, books of high interest with a low reading level, in the *Literary*

Market Place and *Writer's Market*. If you write to these publishers they will tell you which readability scale they use. There are also computer programs to help you determine which grade level a text is written for, based on the complexity of sentences, vocabulary units, length of paragraphs, and any other criteria that some expert dreams up.

PUBLISHING BOOKS FOR YOUNG ADULTS

If you are interested in writing nonfiction for the teenage audience, a good starting place is a study of the school curriculum—the curriculum guides mentioned in Chapter 1. Also study the magazines aimed at teenagers where current interests—such as health and appearance, sports, video games, and hobbies—are played up. Television can give you insight into teen interests, especially problems that plague teenagers and their families.

What most adults writing for teenagers forget is that teenagers are NOT children. They aren't adults either. Publishers have tried to pay lip service to this, but since young adult books are generated by children's departments, they tend to serve the adult's view of the adolescent, rather than the adolescent's self-view as a new adult. For this reason, more and more publishers are publishing hardcover books—bought primarily by schools, libraries, and adults shopping for presents—with the "Adult Books Recommended for Young Adults" designation. *Go Ask Alice* was published in this way, as are other perennial favorites, Gerald Durrel's *Animals of the Ark*, and *The Diary of Anne Frank*. Especially when these books are adapted for movies or television documentaries, the appeal sometimes filters down to even younger readers, sophisticated kids as young as nine or ten. Stephen Roxborough, the juvenile editor of Farrar, Straus, and Giroux, points out that his nonfiction young adult program is promoted to both markets. Roxborough figures that anything that won't interest an adult won't interest a teenager on the verge of young adulthood. Herbert and Judith Kohl's *The Social Life of Animals* is a prime example of a subject that appeals equally to the two markets.

If you feel your book has appeal to adults as well as teenagers, you are best off publishing with an adult department, which will sell your book to bookstores and to adult collections in libraries. If, however, you feel that your slant and your subject are best understood by teenagers, then you are wise to publish a young adult title through a juvenile department where a much more thorough job is done of promoting your book to young adult collections in public libraries and especially to school libraries.

In any case, as a writer for teenagers you can capture a devoted audience and help form ideas that will last a lifetime. The secret is to discuss the complex topics that interest teens in a simple way, introducing background information an adult might take for granted.

WRITING FOR THE AGE GROUP
THAT'S RIGHT FOR YOU—A SELF-TEST

What matters most in writing any book is focusing your interest and talents on the idea that's right for you, but how do you decide which age group to write for? The test that follows isn't a scientific survey or a measure of intelligence, but rather a series of questions that should get you to analyze yourself—what you think about, as well as how you think about it. Take it with a grain of salt, but take it; it will narrow down the nearly infinite possibilities in children's nonfiction and lead you in a direction that is uniquely your own.

1. Your spouse has been elected to public office. Which program will you encourage him to support?
    A. Prenatal care
    B. Alliances between Headstart kids and Grey Panthers
    C. Children's rights
    D. Raising the drinking age
    E. Community centers specializing in family activities

2. You can finally afford your dream house. It is:
    A. Active solar earth-sheltered
    B. A center-hall Colonial
    C. Rehabbed Victorian
    D. High-rise condo with view of the city
    E. Country home on five acres

3. You've just received a $20,000 advance to write a book. Where will you go to work on it?
    A. Beach house with an ocean view on Cape Cod
    B. High on a cliff in Big Sur
    C. In the mountains below the tree line in Vermont
    D. On Lake Powell in Arizona
    E. The Main Line of Philadelphia

4. Your spouse won the lottery and you are to choose the family's third car. It is a:
    A. Restored 1940's Woodie Station Wagon
    B. VW Vanagon
    C. Cadillac
    D. 4-wheel-drive jeep
    E. 12-cylinder Ferrari Testa Rossa

5. Your acting coach tells you have a great future on the stage. Which direction will you pursue?
    A. Shakespeare

B. Musical comedy
C. Henrik Ibsen
D. Neil Simon
E. Harold Pinter

6. Your employer thinks you have great managerial potential and is sending you to grad school. Which course will you follow?
A. Ph.D. in industrial psychology
B. M.B.A., concentration in finance
C. Law school with supplemental courses in art history
D. M.F.A. in creative writing
E. Master's degree in speech

7. Five women want to marry you. Which one will you choose?
A. The heiress who wants to establish herself as a poet
B. Six-foot blonde with the demanding MTV career
C. The witty school teacher you met in the supermarket
D. The single-minded animal rights activist
E. The ambitious editor of your last book

8. You've inherited two million dollars with the stipulation that half must be given to charity. Who will be the lucky one?
A. Women's Action for Nuclear Disarmament
B. The Sierra Club
C. MADD (Mothers Against Drunk Driving)
D. The Corps of Literacy Volunteers
E. American Cancer Society

9. What is your next purchase for your home writing office?
A. Cappucino machine
B. IBM PC with WordStar
C. Your fifth four-drawer filing cabinet
D. Joan of Arc bronze bookends from Sotheby's
E. A Prisma clock

10. You have to plan the menu for your sister's wedding shower. Will it be:
A. Dim Sum and shrimp toast
B. Barbequed ribs, potato salad, and dirty rice
C. High tea with watercress sandwiches, petits fours, and Scotch eggs
D. Nachos, guacamole, and margaritas
E. Ice cream cake and hot chocolate with whipped cream

11. It's vacation time and this year it's your turn to choose the spot. Where will you go?
A. Cape Hatteras

B. Club Med in Cancun
C. 21-day Eurail excursion from Brussels to Venice
D. Camping in the Great Smoky Mountains
E. A New York shopping spree with a suite at the Plaza

12. You're buying a new stereo system and take your favorite record to the store to try out. It is:
A. The "1812 Overture"
B. The *Third Brandenburg Concerto*
C. *Doc & Merle Watson's Greatest Hits*
D. Stevie Wonder *In Square Circle*
E. Keith Jarrett's *Köln Concert*

13. Your kids have worn you down. You've promised that this Christmas they can get a pet. Is it:
A. Guinea pigs
B. An Abyssinian queen
C. AKC runt from the neighbors' litter
D. A tank full of tropical fish
E. An Icelandic pony

14. It's finally Friday night and time to unwind. Do you:
A. Watch old movies on TV
B. Invite the neighbors over for bridge
C. Paint the town red with a final stop at the all-night deli
D. Curl up to talk with a friend
E. Do your laundry

15. Your spouse has a convention in Chicago. What spot do you not want to miss?
A. Shopping at Water Tower Place
B. Night life on Rush Street
C. University of Chicago's Oriental Museum
D. Second City's latest production
E. The Art Institute

16. You've finally saved enough for your trip to Ireland. Which do you consult first?
A. *Trinity* by Leon Uris
B. William Butler Yeats's poetry
C. Your psychic
D. Your American Express credit line
E. Road Atlas of Ireland

17. Your daughter has received a National Merit Scholarship. You don't want to influence her choice of college but where would you just love to see her go?

A. Columbia
B. Cal Tech
C. Your alma mater
D. Tulane
E. Wellesley

18. Your mother-in-law just got her degree in landscape design and offers to redo your backyard. What'll it be?
    A. Bonsai
    B. Formal English garden
    C. French boxwood maze
    D. Dwarf cherry orchard
    E. Golf lawn

KEY TO SCORING THE SELF TEST

Circle the answer you gave to each question. If the majority of your answers fell in one or two age groups, it may be that you have a special bent for writing for, say, preschoolers or young adults. But it doesn't matter if you're spread all over the columns. That may simply mean you're versatile and adaptable and can write for many different age groups. In Part Two, you'll learn how to find the book idea that's right for you and how to tailor it to an age group—how to research it, write it, find (or do your own) illustrations, and envision the finished product.

	Ages 2-5	Ages 6-9	Ages 8-12	Ages 10-14	Ages 12-16
1.	A.	E.	B.	C.	D.
2.	E.	B.	C.	A.	D.
3.	C.	A.	E.	D.	B.
4.	A.	D.	B.	C.	E.
5.	B.	E.	D.	C.	A.
6.	E.	A.	B.	C.	D.
7.	A.	D.	C.	E.	B.
8.	A.	D.	E.	B.	C.
9.	D.	E.	C.	B.	A.
10.	E.	B.	A.	C.	D.
11.	A.	D.	C.	E.	B.
12.	C.	D.	A.	B.	E.
13.	A.	E.	C.	B.	D.
14.	D.	E.	B.	A.	C.
15.	E.	C.	A.	D.	B.
16.	B.	E.	D.	C.	A.
17.	C.	E.	D.	B.	A.
18.	C.	D.	A.	B.	E.

PART TWO

The Nuts and Bolts of Writing Your Book

Since boyhood I had planned to write books and illustrate them. I kept notebooks crammed with verses, descriptive phrases and story ideas. Naturally there were sketches to accompany them. . . . The result was publication of my first book.
—Holling C. Holling

This child
was sick
and they called
a medicine man
to cure him.

What magic
is he using?

What special
chants
and dances
and whispered words
and feathered wands
may have helped
a boy
get well again?

And
did medicine
made from
dry roots
and flowers
and wild
yellow grasses
taste
like
pink medicine
tastes now?

Tom Bahti used designs from prehistoric Indian pottery to illustrate Byrd Baylor's When Clay Sings *(Charles Scribner's Sons, 1972), a beautifully evocative introduction to anthropology for 6- to 9-year-olds.*

CHAPTER 7

Good Ideas— And What to Do About Them

I deas are essential. Finding an idea that interests you enough to stick with it through the long process of writing and publication takes a great deal of effort, but you can make that effort a little more effortless with a touch of inspiration.

Ideas are everywhere, and you must be willing to search unstintingly to collect an array of ideas to write about. You won't use every idea you find, but the larger the pool from which you can choose, the better you can create the book you have in mind.

WHERE DO IDEAS COME FROM?

The hunt for book ideas can begin anywhere. Newspapers are great, especially fillers, those odd little blurbs that show up between articles. But local and national news offer many idea opportunities as well. Start by clipping any article that interests you, even an obituary! Throw it into a file, or if you aren't that organized, into an old shoebox or supermarket bag. Do this for several weeks at least, for several months if you can stand to wait. Then take the time to go through them to see if you can sort them according to a common theme.

Television is another natural source for ideas. As you watch soap operas and sitcoms, notice the nonfiction details: the architecture of the houses, the kinds of pets the family keeps, the subjects of conversation in the dialogues. Television also serves as an excellent bellwether for new fads and upcoming trends.

Radio talk shows are frequently forums for book writers. Here you can get a sense of what's new and what adult books are being published on various subjects. Combine this information with your interest in children and you may come up with a honey of an idea.

Or try writing down instructions, in full detail, of things you do every day—repotting a plant, baking bread, changing a tire, mailing a letter, balancing your checkbook, rewiring a lamp. See if there are how-to concept book ideas suggested by your daily routine.

Librarians and parents know what kids are interested in. Librarians can sometimes tip you off on books that are needed, as well as what's especially popular. And kids themselves—your own, the neighbors', the ones you encounter on the bus—can sometimes provide very good ideas. So can a close study of the books and magazines they're reading.

In addition to talking to children, think about your own childhood. What subjects interested you with a passion? What did you like—and dislike—most about school? Did you like to read? What were your favorite books? The answers to these questions may point you in the direction of a nonfiction book idea.

The Bright-Ideas Journal

A journal, one of the most personal forms of writing, is a good starting point for any writer. Buy yourself a beautifully bound blank book or a utilitarian three-ring binder and record your thoughts, flashes of insight, and surges of inspiration as they occur. Train yourself to write down ideas in your journal every day, even when you think you're uninspired or just too busy. Are you really busy, or are you falling into the Next Week's Chores Syndrome, indulging in busywork to avoid the harder work of creation? If you have no special thoughts for the day, seek out some stimulation—walk in the woods, strike up a conversation with a child, visit an art museum, browse through the children's book section of your library.

Writing every day can not only help you acquire some professional habits, it can also release your more outrageous ideas. Furious at your husband, you might recall that the first expedition to the South Pole did not include any women (because you're thinking of sending your husband there). Exhilarated by a handwritten letter from a dear friend, you might be better able to write the dramatic scene where an Indiana family in the nineteenth century receives a letter from Harvard accepting their young son.

Or, if emotion is not your thing, you might approach extraordinary or dramatic passages from your careful descriptions of ordinary events: your daughter's first filling might give you insight into the thrilling discoveries of anesthetics, watching the osprey from the deck of your boat might bring to life the tragedy of total extinction of many marine birds.

The secret of the bright-ideas journal is to refrain from looking back through it, at least for a time. Approaching each new day with a clean sheet, untrammeled by the moods and reactions of the day before, will give you a long view of your recurring interests, your observations on different subjects that dovetail with one another. After you have recorded a month's random notes without missing a day, set aside an evening or an afternoon, free from distractions, and look over what you have written. After you have read it through, it's time to *think*. Try to clear your mind and remember what you have written. What comes to mind first? Why did you think of that one idea before the myriad of others you wrote about? Is there anything in your journal that surprises you?

By thoughtfully reviewing your journal, you will discover things about yourself that perhaps you never consciously knew: that you are more interested in weather than you are in the seasons, or that you have that second cup of coffee every morning because you are fascinated by the never-ending battle between the squirrel and blue jay at the bird feeder. You may create word portraits of people you never thought were that important, or evocative descriptions of places you had come to take for granted, as you scrutinize them more closely.

The Bright-Ideas File

After you have spent a good long time pondering what you've written, you are ready to create a file of bright ideas. You'll need a pen, a stack of 3x5 cards, and a sturdy file box. You will also need a lot of discipline and no distractions, because you will be arranging your ideas with the detachment and precision of a researcher tabulating statistics. This is a step that is particularly important because each idea has to be book-sized: not too slight, not too unwieldy.

On the next page, you will see a list of possible ideas for index card entries. This is not a comprehensive list, or even a suggested one. It's simply a starting point for you to develop your own categories, based on your own interests and experiences.

In contrast to your spontaneity in jotting down observations and ideas in your journal, you will want to set up your card file with a tough professionalism. The cards should be kept in their own box, alphabetically arranged.

After you have systematically arranged the thoughts of thirty days, you will almost certainly find that you have chosen certain themes, like sports or social situations, as ones that hold day-to-day interest for you. Some people who have captured your interest may even have been growing into full-fledged biographical subjects right there in your journal.

If you are lucky you have a spouse like Gardner Soule's. Janie Soule has compiled an extremely well-organized card file system that starts with general entries like "fish" and ends up with an entry for the most uncommon deep-sea creature. "We try to know anything about an animal we write up, or about any phase of oceanography," says Soule.

Every three weeks, look over what you've collected in your journal and transfer your ideas to cards. As you're doing this, look for subjects that recur in different ways: motorcycle safety, history of motorcycles, engines and motorcycles as machines; lightning as electricity, simple wiring and fuse systems, stage lighting; history of headgear, shoes of many nations, how to sew a jumpsuit. Also try out combinations: ethnic holidays and their crafts, battles and their heroes, taxonomy and giraffes, the Underground Railroad and astronomy, the reasons for your area's weather.

SAMPLE CARD FILE ENTRIES

SUGGESTED CATEGORIES	SPECIFIC EXAMPLES
Current Events	Children as the Peacemakers Who's Who in the Middle East What's the World Population?
Daily Routines	Supermarket: Where Food Comes From Housework—a Guide for Kids Manners for Modern Children
Geography	A Child's Guide to the U.S.A. Swamps of the Southern States Oceans of the Earth
Health	Nutrition and What It Can Do for You Groomed for Success (YA) Hygiene for Preschoolers
History	History of the U.S. Mail To Be an American: Immigrant Stories Growing Up Long Ago
Arts and Crafts	Simple Musical Instrument Construction Make Masks Out of Papier Mâché Christmas Presents You Can Sew
Animals and Pets	Your Very Own Kitten All About Fish How to Identify Wild Animal Tracks

Biography	Religion and Rock 'n' Roll
	Pete Rose, Cincinnati's Favorite Son
	Buckminster Fuller: Renaissance Man
Changes and Transformations	Building a Bridge
	Why the Seasons Change
	Growing Up
Math	Math Problems in Everyday Life
	Geometric Puzzles You Can Make
	Country Counting Book
Psychology/Self-Help	Divorce: A Teen Survival Guide
	Death of a Grandparent
	What Makes a Person *Good?*
Science	Our Solar System
	Spore Reproduction
	Rocks All Over the World
Social Studies	Born on a Farm
	Series Idea: Children of the World
	What's It Like to Live in Russia?
Sports/Recreation	Ballooning
	Soccer Techniques
	Campfire Cookery

After you have built up the card file over a period of three or four months, you are ready to choose a subject to write about. Look back over your card entries, and find an idea that captures your imagination—something that excites you so much your fingers itch to write about it. Then give yourself time to *think*—play with the idea for a while. A long walk, a few laps around the pool, or even mopping the floor can give you the space you need to develop that idea floating around in your head. Think about the different ways the idea could be handled, think about how you would most like to present it, think about who the idea is for.

The age group you want to focus on will also be an important consideration, but getting a clear idea of what you want to write is the heart of the matter. Getting a clear idea of *why* you want to write it—i.e., why you want to write for a children's rather than an adult audience—can also be of benefit in getting the creative motors running.

Following are ten reasons you might consider for writing your book, and examples of authors whose books have expressed these ideas.

TEN REASONS FOR WRITING FOR CHILDREN

1. **As a teacher, parent, librarian, or other interested adult, you see a subject that's been neglected and about which you have something to say.**
Cathedral: The Story of Its Construction by David Macaulay (Houghton Mifflin)
People by Peter Spier (Doubleday) Grades 1-3
Ham Radio by Louis I. Kuslan and Richard D. Kuslan (Prentice-Hall) Grades 7-up

2. **You are not satisfied with the way a much-published subject for kids is handled; this lack fits an interest of yours and you have an original approach.**
One God: The Ways We Worship Him by Florence Mary Fitch (Lothrop)
A Puppy is Born by Heiderose Fischer-Nagel and Andreas Fischer (Putnam Publishing Group) Preschool-Grade 2
The Joy of Chickens by Dennis Nolan (Prentice-Hall) Grades 7-up

3. **You can present a difficult subject simply and objectively.**
Anti-Semitism: The Road to the Holocaust and Beyond by Charles Patterson (Walker & Co.) Grades 8-up
Abraham Lincoln: For the People by Anne Colver (Garrard) Grades 2-5
A Tree Is Nice by Janice M. Udry (Harper Junior Books) Preschool-Grade 1

4. **You see ways of introducing kids to "deadly" subjects in an interesting way.**
The Paper Airplane Book (physics) by Seymour Simon (Viking) Grades 4-6
The Popcorn Book (botany) by Tomie DePaola (Holiday) Grades K-3
Zero is Not Nothing (mathematics) by Harry Sitomer and Mindel Sitomer (Crowell Junior Books) Grades 1-3
Mojo Means One: A Swahili Counting Book (foreign language) by Muriel Feelings (Dial Books) Grades K-up

5. **You see an easy way for kids to master adult skills.**
Photography and Film by Jonathan Rutland and Terry Collins (Silver Burdette)
Sewing with Scraps by Phyllis Guth and Georgeanna Goff (TAB Books) Grades 10-up
Eight Ate: A Feast of Homonym Riddles by Marvin Terban (Houghton Mifflin) Grades 1-3

6. **You want to share your own growing up—its similarities and differences.**
Lumberjack by William Kurelek (Houghton-Mifflin) Grades 1-up
My Animals by Nan Hayden Agle
Homesick: My Own Story by Jean Fritz (Putnam Publishing Group)

7. **You have a strong commitment to a political, religious, or ethnic theme that you want to share with kids.**
In Their Own Words: A History of the American Negro, 1619-1865 by Milton Meltzer (Crowell Junior Books) Grades 5-up
Little Witch's Christmas Book by Linda Glovach (Prentice-Hall) Grades 1-4
To Be a Slave by Julius Lester (Scholastic) Grades 7-up

8. **You want to explain to kids why rules exist.**
A Tale of Two Bicycles by Leonard P. Kessler (Lothrop)
Arson! by Arnold Madison (Watts) Grades 5-up
How We Choose a President by Lee L. Gray (St. Martin's)
Dinosaur Do's and Don'ts by Jean B. Polhammus (Prentice-Hall) Grades 1-up

9. **You have an inspiration that just happens to be a children's book.**
Alphabet Sheep by George Mendoza (Putnam Publishing Group) Grades K-2
Tall City, Wide Country: A Book to Read Forward and Backward by Seymour Chwast (Viking) Preschool-Kindergarten
An Edwardian Summer by John S. Goodall (Atheneum)

10. **The research you're doing for a novel, picture book, movie script, or magazine article gives you an idea for a children's book.**
Lila Perl spun off her novel, *Me and Fat Glenda*, to a children's book, *How America Eats*.
Writing *Number Twenty-Four*, a fantasy about traffic accidents, inspired Guy Billout to explore transportation in his nonfiction book, *By Camel and By Car*.
Higgelty Piggelty Pop: Or, There Must Be More to Life starred Maurice Sendak's beloved sheepdog Jenny. He enjoyed drawing dogs so much that he created *Some Swell Pup*, a book about dog care.

Little Brown Bat

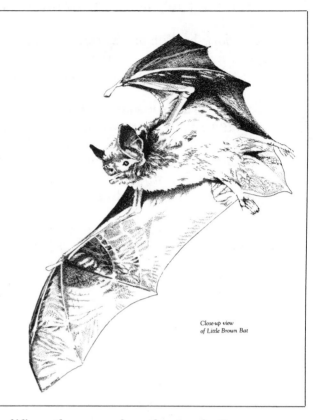

Living everywhere in the United States is another kind of bat called the Little Brown Bat. Some types are 2 or 3 inches long. Others are even more tiny. Their head and body measure little more than 1 inch. Six of them together will weigh about 1 ounce.

Little Brown Bats are born in spring and summer. At that time, the mother bats all roost together in a group, away from the male bats. This is called a *maternity colony*. Sometimes there are 10,000 bats in one colony.

Red Bats and Little Brown Bats eat insects. Some bats eat other things.

6

*Close-up view
of Little Brown Bat*

Even after scores of books, this prolific author never loses her touch. Here, Walter Kessell's beautiful, detailed line drawings complement Miriam Schlein's descriptions of a variety of bats in Billions of Bats *(J. B. Lippincott, 1982).*

CHAPTER 8

Researching Your Subject

I f you are afraid of research, forget writing nonfiction for children." This advice comes from Jean Fritz but is echoed by all the writers I interviewed. Indeed, there are few authors who do not *enjoy* research, and many are keenly aware that good research almost always creates ideas for new books. But most of all, research for children's nonfiction is quite special, and often tougher than research for adult books. In order to arouse and keep youngsters' interest you have to dig for facts that differ from those usually presented in textbooks and encyclopedias. You are looking for interesting, funny, even trivial details that especially appeal to children. Here's how to do research with young readers in mind.

First, it's helpful to consult several encyclopedias: one designed for children, such as the *World Book;* one for the general public, like the *Encyclopaedia Britannica;* one for experts in a field, such as the *Encyclopedia of Social Sciences*, or the *World of Mathematics;* and handy reference, like *The World Almanac.* Once you have done this, and have an overview of your subject, stay away from those books. An encyclopedia has a purpose: to convey the most information in the shortest space. Kids love encyclopedias, learn to use them in the second or third grade, and often have them at home as the only books the family owns. A nonfiction book for children is NOT a rehash of an encyclopedia article, becomingly illustrated; it is a book by a big person for a small person, with due respect for the small person's curiosity and the big person's experience paid in full.

SOURCES

Research makes use of original sources and secondary sources, and while it is possible to base a book solely on either one, in most cases a combination of both is necessary. Usually, too, the combination will produce a superior book.

Original sources consist of anything that has never been published, and can include interviews; observations of places, natural events, and human endeavors; personal experiences from doing-it-yourself and/or teaching; or contents of certain documents (which might be found in a library or museum).

Secondary sources are materials someone recorded first, i.e., books, newspaper and magazine articles, letters, manuscripts, videotapes, film clips, etc. The library, of course, is the most common center for research of secondary sources. Some authors have the privilege of using a special university library or have easy access to a big city library.

On the other hand, the absence of a large library doesn't have to be a handicap. Daniel Cohen, who is only in his mid-forties and has already written more than sixty books on science (*Intelligence, What Is It?*), animals (*Watchers in the Wild, Night Animals*), paranormal and mysterious matters (*The World of UFOs, The Body Snatchers, Curses, Hexes and Spells*), and religion (*New Believers: Young Religion in America*), lives in the small town of Port Jervis, N.Y.. He is happy with the local library which has, through interlibrary loans, access to other larger collections. A former long-time managing editor at *Science Digest* magazine and a member of the Committee for Scientific Investigation of Claims of the Paranormal, Cohen relies heavily on his own experience, his vast files, and his menagerie of cats, dogs, and other animals—that he claims makes his roomy house a "combination office and zoo."

Even if your research isn't from books and records, you will find places that can help you. If you like to write about such specialties as Janet and Alex D'Amato did in *Italian Crafts: Inspirations from Folk Art; Algonquin and Iroquois Crafts for You to Make;* or *Colonial Crafts for You to Make*, you may prefer a museum to a library. One of Janet D'Amato's favorite research places is the Museum of Primitive Art, now a part of the Metropolitan Museum of Art in New York City.

Many people think that "library" research is identical with "secondary" sources. However a library, museum, zoo, or historical society can also offer original material. The American Kennel Association has marvelous volumes on purebred dogs. A diary by a North Pole explorer or an original sheet of music with the composer's annotations is an original source. Say you want to write about the San Francisco earthquake of 1905. If you find contemporary reports about the disaster in a library you'll be dealing with original sources. In his widely acclaimed books portraying America's past, Milton Meltzer used innumerable original contemporary records of what common people have thought, felt, and done. Thus, books like his *In Their Own Words: A History of The American Negro, 1865-1916* or *Taking Root: Jewish Immigrants in America* offer a lot of first-hand material and make fascinating reading. He uses the libraries of Columbia University as well as specialized collections like YIVO and the Schomkerg Collection in New York City.

What you don't find in a public library you might find in private libraries of foundations, corporations, or individuals. Most of them will open their doors if they feel that your request is legitimate. That is, if you know what you want, what you plan to do with it, and why you are interested in the subject—what your angle is.

Organizing Your Material

Organization is the key word while doing research in the library. Most authors use a file system consisting of cards and folders. They put every fact they intend to use on a reference card and note the source of the fact. Cards make it easy for you to go back to the library to study the topic further if needed. You can organize your cards by subject matter coordinated with your book outline. Then you can file these cards, along with more detailed information, in file folders that are organized and coordinated with your book chapters. If the information on a card is necessary in more than one chapter, you can make a duplicate of that card to file in the folders for each chapter in which it applies.

Many newcomers to writing think of original sources as the more exciting research. There *is* an advantage to the use of original sources. If you yourself visited historic places in Great Britain as Jean Fritz did for *Can't You Make Them Behave, King George?*, or if you dived with sharks and whales—experiences that led to Ann McGovern's *Sharks; Little Whale*, and *The Underworld of the Coral Reef*—your writing certainly will be more vivid. Still, even first-hand experience can be enriched with added library research. An astronaut describing her travels in space could add historical anecdotes about strange ideas men had about the stars centuries ago. An author writing a simple manual about how to fix bicycles from his own experiences could research little-known facts about the invention and development of the bicycle—facts that might catch the imagination of young readers. As exciting as original research might be, there are barriers: You may not have the money to study computer factories in Japan; you don't have the time to visit Colonial Williamsburg; or you don't have an "in" to interview Joe Namath.

Often, secondary research in a library seems to be all you really need. There is no point interviewing every automotive engineer in the country if you simply want to write a book on how a combustion engine works. But in contrast to the astronaut or the bicycle expert who spice up their personal experience with library research, you might want to keep your readers' attention by adding a first-hand report from a tinkerer who just averted disaster with his speedster's engine. Primary research is not just crumbling, illegible documents—it is the exciting interview, the fascinating trip abroad, the study of an archaeological site or graveyard.

THE INTERVIEW

Books for children in the lower age groups are usually too short to offer much space for interviews. Writers for young adults, on the other hand, will almost certainly be improved by the use of interviews. And interviews become almost a must when you write biographies of living persons, as James Haskin has done with black politicians (*Andrew Young; Adam Clayton Powell; Fighting Shirley Chisholm*) or sports stars (*From Lew Alcindor to Kareem Abdul-Jabbar; Bob McAdoo, Superstar*).

The majority of your interviewees will be adults. And though you are not doing the interviews as a journalist for newspapers, radio, or TV, many of the journalists' techniques can certainly be applied. But explain to the interviewee immediately that you write nonfiction for *children*, that you are very conscientious about informing and educating them—in other words, that you are not the investigative reporter with hidden cameras and microphones who is out for a sensational story.

If circumstances allow it, a face-to-face interview is usually most fruitful. However, depending on how much information you want to get from a person, a phone call or a brief questionnaire to be returned by mail will do, too. It is important, though, that you introduce yourself properly. If you are already an established author, a reference to your published works will do the job. If this is your first book, a commitment from a publisher to consider it for publication definitely will help: Your interviewee will be assured that he or she is not wasting time talking or writing to you. "I want to write a book on the activities of Mt. St. Helens," is certainly not enough when you are an unknown and are asking a top geologist for an interview. You need to describe the background and special experience that enable you to write on the subject, explain why you want to write it, and, perhaps show some of your outline. (Don't worry that the geologist will steal your idea.)

Often, business executives, sports stars, entertainers, and celebrities of all sorts will claim initially that they have no time—especially since your book is "only" a children's book. Scientists, especially doctors, are very protective of the their profession and their colleagues; interviews with physicians for a book on malpractice, for example, would be hard to come by. But if you're patient and explain your case well, i.e., point out ways in which young readers would profit from the professional's knowledge, you'll be surprised how many busy or reluctant people will finally agree to be interviewed. Selling yourself as a researcher is as important to the final book as selling yourself to an editor as a writer.

And expect the unexpected. Ann McGovern had already done several "if you . . ." books *(If You Lived in Colonial Times; If You Grew Up with Abraham Lincoln)* when she set out to talk to members of the Ringling Brothers circus in Florida for her book *If You Lived with the Circus*. The circus people did not mind talking but the manager got the idea that Ann should pay some kind of royalties for the interviews. He began chasing her around the circus grounds so threateningly that she had to hide behind an elephant. However, in most cases the question of *paying* for an interview in connection with a children's book will not come up.

Do Your Homework

Everyone who grants an interview usually does it with some time limit in mind. It's up to you how much you get out of this time. Generally, the more time you are willing to spend on your homework, the more information you'll get in the actual interview.

If you intend to write a biography of your interviewee, read everything you can find about the person's background. Besides the *Who's Who* for world-famous celebrities, there are also numerous *Who's Who* editions broken down by regions or professions. You can check with Chambers of Commerce for information on local businessmen, or consult professional magazines for scientists or lawyers. Very often you'll find the archives (also called the "morgue") of local newspapers an especially rewarding source for small-town personalities. If you have an entertainer in mind, don't overlook gossip magazines or gossip columns.

Many celebrities expect you to be familiar with their fame. A well-known professor might be polite enough to answer all your questions about his background, but deep inside he'll resent the fact that you don't already know about his brilliant academic career. He will certainly notice that you came unprepared and treat your questions accordingly. Sports people and entertainers might react more impulsively. They have been interviewed so many times and their personal life has been recorded so often in the media that a boxer, for instance, might blow up when you ask him if it's true that he was born in the slums and end the interview. Ava Gardner once said of reporters: "It's always the same old stuff. 'Tell us about the dancing on the table tops. Tell us about the bullfighters. Tell us about Sinatra.' God, haven't any of them got any imagination at all?"

Most of all, bear in mind that you're writing a biography for *young* readers and don't get carried away by the interviewee's success. His or her career statistics might be impressive to you but rather dull to children. Get your subject to talk about struggles he had to overcome as a youth or about funny events she likes to remember. "The child is the father of the man," and kids with their unerring instinct for the truth know this. You can often encourage the interviewee to open up by mentioning experiences from your own childhood—experiences he might want to outdo with his own.

For nonbiographical interviews, study the person's work as much as you can. Even if you are not familiar at all with that profession (whether it's science, business, or entertainment), you can read up on it to a certain extent. This will convince your interviewee that your request and interest are sincere. But don't hesitate to tell your subject if something is confusing or unclear. Ask him for examples that explain the problem. A paleontologist accepts the fact that he's not being interviewed by another scientist. A business leader assumes you don't have the same inside information she has. But don't be so unprepared as to ask a marine biologist where the Galapagos Islands are or a business executive what the standing of his company stock is.

If you want to interview children, don't take the task lightly. Anyone who has been in daily contact with children—parents, teachers, librarians—knows that interviewing youngsters is not necessarily different from interviewing adults. You might not need to do as much homework as for interviews with adults, but be sure never to talk down to them or to use baby talk. In *The Craft of Interviewing*, John Brady reports how an interviewer once approached a nine-year-old with the question: "If a fairy came in the door and offered you three wishes, what would you say?" "A fairy?" was the response. "I would ask him if he thought I was a queer." Brady recommends child psychiatrist John Rich's *Interviewing Children and Adolescents* for dealing with kids. "The key to successful communication," writes Rich, "is having a common ground with the child. Some interviewers interpret this as meaning that they should be childish and pretend to have interests and an outlook they do not have. This is ruinous—children are quick to spot such a phony approach."

Adults are ex-kids, as Ezra Jack Keats used to say; and kids are potential adults. The interviewer is no better—and no worse—than either of these. However, the interviewer knows something important: that the gap must be bridged, that outside of the apparently oppressive and certainly inhibiting grown-up/kid dichotomy, there is a tremendous opportunity for communication.

How to Make a Lasting Record

Whether you use a pen or a tape recorder is not always up to you. Some people still don't like the idea that each and every word of their conversation is being taped. But if they agree to a tape recorder, you must decide for yourself about the advantages or disadvantages of either method.

Pen: The more complicated the subject of your interview, the more you will have to concentrate on writing down as much as possible. Unless you know shorthand, this can become distracting for you and irritating for the interviewee. The scene will be not unlike that of a classroom where the professor lectures and the students try to write down every word—it's not the desirable atmosphere for an interview, where rapport between the two parties is essential, and where listening closely to your subject's answers may suggest questions that may lead in interesting and unexpected directions.

Some interviewers take very few notes and sit down immediately after the interview to write about it. This way they have much more time to listen to their interlocutor and to get a real conversation going. But obviously a good memory is all-important!

Tape Recorder: The advantages are clear: No worry over taking notes, less chance of the interviewee denying things later. The setbacks are equally clear: It may take hours to transcribe a tape; a recorder can fail without your noticing it (therefore it's advisable to take at least some notes anyway), and worst of all, it can lull the interviewer into complacency. You know that everything will be on tape and instead of listening carefully to what the subject has to say, your thoughts stray, either to the next question or last night's TV program. There is, however, one advantage a tape has even over the word-by-word shorthand record: By playing the tape, maybe over and over, you will be able to recall the details of the interview much better than by just reading your notes.

Make Your Interview Foolproof

However you choose to conduct your interview, make sure the finished product is absolutely accurate. You may want to double-check facts reported by your subject. If you have any doubts—you can't read your notes, the tape is not clear—get in touch again for verification. If you use direct quotes, most people will demand that you check back with them before those quotes go to print. Even if people don't demand it you're better off with a checkback to avoid embarassment or even legal action later.

FIRST-HAND OBSERVATIONS

If you like to write about nature, countries and their people, sports, or science, the most valuable observations will be your own. You'll be involved in field trips, traveling, in participating in or watching all kinds of physical activities, or in laboratory experiments. And don't feel this wonderful kind of original research is something you might not be able to afford.

Of course, studying elephant herds in Africa *is* expensive. But if nature intrigues you and you don't have the money for an African safari, you can choose subjects to observe much closer to home. Common animals you might study by driving a few miles away—owls, snakes, rabbits, raccoons, beavers, or alligators—are animals young readers might love and want to know better than far-off elephants. The success of veteran writer Herbert Zim (of his roughly hundred books, *Birds* sold more than five million copies and dozen of his other titles sold over one million each) and of many younger authors who have written about animals close to home is the best proof.

Likewise, studying exotic tribes along the Nile and Amazon rivers, though exciting, doesn't come cheap. But America is rich in rare religious sects and ethnic groups, and it's a rare area that wouldn't yield some intriguing and unique lifestyles. With a bit of research you might discover Sephardic Jews, Dutch descendants who have preserved their heritage, Native Americans adapting to modern ways, Mennonites, or other interesting people with fascinating customs in your vicinity.

Sports and science also offer a choice between expensive and affordable observations. You can follow the Oakland A's baseball team all around the U.S. and Canada, but you can also watch the Little League close to home or swing your own bat. You might be permitted to observe a geological expedition to the Antarctic if you paid your way, but you can also peer through a microscope at home.

Curiosity is an observer's most important asset. Gardner Soule was only eight years old when he compiled a book of ocean-going ships, just for his own instruction. He studied the ships carefully when he accompanied his father, who at that time was U.S. consul in the South American harbor town of Cartagena. One of the senior Soule's duties was to check the cargo of every vessel. Though at the time it was just a boy's hobby, the entries in Gardner's book proved useful in the discipline of meticulously observing that he carried into later life as a writer.

Soule's early work was never published. But he says: "I suppose my greatest love has been the ocean, which is always fascinating in all its aspects"—a love that has led to almost a dozen books on the ocean. Love alone, of course, is not enough. "I try," explains Soule, "to be a careful observer, always an observer, and to put down on paper, as best as I can, accurate (and, if possible, interesting) descriptions of what I have observed."

Soule's observations are not restricted to the tangible. Later he recorded equally meticulous information about less verifiable phenomena. His *UFOs and IFOs: A Factual Report on Flying Saucers* became Putnam's #2 all-time best seller. His *Trail of the Abominable Snowman* and *Maybe Monsters* are other examples of books based on subjects questioned by science but loved by mystery-hungry youngsters.

The best observations, however, don't do much good if they are not carefully recorded and preserved. When making your own observations, be prepared to take copious, and perhaps tedious, notes. It's up to you how you want to preserve what you have seen or heard. Talking into a tape recorder or writing a diary every night on travels or field trips is a common method. Other ways of recording your observations can include making photos or drawings for future reference, making tapes of aural impressions such as animal or bird calls, or collecting physical reminders in the form of shells or rocks.

GENERAL GUIDELINES

Solid research is more than just finding the right source and knowing how to use it. Before you get too involved and sometimes happily lost in the search for details, keep in mind some general guidelines:

Look for the Truth

Nothing sounds more simple than telling the truth. But finding the truth can easily become a serious challenge. Even more important: Never forget your responsibility to children. They trust you and take your word for granted. Even if you don't *intend* to mislead them, a lack of thorough research on your part can result in half-truth or misrepresentation.

Imagine that you interview a promising and ingratiating college basketball player. Glowingly he tells you how basketball led him to a scholarship and thus the opportunity to go through college and afterwards build a career that will take him out of the ghetto for good. As a truly curious writer, however, you check further and discover a far less rosy picture: The chance for ghetto kids to get rich through college basketball is minimal. Only very few kids (as a percentage) get a scholarship based on basketball to begin with. Once in college they may have to neglect their regular studies to make the team. If at graduation they cannot make it to the pros—and the percentage of those who do is minuscule—they have achieved little or nothing: Often neither a meaningful degree, nor a chance for a job outside of sports. The player you interviewed did not lie—but he was a very lucky exception. If you had *not* checked further but just told the student's story as you heard it, many of your young readers would take it from *you*, the writer and authority, that sports was a sure road to riches.

In *America Revisited,* an analysis of school history textbooks, Frances Fitzgerald questioned how much information the author can withhold without becoming guilty of misrepresentation. She cites books about the Spanish conquest of Central and South America that do not mention slaves, gold, or Indian massacres. Why? Because the various committees that decide whether or not to recommend a textbook for the classroom were obviously afraid that Hispanic-American schoolchildren and/or their parents might be offended by the mentioning of slaves, gold, or massacres.

As an author of nonfiction *trade* books you might run into similar problems with a timid publisher. Try to stand fast. Maybe you'll be rewarded as Jean Fritz was. She tells of one of her favorite fan letters, "from a boy who had just finished reading my biography of Paul Revere. 'Mrs. Fritz,' he wrote, 'I like the way you tell the *very* truth.' He especially appreciated knowing what the British officer said when he stopped Paul Revere on his midnight ride. In my notes at the end of the book I explain that the source for the quotation was Paul Revere himself. 'Damn you, stop!' the British officer said, 'If you go an inch farther, you are a dead man.' My correspondent believed my book, he wrote, 'because that's the way men really talk in war.' " Not only has the "damn" been deleted in a reprint in a current textbook, but teachers have criticized her for using it.

Another crusader for truth, Ann McGovern, says: "Even though the truth may not be popular, I think it important to tell it like it was." And so, in *If You Sailed on the Mayflower*, she shows that the Pilgrims got seasick and threw up, "like ordinary folk."

Accuracy vs. Bias

With things like height, length, weight, and other quantifiables, it should be easy to provide accurate figures. But there are many fields where two or more parties can come up with different and contradictory figures and it's very hard to decide who has the exact proof. Take the coyote, for example. Western ranchers will come up with all sorts of statistics to show the extent of their losses of sheep and other livestock from coyotes, and will ask for an unlimited license to kill them. Conservationist groups will counter with a different set of figures which they say points to the need to protect coyotes. As an author you can make a passionate argument in your book for either side depending on your own conviction—and your nonfiction could not be called biased as long as you mentioned the claims of the opposite side.

If you feel that stereotypes have had a damaging effect on, say, American Indian tribes, you are entitled to try and persuade your readers to believe otherwise. Ann McGovern did this in *If You Lived with the Sioux Indians*. Many people know that the Hopi Indians always have been peaceful farmers, but frequently see the Sioux depicted in TV and movies as fierce and vengeful warriors. In her book, Ann McGovern, convincingly emphasizes the Sioux nation's peaceable nature.

Vivid Details

Just because you are writing a nonfiction book does not mean you have to write a dull one! From the start of your research (in the field or in the library), keep an eye open for vivid or unusual detail. If you write about mountain climbing in the Himalayas, don't just talk about hardships, weather, or your daily progress. Surely the sherpas who carry equipment are a mine of fascinating lore. Give more than just the number needed for an expedition. How much do they earn for their hard work? While the mountain climbers from abroad wear hundreds of dollars' worth of clothes, what do the sherpas wear? (Their footwear is often sneakers without socks.) What do sherpas do when they aren't carrying equipment for foreigners? What are their religious beliefs? The kid who's going to pick up your book on mountain climbing is already interested in this subject; by adding meaningful and vivid detail you can widen his knowledge and imagination.

What school child doesn't study the major achievements of Benjamin Franklin? But is he or she intrigued by those facts alone? It's hard to imagine that a youngster wouldn't love some of the little-known facts from Franklin's childhood as told in Jean Fritz's *What's the Big Idea, Ben Franklin?* Here the reader learns, for instance, that young Ben Franklin decided one day to become a vegetarian. It wasn't that Franklin didn't like the meat he got at meals at his older brother's table. But he had to pay for the meals because that brother was also Ben's employer. Cutting out meat, Ben was allowed to pay only half and to eat by himself. Munching on a biscuit and a handful of raisins, with a glass of water, he could read while eating and buy books with the money saved. It's details like this that make nonfiction attractive for children.

Do-It-Yourself All the Way?

Theoretically you can do research either way: all by yourself or with the help of hired research assistants or, if you are a teacher, with the help of your students. Some writers might be terrified of entering the labyrinth of a huge library, fearing they'll come out empty-handed. And it *is* frustrating to look through catalogs and file cards only to find that the crucial book is not on the shelves.

But nevertheless, the overwhelming majority of children's book authors vehemently rejects outside help. As said before, they *enjoy* research and they all look forward to the serendipity effect—known in research as finding as "unexpected byproducts." After all, America was the unexpected byproduct of Columbus's search for a route to India. Authors also point out that even the most enthusiastic and loyal helpers cannot always think along the lines the author does.

As Jean Fritz summed up her own and her colleagues' attitude: "If you collected shells, would you send someone else to the beach?"

How Many Facts—And When to Stop

Research can often carry you away—and it should. An author who stops his research exactly when she or he figures there is enough material to fill so many pages inevitably will come up with a poor book. You can't set a specific statistic on how much *more* an author should know than he or she actually puts in writing (opinions vary from twice as much to forty times as much), but it is only logical that you will write a better book when you have a large pool of facts from which to choose. And the more opinionated you are, the more facts you need to prove that your opinion is justified and not just a flimsy bias.

"I never know when to stop," you often hear from authors doing research. And yet, at some point they do stop, of course. (What extra information they might decide to carry over for another book is another question.) You have usually developed numerous questions during your research. If you feel these questions have been answered in a satisfying way and to the best extent possible, and if you cannot come up with any more, then this might be the time to stop researching and start writing.

Finally, no matter how much research you devote to your nonfiction, let your young readers know that the adults in this world do not know *everything*.

Should You Write During Research?

Unorthodox as it may sound, it *does* make sense to write a draft of your manuscript, or at least an outline, before you start to do serious research. If you're writing about an event in history, for example, a quick look at the reference books will give you some useful parameters: when your subject happened, who were the most important people involved, where they lived, and why your subject is still interesting however many years after it happened.

When I was working on a book on greeting cards, I began by making a list of holidays and special occasions, from my own experience. Then I went to a card shop and talked to the owner. Finally, I went to the library and studied the many books about greeting cards. Since the outline had already been written off the top of my head, I had a structure into which I could place facts, a pudding into which I could drop my sugarplums.

It's strictly up to you whether you want to interrupt your research to write some of the manuscript, and here there's no consensus at all among authors. The desire to get it down on paper sometimes pops up when you are in the midst of some fascinating research. You are hot and think you'll never write it better. This is probably true from the point of writing. But later on you might find facts that contradict the earlier research and you might have to drop or rewrite entire passages. Never mind that—write when the spirit moves you. Alternating *spontaneity*, which will give your writing life, with *rigor*, which will give it structure, is the secret of writing a book manuscript that meets professional standards.

CHAPTER 9

The Writing Process

Slowly but surely the world at large is beginning to recognize that presenting facts to children is NOT a watered-down version of writing a college textbook on office automation or a five hundred-page exposé of the cosmetics industry. It is an exacting and important form.

The writer of a children's book must work within severe limits. Some writers welcome these limits; others curse them. My aim in this chapter is to show you why and how to work within them without *sounding* limited.

There are three unbreakable rules of writing nonfiction for children which I will mention once in the hope that the last-chance challenge will imbed them permanently in your mind.

1. *Write about what interests you.* If you aren't interested in computers, don't write about computers. If you *are* interested in chickadees, even if there are already seven good books about chickadees in print, write about chickadees. Norma Jean Sawicki, the editorial director of Four Winds Press, says it from the editor's perspective: "The market is in too much of a flux now for publishers to predict with certainty what will sell. We identify and encourage talent, and publish books that represent the best of their kind. Quality always finds an audience."

2. *Stay interested.* If you meet a mechanical engineer who tells you that Boss Kettering is far more fascinating to the contemporary audience

than Tom Edison, and you've just spent eight months researching Edison's life for a book, smile politely, listen to what he has to say, then change the subject. When you're done with Tom, you can consider Kettering. Distraction is a dangerous thing.

3. *Write ideas down as they occur to you*, and don't throw away anything you've written until the book is printed. The insane thought you had in March might make the perfect caption in June. Allow your book or article to live with full privilege of expression.

Writing at least a rough draft before you begin to do research will free you to ask the questions to which you want answers, rather than those to which answers have already been published. Asking questions as you write puts your audience's needs ahead of the demands of the subject. Within bounds, this is the key to writing for children: you are writing a book *for them*. You aren't writing for yourself or the reviewers; instead, you're stepping into smaller shoes and imagining what children are interested in and more especially, what they can be *made* to be interested in, through your writing skills.

When I was editing *On Reading Palms*, an introduction to palmistry, I asked the author what a monkey's palm would say about his life and fortunes. The enterprising author, Peggy Thomson, got in touch with the Yerkes Primate Research Center in Atlanta to get the palm print of a chimpanzee. The researchers were tickled by this unorthodox request. They supplied the palm print, and the author analyzed the chimp's hand just as palmists analyze people's hands. This gave the readers, in the 8 to 12 group, a more objective perspective on the art and science of the palmist's practice. If it hadn't been for my silly question, based on zero knowledge of palmistry, and the author's adventurousness, this never would have happened in print. I believe the book is better for it. Nobody knows how accurately she predicted the chimp's marriage prospects. Nonetheless, by being loose enough to ask what you really want to know, you can, like this author, include some interesting and occasionally astonishing approaches in your book.

STRUCTURE BEGINS WITH SELECTION

In a nonfiction book for children, structure is very important. The exacting task of outlining your book for a publisher will be covered in Chapter 12, but for now you need to get a grip on how you will actually *write* the book. Because you don't necessarily have the space to develop every idea fully, selection is an important key in arranging ideas so that questions raised in the text don't go unanswered.

First, you must select your facts. You have recorded your information and sources on file cards or floppy disks and have enough material for twenty books. That's great, but you're only writing one at the moment. You consider the question: How specific do I want my book to be? Do I want to explain the influence of Copernican laws on Galileo's theories, or do I want to concentrate on Galileo's childhood? Do I want to explain that Francis Parkman died while dreaming of wrestling with a bear ("I killed him," he shouted to his housekeeper, and fell dead on the bed), or will that spook nine-year-olds? Do I want to mention Michael Jackson's cosmetic surgery in an article for a religious magazine?

Once you have created a preliminary focus for your writing, you need to break the manuscript down into manageable chunks. For the youngest child, this will be little more than a caption. For children who have just started to read, it will be a short paragraph. For children who have mastered basic reading skills, it will be chapters of five to ten pages.

For preteens and teenagers, the nature of your subject matter will determine the size of the units into which you break up the book. Science subjects almost always require diagrams to reinforce concepts. Biographies for older children usually include some photographs, to bring the subject to life. History books are more fun when the author includes illustrations from the period the book covers. If you have a lot of pictures in a chapter, you may want to write shorter. If you can't find illustrative material, your writing will have to illustrate your points, and therefore be longer. "Writing short," the author of over a hundred books for children confessed to me, "is hard. It's so easy to read, readers tend to think it's easy to write. Wrong!"

Chapters can be of any length. In *Bolivar*, Ronald Syme is discursive, providing easy-to-read information in long chapters. In *Witches, Pumpkins, and Grinning Ghosts*, author Edna Barth opts for short sections of two or four pages to make her book "browseable." Whatever way you slice it, it's important to break up your book for the young reader, whether it be sentences for the picture book age, paragraphs for the six- to nine-year-old, or chapters for older readers.

Anecdotes are a way of breaking up a text that might seem long for a young reader. In *My Animals and Me*, mentioned earlier, author Nan Hayden Agle writes about the pets that she kept during her growing up in the first World War. The steady stream of anecdotes mixed with information about animals brings the reading level down a notch.

Increasingly, publishers are looking for younger and younger treatments of nonfiction subjects. "Give me a good manuscript," says editor Joe Ann Daly, "and I will edit it for the appropriate age group." One way you can make your manuscript eligible for this editing-down process is to isolate information in discrete units. In *Metamorphosis*, by Alvin and Virginia Silverstein, a pronouncing glossary provides much-needed information without cluttering up the text.

Thinking Ahead

Illustrations will be covered in depth in the next chapter, but envisioning illustrations as you write can make the job easier. When writing about Venezuela, it might be awkward to describe that country's proximity to the Central American islands of Trinidad, Tobago, and Grenada. But a map showing how close the countries are can make this clear at a glance, leaving you the space to discuss how these countries work together to produce oil for America. The map is not worth a thousand words, but it would be worth a hundred or so.

If you were trying to describe Eleanor Roosevelt's appearance, a photograph could speak volumes. It saves the writer from two traps (1) detailing a description that is peripheral to Eleanor Roosevelt's life (she's one woman whose appearance was not considered an asset) and (2) passing judgment on her appearance which might include some apparently negative observations. A photograph saves the author from the mire of opinion as well as the mire of descriptive writing with which children have little patience.

But there are also times when a verbal description is more effective than an illustration. At the beginning of a text, for whatever age group, you want the reader to *hear* you, to fall into your rhythm, to march to your drum. Here a prose description is almost always more effective than an illustration:

> Exploring space is a great adventure—so is exploring the kitchen. Put the two together and you have the daring astrocook, the most important member of the space crew. Astrocooks prepare wholesome meals that are as important to the astronauts as fuel is to the rockets.

In this introduction to *A Space Age Cookbook for Kids*, the authors ease up on the illustration until they have hooked their readers into hearing what they say. The tone of the writing is aural; the difference between a text and captions is that the text is heard, whereas captions are seen. The writer establishes his voice and THEN the illustrator introduces his vision. The author's voice can be very individual, as is Sidney Lanier's in *King Arthur and His Knights of the Round Table:*

> It befell in the days of the noble Utherpendragon, when he was King of England, that there was born to him a son who in after time was called King Arthur. Howbeit the boy knew not that he was the King's son.

Or it can be neutral, as is Christine Chaundler's voice, in *A Year Book of Legends:*

The universal appeal of legend, whether to children or even adults of ripe age, shines in this treasury of folklore from various sources. The best-known legends are attractively rewritten, but some of the stories will be unfamiliar. The arrangement is by the months, so that there is something for all times and seasons.

In many cases the writing comes before the illustration, so that the young reader gets a sense of the starting place, which is what the writer has to say. Librarians, in their professional evaluations of books, always apply the text test—how a text sounds, reads, and wears—before they evaluate the pictures. Although a strong text can carry a weak format, the reverse is not necessarily true. Consider how many different editions and revisions have been made of great pieces of writing. If the test of great literature is the uncanny ability of a piece of writing to inspire diverse interpretation, the secondary nature of illustration can be better understood.

EMOTION AND CLARITY

Emotion has a far more important place in juvenile nonfiction than in adult nonfiction. That doesn't mean that you have to gush, or be unrelievedly optimistic. All it means is that you need to look on the inspirational side as well as the down side. In Larry Pringle's books for ten- to fourteen-year-olds on man's destruction of the environment, he emphasizes how kids can put a stop, or at least a slowdown, to the wanton practices that are polluting our rivers and skies. Part of his inspiration is to clue kids in on how bad the situation is. He makes them want to help, and then shows them how they can.

Emotion, carried to an extreme, can be the enemy of clarity. Clarity is important because it's basic. Clarity is the cake, emotion is the frosting. Clear writing for children is painstaking: there are no shortcuts.
Be direct—use the active voice, not the passive voice:

> He hit his brother in front of the whole group.
> NOT
> His brother was hit by him in front of the whole group.

But remember, too, that direct is not always clear.

> The referendum to the legislature proved Scott's popularity with the people.

is not clear to children of any age.

> When he retired from the army, Senator Scott thought he would like to run for President. He was popular with the people of Oregon, just

as he had been popular with his soldiers.
would do for the 10 to 14 age group, whereas

> He was a good leader. The soldiers in his regiment liked him. The people in his town liked him. The people in his state supported his idea of building ten new schools.

would be better for the 6 to 9 age group.

You will notice that the younger the age group, the more repetition is required. It doesn't have to be repetition of the same words, but it should be a recap or reinforcement of the same ideas. You may remember from your reading primers, " 'See Spot run,' said Dick. 'Run Spot run,' said Sally" as the reason that a whole generation of Americans can read the word "run"—and indeed many of them run themselves.

For the older age groups, from third grade on, reiteration is most effectively handled by the use of anecdotes that are amusing, exciting, or merely illuminating. "I've been interested in comics all my life," the entrepreneur says in Steve Berman's *What to Be*. Then Berman goes on to explain the entrepreneur's first favorite comic was the Classics Illustrated version of *The Prince and the Pauper*, for which he paid 25 cents in 1956. Further on, Berman mentions that the entrepreneur sold this comic last year at a comics fair for $250. The young reader gets the message, through repetition, that a childish interest can become an adult occupation—indeed a rather lucrative one.

RESOUNDING CONCLUSIONS

The emotional climate of a children's manuscript is just as important a determinant for the age group as the length of the sentences, length of the paragraphs, and lengths of the chapters. You want your conclusion to have emotional as well as intellectual impact, and the emotion comes out of the writing, NOT the research. For the YA audience, Dennis Nolan writes in *The Joy of Chickens* the concluding paragraph:

> Chickens have been bred in an infinite and dazzling array of sizes, shapes, colors and patterns. Whether proud, fierce, comical, plain or fancy, it is always a delight to hear and a pleasure to behold a chicken.

For the 8 to 12 audience, Shirley Parenteau and Barbara Douglass write in *A Space Age Cookbook for Kids:*

> Many mysteries remain in our universe. Many learned guesses are still to be proved true or untrue. Perhaps one day *you* will help solve some of those mysteries.

To master these writing skills for the age group and subject of your choice, it is necessary to do two things: read and write. Reading is called "research" and is discussed in the previous chapter. Reading is also market research; this is covered in Part III, "A Practical Guide to Publication." But writing comes in two forms, too: writing and rewriting.

Be a Pro

Writing is hard to start for some people, hard to stop for others. It is important to learn whichever part is hard for you. Writers vary in many habits, but the successful writers I know all agree that it is essential to write every day. Some people set strict limits for themselves, others settle for a jotting in a diary one day and twenty perfect pages another.

Professional writers think professionally as well as creatively. If you're nervous about writing query letters to publishers, write a sample query letter every day for a week. If you are frightened of how your manuscript will seem to an editor, write a sample manuscript page at the end of your writing day so that the routines of publishing are second nature to you. That's what being a professional writer is all about: getting comfortable with the conventions of book publishing.

Writing every day has another advantage, besides making you comfortable with professional standards and testing your creative limits. Your mother was right; you really do learn something by practicing. It's thrilling to look back on what you wrote last week, or last year, or three decades ago, and smile at your progress. And learn again from your earlier mistakes.

Mistakes are fun. Properly shined with discipline and rewriting, mistakes are good ideas, first drafts. Making mistakes is something writers can do to good advantage. This can't be said for many professions.

WHICH WAY TO ALGEBRA I? TO THE GYM? TO THE COUNSELOR'S OFFICE? TO MY LOCKER? TO THE CAFETERIA? TO THE LIBRARY? TO THE . . . ?

Even though changing schools causes concern, changing isn't necessarily bad or difficult. On the contrary, one sociologist, Mildred Kantor, says that it can be very good. Her studies indicate

71

In Help! We're Moving! *the chapter opener reflects the personal tone of this self-help guide.*

CHAPTER 10

The Book
as a Physical Object

I f you think back to your own first encounter with books, you may be
surprised at the images that come to your mind. An adult reading quiet-
ly in the corner of the porch while you played cops and robbers with
your brother; a minister reading from the pulpit; or, you yourself deciphering the sounds of g-e-t from your first-grade primer. All of these are physical activities, much as playing an instrument is. The book is an object, just
as a painting in a frame is an object. That it is infinitely evocative, subject to
your interpretation and that of others, is not to discount it as a physical
object.

Anyone writing for beginning readers, whatever their age, needs to
understand what a book can be. To the uninitiated, a book is not automati-
cally recognized as a good read or mine of information. It is a *thing*. Encountering this thing is where reading begins.

The writer for children needs a highly developed sense of the book as
a physical object. This poses some problems, since writing and its practitioners, often abstract people, are using the limitations of material to convey limitless vistas. But the next time you pick up a book, notice your response. What leads you to it? Is it the fact that it is a book? Is it the fact that
you are looking for something to do, something to think about? Does the title catch your eye? Or the picture on the cover? To discover what makes a
book inviting, think about what books do to invite you. Here's a list of possibilities to get you thinking:

- a brand-new book, never opened.
- a dog-eared book, read and loved.
- a plain Penguin paperback with the title starkly printed and no further advertisement required, as though people *know* this is a good one.
- an appealing picture on the cover.
- something you recognize—an author's name, a place you've been, a subject you studied in school, a problem you thought your exclusive property.

As an adult who has been reading and writing long enough for the book as a physical object to have become second nature, you need to go back to the beginning and recapture your first encounters with books. It may be, as it was for me, that it wasn't the first meeting that inspired the enthusiasm. For many people, being read to was one thing, but reading on one's own came later, much later, after the reading books were chucked, the textbooks returned to the bookstore, the books everyone else was reading were read, dissected, and forgotten. The moment a person reads a book is not always the moment one becomes a reader, but a single reading experience can pave the way for a full literary life.

Teachers and librarians understand this phenomenon, and try to use it effectively in getting children reading and keeping them reading. For most children, the first hook into the world of reading is the story hour, in the library or the classroom. Young children hear a whole book, and request it for perusing on their own. Older children enjoy hearing part of a book, and then finishing it and perhaps re-reading it on their own. Kids don't have enough solid experience with books and reading to know that the process is one they can enjoy because they control it. Adults can help children shore up their self-confidence and attack a book by themselves by showing them how easy it is to pick up a book and put it down. Or keep it, as the child chooses.

The writer has a tougher mandate. No writer worth his ink wants his book to be put down. Keeping readers is a lot harder than getting them. And keeping young readers, accustomed as they are to two minute and forty second television segments, three minute pop songs, fast food, and electronic feedback, is hard. One of the tricks you can use is illustrations.

PICTURE PERFECT

Kids are impressed with appearances. They like colorful TV graphics, snappy candy wrappers, cereals with funny pictures on the box. And kids, who spend much of their school day poring over the tightly designed, never controversial, textbooks, welcome a book that *looks* interesting. Whatever age group you are serving, you can create a book that has appeal from the cover on (and children do judge books by their covers!) with illustrations.

As noted in the last chapter, you will find it helpful and inspiring to consider what illustrations would work best with your words to first introduce and then reinforce your points. Some guidelines exist to help you ascertain what's possible in a published book. But don't look at these guidelines as limitations. Look at them as possibilities and bear in mind that there are trade-offs, both economic and artistic, to get your writing the stage setting you want.

The subtleties of visual presentation are such that the editor, author, and illustrator of books that *depend* on illustration to capture and hold the child's attention have to have long experience to make decisions that are both artistically effective and economically viable. Each book is a unique case. But there are general principles from which professionals work, and you can use them even though you are new to this exciting field:

1. Illustrations should be spread evenly throughout the text. The clumps of photographs that one finds in celebrity biographies or the beautiful frontispiece that you see in a novel have no place in the informational book for children.
2. The writing style, the typography, the layout, and the illustrations themselves should express the same mood. If you're writing a serious book about laboratory animals, for example, you don't want cartoon illustrations. If you're writing a biography of Mary Lou Retton, an old-fashioned typeface like Caslon will be less appropriate than a modern one like Times Roman, (the standard newspaper face) or Helvetica (a popular face for advertising, because of its bare-bones simplicity). . . . Look at the type chart on pages 170-171 and you'll see what I mean.
3. The illustrations, as much as the text, should reflect the abilities and interests of the age group the book is aimed at. Maps, diagrams, and charts don't belong in books for the very young; nor do highly stylized and simplified illustrations belong in books for teenagers who want action, involvement, and plenty going on at once.

Photo Realism

Connie Epstein, editor of Morrow Junior Books during its heyday as a publisher of juvenile nonfiction, found that photographs were the favorite kind of illustration with children. "When a child sees a photograph, he can point to it and say 'That's real!' whereas drawings, no matter how realistic, seem contrived." Finding photographs that can be reproduced in book form (with its constraints of small size and cheap printing) is a gigantic task for the writer.

There are several ways to go about finding photographs. You can call on a stock photo collection, like the Armstrong Roberts Collection in Philadelphia, or you can write or visit museums, government agencies, libraries, and schools with collections in your area, you can hire a professional photographer, or you can take the pictures yourself. Stock photo houses are listed in *Literary Market Place*. If you live in a metropolitan area, you can find photographers listed in the Yellow Pages.

Taking the photographs yourself, or asking a talented friend or family member to take them, is time consuming but ultimately rewarding. You should be forewarned, however, that the standards required for book reproduction are very high. Usually, art directors ask for 8x10 glossies, rather than Polaroid snapshots. If you compare the difference between the reproduction quality of the common 35mm snapshot and the 8x10 photo taken with reproduction in mind, you will see why the art director fusses.

If you decide to get your photos in part or in full from photo archives, you have a monumental task in front of you. In the search for just the right picture, you will find scores of pictures that will "do." Choosing the best one will mean combing through public library picture collections, private archives, and museums. It's fun work as long as you keep interested, but after awhile, even the most seasoned professional picture researcher begins to flag. It's important to keep going, to keep looking for photos that are consistent, interesting, and keyed precisely to your text before you give up.

The other problem with photo research is that photographs are not cheap, even for one-time reproduction. Expect to pay from fifty to one hundred dollars per photo, and this money comes out of your pocket. When you negotiate for photo rights, try to cover all rights in one shot: ask for non-exclusive world rights so that if your book is sold to England or France, you won't have to go back and negotiate again—from an impossible bargaining position—for additional rights.

Illustration Savvy

Until fifty years ago, it was standard for adult books to be illustrated. Bibles, novels, travel books, and cookbooks all featured some kind of illustrations. But the fashion for the most possible information, the no-nonsense, most-text-for-your-money attitude has all but removed artwork from adult books. A movie star's biography might feature a small section of stills, a textbook might have charts and diagrams, but the beautifully integrated interplay of words and pictures has in the last three decades been confined to children's books.

There is a practical reason that illustrated books have become the sole province of the juvenile divisions of book publishers: the training and skill required to put such a book together. Editors have some appreciation of the occasional illustration (as a pie graph in a business book or a cartoon

Rolag after rolag Carolyn spins into yarn. When a bobbin is full, she winds the yarn onto her *kniddy knoddy* into a skein. There is a special sound to this as the bobbin turns and the wool yarn whispers while passing on to the kniddy knoddy. But the best sound of all is the flutter of the wheel when Carolyn spins. If butterflies had wings of wood as thin as paper and flew in perfect circles, this would be the sound of a spinning wheel.

"Spinning!" says Carolyn. "It's almost magic!"

Kathryn Lasky's you-are-there text provides a lively counterpoint to Christopher G. Knight's clear and uncluttered photographs.

illustration in a humor book) or the occasional text (as in the running text in art books or the captions that tell the narrative in a photo-documentary volume.) But the illustrated book, with its careful balance of typography and illustration requires (1) knowledge of typography, (2) knowledge of illustration placement and (3) knowledge of page layout. Although both art schools and colleges offer courses in these disciplines, the field is so new and so complex that on-the-job exposure is the only sure route to the mastery of this arrangement of elements. Every book really is different, even if it's a series. When I first began publishing the "Basics" games series with Arvid Knudsen's packaging group, we worked up a combination of diagrams (to show court size, scorekeeping, and the dimensions of equipment), line drawings to schematize techniques, and photographs to give an idea of how the games are actually experienced by their young participants.

The series was so successful that we expanded it to include that great indoor sport, electronic technology, including high-fidelity recording, video, and computers. Although the three-pronged approach to illustration still held, we were amazed to see that the functions differed: the diagrams were useful for showing wiring diagrams; the photographs were indispensable in showing the various forms of equipment, but we really counted on the drawings to show the use of the equipment because *anything* is more arresting than a picture of a kid at a computer, or watching his video, or listening to a record. It would have been about as interesting as showing people standing on the train at rush hour. So even using the same format, the approach had to differ radically.

BOOK DIMENSIONS

A book can be any size, but for practical purposes, it is usually at least three inches wide and rarely more than twelve inches high. Within this

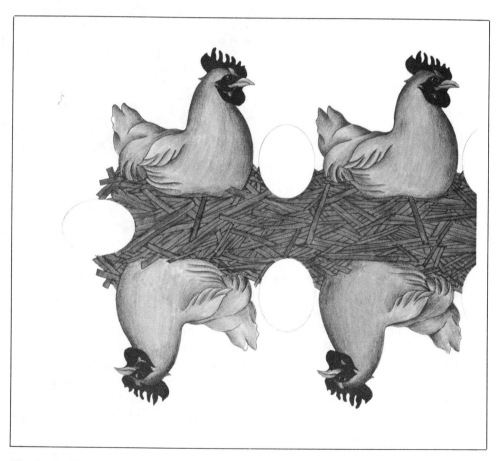

The beautiful endpapers of Chickens Aren't the Only Ones *by Ruth Heller (Grosset & Dunlap, 1981) tie together this lively and informative book.*

range, there are the physical facts of a book's cover, its pages, and its illustrations. Writing and research quality are the first and last tests of a book's worth, but in order for the writer to find the audience, the facts of a book's physical presence must be studied and the conclusions absorbed in the basement of the writer's mind.

Once you have a vague idea of your manuscript's word count, consider how those words are going to be displayed on the individual page. Here is where your graphic ingenuity will help your writing. You may not count yourself an expert on layout and typography, but all experienced readers have a store of reactions to what they like and what they don't like. You want a book to be something that represents *you*, and the visual representation is just as important initially as the words themselves.

The consideration of the book's physical existence will help you develop an angle in the actual writing. If you know that the book will be sixty-four pages long, and contain thirty pictures, you have to consider what you want the pictures to do. Do you want the text itself to serve as captions, or do you want to have the captions and pictures separate from your text? The answer you come to will depend on the kind of writer you are. If you are discursive, and write close to the way people—in this case young people—talk, you will probably elect to have the captions and pictures separate from the text. A little knowledge of typography, the choice of typeface, spacing, and other design elements will help you rough out the idea of how you want your book to be read, digested, and enjoyed.

Typographical Tactics

Type size has conventions for certain age groups: generally the younger the reader, the larger the type. But as reading levels vary increasingly, the bright teenager may be just as comfortable with large type as his equally bright first-grade sister who's just learning to read. The secret in type-size selection is the effect you want: if your book is a pop biography, then large type and nearly adult subject matter go together well. If your book is a "family reading" book on natural science, the type can be small, because you want to emphasize the aural experience as your text is read aloud as much as the visual experience as the book is examined by a range of people of different ages.

Publishers have traditionally asked their typesetters to submit sample pages of prospective books. These sample pages include complicated juxtapositions of type, as are found on chapter openers (the pages that begin each chapter), the title page, and an illustrated page. You aren't a typesetter, and you may not know kerning from kippers, but you do know what you like. If you start by making a dummy of a few pages from your book when the first bright idea hits you, your research and writing will be easier. Here's how to do it: fold a sheet of 8½"x11" paper in half crosswise. Using a

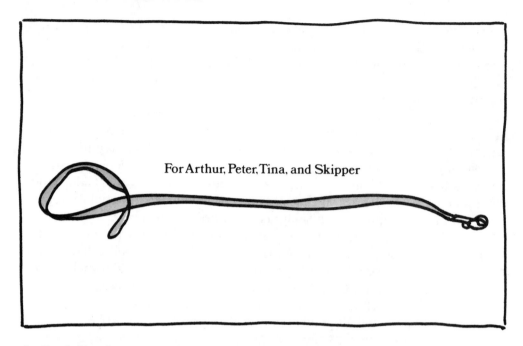

In the dedication page to Some Things You Should Know About My Dog *by Muriel Batherman (Prentice-Hall, 1976), simple elements are elegantly arranged.*

pencil with a good eraser, sketch in the title page on one or more of your "book's" pages. You have a couple of good ideas for titles and you know what your name is so just go ahead and play around with these two simple elements. You'll find it relaxing as well as fascinating.

If you consider carefully—especially with the help of a journal, a clip file, or an index of bright ideas—you will be able to isolate the nuggets of information that inspired your interest in the subject you are writing about. Make this seminal inspiration a chapter title, and design a page, with or without an illustration, showing what you want it to look like. If your ideas for chapter titles are snappy, you might want to use letters at an angle, or a fancy type face you've seen in a slick magazine. If you're adept at lettering, you might try drawing the titles yourself. Art supply stores also sell press-on type lettering which you can use to illustrate these preliminary titles.

Now put these rough sketches in a file, and with them firmly but unobtrusively planted in your mind, continue your research and think about the structure of your writing. Look at other books for the same age group, on the same subject, and compare your ideas with what others have done. The idea is not to *copy* but to compare. Are the square black-and-white photographs stiff? Are the blocks of text formidable in length? As you imagine the book you will write, put yourself in the reader's shoes. What would you, as a reader, like to write if you had the chance? S. E. Hinton wrote her first

CONTENTS

In A Space Age Cookbook
for Kids *(Prentice-Hall,
1978), Shirley Parenteau
and Barbara Douglas cap-
ture a space theme as they
present the possibilities to
aspiring celestial chefs.*

PACK, BAND, AND COLONY

The World of Social Animals

JUDITH & HERBERT KOHL

Pictures by Margaret La Farge

Farrar · Straus · Giroux

NEW YORK

In Pack, Band, and Colony, *the dignified design of the title page incorporates Margaret La Farge's vivid portrait of wolves with the straightforward title and subtitle.*

book as a teenager because she wanted something to read. Marvin Terban wrote his first book as a sixth-grade teacher because he wanted a way to show his students that words are a scream. Ruth Belov Gross wrote *The Money Book* because she felt that adults wanted to spare children their own financial worries, but at the same time expected kids to show some responsibility about money. Her approach had to be light enough not to threaten parents or bore kids, but it had to have enough substance to serve the purpose of educating her audience. Gross used the *format* to convey the lightness, so that her text could be straightforward and informative.

THE BOOK'S THE THING . . .

Aside from the page layout, with its elements of typography, white space, photographs, and design, the book-object offers a promise that the subject will be adequately covered. A newspaper article or TV clip can get away with a "to-be-continued" close, but the book reader wants those covers to enclose a complete body of information. You have no doubt encountered various offerings in response to this expectation in your reading life, from the multi-volume study to the slick quick introduction. Writing for children is serving up food for thought, and there is a lot of maneuvering room in what will be on the menu. Some books are "starters," first course, appetite-whetters, introductions to the world of your subject. Some are "main course" books, not always for older children, since an eight-year-old's curiosity can outdistance a sixteen-year-old's, given the right subject and the right child. And others are "dessert" books—just plain fun, like S. Carl Hirsch's *Stilts* or Ray Broekel's *Candy Bar Book*. Your book endures in the child reader's intellectual life as a piece of writing—the precise expression of *your* thoughts in the framework of your experience and feelings—but the physical book is, in itself, an entity.

Two constant reminders to the young reader are "You can't believe everything you read" and "Don't judge a book by its cover." The reason these tired old clichés are trotted out so often is that children *want* to believe everything they read, they want to be able to select a book by its cover. No author can be absolutely certain about the truth of what he says, since we are discovering things about the past we didn't know before while we explore the present and fuss over the future. And no author, especially one working with the editorial, art, sales, and marketing departments of publishing companies serving children, has control over his book's cover. But if you think about integrity and honesty as you write, you may be surprised at how satisfying the results can be.

Acting as an Architect

While it's important, even essential, that the author have the final realization of his manuscript into a book in his mind as he writes, no publisher is going to invite you to be the art director of your book. Here's an excerpt of a letter from an editor to an author:

> I should warn you that few illustrators will want to be so closely guided by an author's vision of how the pictures in a book should look. If an element of the picture is essential to making some sense of a fact not spelled out in the text, that is one thing. But to specifically detail that which is beyond the actual manuscript is very constricting to an artist, part of whose job and pleasure it is to add his own creative interpretation to your text.

Here the author has to make clear to his editor that he is like a good architectural client, in that he jots down what he thinks he wants to give the builder (in this case, the editor) as a starting place.

The author's concrete interpretation of the text in terms of format and illustration gives the editor a starting point from which to generate his or her own idea. If your editor balks at your suggestions—and very few editors of nonfiction books for children will do that—simply explain that you offered them in order to inspire, not to instruct the artist.

In nonfiction far more than fiction, the publisher's imprint bears more heavily on the author's approach. Many publishers have nonfiction series with a given format: these series can be figured down to the last character of type, like the Harper "I Can Read" books, or they can be loosely arranged in a standard format with lots of leeway, like the Dodd, Mead "Wonders of Auks, Wonders of Stars," series. For this reason, you want to keep your manuscript submission separate from illustration and design suggestions. I always prefer to look at a manuscript on its own: if I'm interested, it's very nice to see the author's conception of how her book can look in a separate manuscript. I suggest a photocopied manuscript, either arranged to show various illustration suggestions or marked with ideas for art. But the text alone should be made available for the artist, designer, and editor to work with independent of your good ideas.

Trina Schart Hyman was very pleased when she was asked early in her career to illustrate a picture book on a little girl's adjustment problems. Hyman was even happier when the best-selling author requested that she be asked to illustrate the next book in this successful series. The author wrote to Hyman, praising her work. Thrilled, Hyman wrote back and thanked the author for suggesting her for future books. Then the author sent Hyman a package—435 color snapshots of the author's daughter, whom the author wanted Hyman to use for a model in the next book. Hyman wrote back to the author returning the pictures and to her editor returning the advance. Opinions and advice from the author to illustrator should be given in the same spirit as the author would like to receive advice from the illustrator. When the illustrator suggests that you talk about mice

BY CAMEL OR BY CAR

A LOOK AT TRANSPORTATION
BY GUY BILLOUT

Copyright © 1979 by Guy Billout
Library of Congress Cataloging in Publications Data
Billout, Guy. By Camel Or By Car.
Summary: Text and illustrations describe 16 types of water, air, and land transportation.
1. Transportation-Juvenile Literature (1. Transportation)
I. Title. TA1149. B54 1979 380.5 78/26120
ISBN 0/13/109603/6

PRENTICE-HALL, INC.
ENGLEWOOD CLIFFS, NEW JERSEY

The title page of By Camel or by Car: A Look at Transportation *by Guy Billout (Prentice-Hall, 1979) is graphically controlled to call attention to the evocative illustration.*

NOTES

7   Franklin Field belongs to the University of Pennsylvania and is in Philadelphia. Franklinia is a tree with a white flower. It is extinct now except for a few cultivated plants in Washington, D.C.

8   Franklin also had 6 sisters.

22 James Franklin could no longer legally claim Benjamin as an apprentice although he considered this only a technicality. Because of trouble with the government, James had been ordered to suspend his paper, but instead he made Benjamin the temporary editor. James had been forced to tear up the old apprenticeship papers but secretly had made a new contract just between the two brothers. Benjamin considered himself morally obligated to James but still when he escaped, there was no way for James legally to get him back.

24 Franklin gave up vegetarianism on the way to Philadelphia. One reason Benjamin visited Boston was that he wanted his father to set him up in his own printshop. Governor Keith of Pennsylvania had met Benjamin and had made this suggestion. When Mr. Franklin refused, the governor offered to raise the money and sent Franklin to London to buy the equipment. But the governor did not keep his promise. Benjamin stayed in London 2 years, working for a printer.

31 Later the Leather Apron Club was called the Junto.
    No one knows who William Temple's mother was. He was born before Benjamin married; Debbie became his stepmother.

34 The bottle was know as the Leyden jar.

36 Franklin was lucky that the bolt of lightning that hit the kite was not stronger. He could have been another dead scientist.

42 "We hold these truths to be self-evident," the Declaration says.
    William Temple went to London with Benjamin and later was appointed governor of New Jersey. When war came, he decided to support England instead of America. This was the bi
    Sick as he was on the trip to France scientific experiments. While the lowered a thermometer 2 to 4 tim found that ships which crossed the those which ran against it, Benja exact location.

46 It is only fair to point out that Frankli ment as well as friends. John Adam Franklin was secretive and lazy.

The appendix of What's the Big Idea, Ben Franklin? *by Jean Fritz, illustrated by Margot Tomes (Coward McCann & Geoghegan, 1976), left, provides valuable information on sources that would disrupt the flow of the text.*

Index

60

The index of Album of Dinosaurs *by Tom McGowen, illustrated by Rod Ruth (Rand McNally, 1972), is spaciously laid out for easy reference.*

instead of rats in your book on household pets because he draws from life and he doesn't want to keep rats in his studio—do you, as the author, say yes or no? The illustrator is in a similar position when you ask him to draw a landscape of the Ural Mountains instead of a relief map because it fits better with the tone of your book. Editors are known—and mocked—for keeping authors and illustrators as far apart as possible. But experience has taught every publisher that good fences are in this case the only sure-fire way of creating good neighbors.

The writer for children uses illustration to inspire the reader to come into the book and text to invite the reader to stay and come back. Sandy Peele, the manager of The Corner Bookstore in a family neighborhood in New York, has to utilize his teaching experience some afternoons when the older children come in and, instead of reading as their ambitious parents would like (and for which reason the children have charge accounts at the store), they curl up with Richard Scarry's *What Do People Do All Day?* or Brian Wildsmith's *Shapes*. When they are older, these children will find a more respectable outlet for their passion for pictures in the expensive art books on the second floor gallery of this bookstore, but the private world of looking at pictures is a luxury for the school-age child. A writer can take advantage of this passion by using the pictures in his book to (1) seduce the reader, (2) verify the reality of his subject, (3) create a climate for his exposition, and (4) introduce new forms of illustration to children (for example, diagrams, maps, or exploded drawings). These are not the province of the writer: the designer lays out the page, the artist draws the pictures, the photographer arranges the photographs, the editor decides where illustrations are required, but it is the writer's obligation to keep the layout needs of his ideas in the back of his mind.

You know from the books you enjoy reading and owning that appearance *does* matter. And to the child whose abstracting powers are not fully developed, the look and feel of a book can give it a reassuring reality before the child reads it. Illustrations that are comical, like Leonard Kessler's light-hearted illustrations for easy readers or Paul Coker's zany cartoons for middle-graders can be nonthreatening accoutrements for such deadly subjects as bicycle safety (Kessler's *Tale of Two Bicycles*) or statistics (Coker's hilarious cartoons for *Winning with Numbers*). Ann Ophelia Dowden's beautiful color paintings add dignity to her book about weeds, *Wild Green Things in the City*, whereas Jean Zallinger's beautifully detailed black-and-white illustrations add volumes of information to her natural science texts.

Whether accompaniment or reinforcement, illustrations in a children's book are one of its hallmarks, and the illustrator and author can work together to achieve a whole that IS greater than the sum of its parts.

Words about BOWLING

ARMSWING: The back-and-forth motion of the arm as the bowler approaches the foul line

BALL RETURN RACK: The stand where balls are placed between turns

FOLLOW-THROUGH: The continued swinging arm motion after the ball is released

FOUL LINE: The line painted on the lane which bowlers must not cross when releasing their ball

FOUR-STEP APPROACH: The continuous four-part motion made before releasing the ball

FRAME: One turn in bowling; also, the squares on the scoresheet in which the score for each player's turn is listed. A game is ten frames.

GUTTER: The grooved space running the length of the lane on both sides

HEADPIN: The number 1 pin at the front, or head, of the triangle of pins

LIFT: A force given to the ball as it is released which helps keep the ball spinning down the lane

PENDULUM: The object on a clock that swings evenly back and forth. In bowling, the arm holding the ball should swing like a pendulum.

PICK UP: To make a spare, or knock down all of the remaining pins on the second shot

PIN-SETTING MACHINE: The machine behind the lane that clears away knocked-down pins and sets them up again. The machine also sends the ball under the lane and back to the ball return rack.

PUSHAWAY: The first part of the four-step approach; the ball is pushed out, away from the body, and down

RELEASE: Letting go of the ball and sending it rolling down the lane

SCORESHEET: A sheet for keeping a record of the scores in a game

SLIDE: The last part of the four-step approach, done as the ball is released

SPARE: Knocking down all the pins on the second shot. A spare adds 10 points to the score, plus the number of pins knocked down on the first shot of the next frame.

SPLIT: Two or more pins left standing on the first shot with more than a pin space between

SPOTS: The seven arrows painted near the middle of the lane, used to help bowlers aim the ball at the pins they want to hit

SPOT BOWLING: Aiming for the pins by rolling the ball over the spots on the lane; different from **pin bowling,** or aiming at the pins themselves rather than at the spots

STRIKE: Knocking down all 10 pins on the first shot. A strike adds 10 points to the score, plus the number of pins knocked down on the next two shots.

TAKE OUT: A pin knocked down by another pin

Technical terms printed boldface in the text are defined in the glossary of Bowling is for Me *by Mark Lerner (Lerner Publications, 1981). This book is part of a series entitled "Sports for Me," which covers everything from archery to wrestling.*

The moon is so close to Earth that we can see many details on its surface. But this photograph of the moon was taken through a telescope. The brighter parts are hills and mountains covered by large holes called craters. The dark parts are flat lands that are called seas. Early peoples thought that these dark spaces were covered with water. Today we know that they are really dry lands, but we still call them seas.

Until a short time ago no one had ever seen the other side of the moon. That's because the same side of the moon always faces Earth. Then, a few years ago, spaceships from Earth passed behind the moon. Here is a photograph that shows part of the far side of the moon. It has craters and mountains, much like the side we see from Earth. But it has few flat lands, or seas.

Author Seymour Simon obtained these photographs from Hale Observatory and NASA to illustrate The Long View Into Space *(Crown Publishing, Inc., 1979).*

STAGES OF CREATION

The following checklist is a recap of what we've covered so far in Part II. You may not be able to answer all these questions now, but let the ideas percolate in your mind and see what comes up. Selling your idea to a publisher will be covered in Part III, and you'll be better prepared to market your manuscript in a professional way if you have a firm grasp of this information.

Stage One: "I have a great idea for a book!"

1. Test your ideas. Ask yourself, does the idea justify a book? Does it appeal to a broad audience?
2. What age group will your book be for? Does your idea fit with the interests of this age group? What's the cognitive level required to understand your treatment?
3. How traditional, or timely, is your subject?
4. Check *Children's Books in Print* at the library for similar books. When were they published? How does your angle differ? What developments have occurred in the field since their publication?

Stage Two: Researching your subject

1. Don't stint on research just because your book will be short. See Chapter 3 for reasons to learn as much on your subject for baby beginners as you do for learned teenagers. Your selection will only be as good as your collection of data.
2. Look for quotes, slogans, events that will break up your narrative into manageable parts. Questions and answers, categories, personalities, and record-breaking happenings all help pull together a body of information. Knowing who your audience is can make this culling process easier.
3. Don't skip over a fact because you've encountered it before. Note all the places you've come across it on a single card: If it's so, your research is reinforced. If it's a phony fact, your "unlearning" mission will become all the more imperative.
4. Whatever your subject and the audience you're aiming for, note sources for books that will interest your book's fans. In most books for the elementary age, sources are not cited in the book itself, but *assume* your book will be so intriguing that your readers will write to you with questions that a reading list can answer.

Stage Three: Writing your manuscript

1. Write about what interests you—pick a subject you're excited about and can stick with for the time it takes to write a book. Young readers are quick to spot a phony, as well as genuine enthusiasm for a topic.
2. Before doing exhaustive research, consider writing a rough draft to see what questions arise. This will help you understand what *your reader* wants to know. Don't be afraid of the offbeat question—it may yield the type of fresh information young minds find irresistible.
3. Determine the focus of your book and select from your research materials those facts which will best lend themselves to your focus. Make sure your point comes across by "recapping"—repeating key ideas for younger readers or using anecdotes to reinforce concepts for older readers.
4. Be thinking about illustrations as you write—how much illustration will be needed to convey the information you want to put across? Keep in mind the age level when deciding on the balance between illustration, text, and captions.
5. What's the mood, or emotional climate, of your treatment? Is your writing clear and vigorous? Have you created a satisfying conclusion?

Stage Four: Envisioning the book as an object

1. How do you picture the title page—sweetly traditional, straightforward, humorous—and how does the combination of your title's content and its presentation in type assure readers that this is the book for them? What will make it more interesting than a box of Kleenex and more distinctive than a cassette package?
2. Imagine laying out a chapter opening for the chapter that you could sit down and write this very minute. Do you want to capture the casual reader with large type, big illustrations, snappy headlines? Or do you want the attention of the more advanced reader with quieter graphics and more room—both on the page and in the reader's mind—for an in-depth exploration in the text itself?
3. Will your book be an introduction, with its emphasis on initiating the reader? If so, you will want to have an accessible format. Or do you want to add to the knowledge a reader already has in a subject? Here key issues should be highlighted to give the intermediate child a sense of where his previously acquired knowledge will take him. This can be achieved with many smaller headlines or sub-headlines. If your book is for the aficionado, concentrate on content, giving yourself plenty of room for text pages, and foregoing the seductive format. The reader is already yours.

Here is a woman who works

as a zoo keeper.

She takes care of snakes,

lizards, crocodiles, and turtles.

She feeds them,

and cleans their cages

and sees that they

are feeling fine.

In Butcher, Baker, Cabinetmaker *by Wendy Saul (Thomas Y. Crowell, 1978), photographs by Abigail Heyman help children look more carefully at the various ways women can make a living. This is in keeping with the publisher's commitment to making available very contemporary books for girls. The front flap of this book jacket includes both the age ranges (top left corner) and the grade levels (bottom left corner).*

CHAPTER 11

The World of Writing

Becoming a writer is an arduous process. The isolation of writing itself and the complex problems of selling what you have written can inspire paranoia, anxiety, and other related, and unwelcome, symptoms. The only antidote for this down side of writing is the company of other writers. Even if your book hasn't yet appeared in print, your experience with the writing life will create the basis for socializing with other writers.

There are two places in every community where a writer can find sympathetic company. One is the library—the public library, the church library, the lending library attached to a local bookstore—and the other is the school. When you have prepared a rough draft of your nonfiction manuscript, stop in at the library and discuss it with the librarian. Librarians know what is being published, and they know what is circulating with the children. In The Dalles, Oregon library the hot book may be one on Tglinkit Indian traditions; in New York City, the best seller might be a book about life under the street—the subways, electrical lines, and water systems. Librarians have been trained to identify the titles that interest their clients. I have found librarians very helpful in making specific suggestions about subject matter, format, and age groups.

The schools in your area are also an invaluable resource. If you have a manuscript that is ready for "test marketing," you may be able to talk a local teacher into lending you her class for an hour or so. In selecting a teacher to talk to, you might want to call the school office and ask for the curriculum guide. That way you can determine what grades are studying what subjects at what time. For instance, if you are preparing a manuscript on the Pilgrims, the end of November might be a good time to present the manuscript to third graders. The teacher may be pleased to hear the nuggets of research you have discovered to add to his or her own store of knowledge. And he or she will no doubt tell you that it's a relief for the teacher, as well as for the children, to have a new personality and a fresh perspective for a change.

Outside of the school and the library, there are many other community centers where interest in writing—and a particular writer—can be drummed up. Church and synagogue programs, especially those centered around the holidays, are good forums for writers. If you've researched your subject adequately, you can also talk to adults who are interested in the subject. And because you have the added advantage of being able to bring the subject down to school-age children, you might address the children during the day, teenagers after school, and the adults in the evening. Since children's nonfiction depends so heavily on illustrations, you might consider developing a slide show, or simply showing pictures as you tell about your subject.

CONTINUING EDUCATION

Your community college is another place to turn for company as a writer. Many community colleges offer creative writing courses. Here you can develop innovative approaches to writing nonfiction for children, even if your classmates are perfecting their blank verse or revising an autobiographical novel. Writing is writing. If you find that a structured schedule is what you need to keep you from getting lonely and discouraged, sign up for a writing class. Tell your instructor what you are interested in—you won't hear any arguments from him, I promise you. John McPhee and Tom Wolfe have done a great deal to restore nonfiction to its proper (and to my mind, first) place in American literature. Your teacher will respect you for the discipline you bring to writing simply and for the enthusiasm that enables you to do the necessary research.

Workshops

I've always been too shy to benefit from a writers' workshop, but many writers find this an invaluable experience. It is generally a group of five to ten people, each immersed in his own writing project. Each reads an excerpt aloud and the other writers in the group make comments and suggestions. These are people who are writers just like you, so their suggestions are likely to be more sympathetic than what you hear from children, or teachers and librarians. I've sat in on many writers' workshops, and I feel that the most valuable part of the experience is the help you get in seeing the forest for the trees.

Writers' workshops are listed in the professional writing magazines, like *Writer's Digest* and *The Writer*. Sometimes they are sponsored by local colleges. Keep your eyes peeled. If there seems to be nothing of the sort going on in your community, start your own. Pat Poling, a writer based in Cleveland, Ohio, found that there was no place in her new suburb to discuss her work. She started her own group, and was delighted to find, through notices she posted in schools, libraries, churches, and penny-savers, that there were writers all around, dying to find a place to share their work.

Correspondence Schools

If your schedule cannot accommodate regular classes or meetings, you might want to look into correspondence schools for writers. *Writer's Digest*, the North American Newspaper Syndicate, and the Institute of Children's Literature all offer courses in writing for children. Although correspondence schools have something of a bad name, all three of these courses offer what they promise: personal attention from a professional staff, and a curriculum geared toward publication.

Because the teaching staffs in both correspondence schools and college classrooms have most likely had publication experience, they are able to guide as well as encourage you. Simply understanding the varied markets for books and articles is more than a full-time job. And since the markets change so rapidly, it's important for a beginning writer to ally himself with a seasoned pro. Your spouse or your neighbor can cheer you on, but only someone who is in the field can give you useful guidance.

BOOK FAIRS

A book fair can be a great way to learn about the many and varied book markets.

If the schools in your area don't have a book fair, you might want to get one started. It can be a moneymaker for the school's athletic program, PTA, or school library. It will give you a chance to see what publishers are promoting in the way of new books. There is nothing like looking at a hundred brand-new titles to inspire you to work on your own project. Book fairs can be arranged through special jobbers (check the Yellow Pages under "Books"), through your local bookstore, or if you're highly ambitious and highly organized, directly through publishers. If you choose this last route, check the books that you feel are the best ones published for children and approach their publishers either by letter or by telephone. This is a fine way to acquaint yourself with the staff of a children's book department.

A book fair often includes speakers. Local authors are sometimes willing to speak for free, some authors are willing to appear for expenses only, and some authors command fees that would break your bank. The only way to find out is to ask. Here you should approach the library promotion director of the children's book department, and inquire. She will be eager to help, I assure you.

If you do succeed in arranging to have a speaker at your book fair, it's a nice idea to host a luncheon or a small party honoring the writer. This will give your guest a welcome respite from her typewriter—and a chance to meet her readers. She will enjoy every minute of it. And it will give you a chance to talk to a Real Published Writer.

It is essential that you be familiar with a writer's work to talk to him or her with any result. If you know how Milton Meltzer approaches the writing of history for children, you can ask him why he puts so much emphasis on original documents, oral histories. If you haven't read the man's work, there's not much to talk about except how much money he makes and how he got started. That's gossip, not a writers' dialogue. I find nothing so annoying as people saying, "I loved your book but I was wondering"—then asking something I covered thoroughly on page 27. I always answer these questions, but often through gritted teeth. Many authors are not so polite—and why in the world should they be?

AUTHOR CORRESPONDENCE

If you read a book that you admire, and it inspires you to try to write one yourself, you might try writing a fan letter to its author. Fan letters are tricky. Some writers don't answer their own fan mail, relegating the task to a secretary or an assistant. Some authors send standard form letters to admiring fans, along with a listing of their books and perhaps a photograph. But there are many writers for children who see the importance of nonfiction, and are happy to help newcomers in the field. The most helpful guide for writing a fan letter appears in William Goldman's *Adventures in the Screen Trade*. In Chapter 7, he compares a fan letter he does answer with a typical example of the kind he doesn't. If you're thinking of writing a letter to an author, you should study this chapter, which is too detailed to paraphrase here. Generally what you want to do is (1) show that you have an understanding of the author's work, not just an acquaintance with it, (2) ask specific questions the author can answer, and (3) make it clear you are looking for advice, not favors. You may discover that your letter still isn't answered—don't take it personally, but instead, try again with another author.

Writers are often readers themselves, and it's really the fellowship of readers that draws writers together. When I worked with Shirley Hughes, the English picture-book creator, we got along fine, discussing royalty rates, production problems, and good hotels in London and New York (a more interesting subject than you'd think). But it was the discovery of our mutual enthusiasm for the novels of George Eliot that sealed our friendship. There are a few writers who don't ever read, but most writers are enthusiastic readers, astute critics, people who cling to their library books with the passion a sailor feels for his ship. Editors are always readers, and one good way to make it into the editor's inner circle is to share reading experiences. You can't go wrong.

The writing life is inherently lonely. Man is a social creature, and God did not mean for us to be lonely. Hobnobbing with insurance salesmen, doctors, and high school math teachers may be a pleasant diversion, but if you are serious about writing, you need to make room in your life for other writers, other readers. Sometimes it feels as though the competition is going to kill you, but it won't. The camaraderie and the comfort of shared misery will help you through the weeks and years of being alone with your typewriter. Writers can be stalwart friends through the dark periods, and there's a special quality of fellowship when you share success with another writer—whether it's being accepted for publication or getting a sentence exactly right.

PART THREE

A Practical Guide to Publication

When I submitted my book to Harper and Row, I thought I was handing my book over to my editor, a simple enough transaction. By the time the book was published, I had worked with sixteen different people! But they never dropped the ball.
—John Donovan

SOMETHING ABOUT THE AUTHOR

George E(dward) SULLIVAN

HOME: 330 E. 33rd St., New York, NY 10016 / (212) 689-9745.

AGENT: Eleanor Wood, Blassingame, McCauley & Wood, 225 West 34th St., New York, NY / (212) 695-3241.

FORMER CONNECTIONS: Popular Library, Inc., Promotion Manager; AMF, Public Relations Manager.

PRESENTLY: Fordham University, Adjunct Professor, teaching "Nonfiction Writing."

MEMBER: P.E.N.; Authors Guild; American Society of Journalists & Authors.

CONTRIBUTOR TO: Leading popular magazines, children's magazines, *World Book Encyclopedia*; CBS Publications.

LEE SNIDER

BOOKS:

Anwar el-Sadat; The Man Who Changed Mid-East History Walker & Co., 1982

Inside Nuclear Submarines; Dodd, Mead & Co., 1982

Quarterback; T.Y. Crowell, 1982

Great Impostors; Scholastic Books, 1982

The Art of Base Stealing; Dodd, Mead & Co., 1982 (Junior Literary Guild Selection)

The Gold Hunter's Handbook; Stein & Day, 1981 (Outdoor Life Book Club, Popular Science Book Club)

The Supercarriers; Dodd, Mead & Co., 1981 (Junior Literary Guild Selection)

Superstars of Women's Track; Dodd, Mead & Co., 1981

Discover Archaeology; Doubleday, 1980 (Junior Literary Guild Selection; Reprinted by Penguin Books)

Better Baseball for Boys; Dodd, Mead & Co., 1980 (Sports Spectrum Book Club)

Gary Player's Book for Young Golfers; Simon & Schuster, 1980 (*Golf Digest* Book Club; A Teen-age Book-of-the-Year Selection, New York Public Library)

Track and Field; Secrets of the Stars; Doubleday, 1979 (A Teen-age Book-of-the-Year Selection, New York Public Library)

Run, Run Fast; T.Y. Crowell, 1979

Modern Olympic Superstars; Dodd, Mead & Co., 1979 (A Book-of-the-Year Selection, Child Study Association)

Amazing Sports Facts; Scholastic Books, 1978

Wind Power for Your Home; Simon & Schuster, 1978 (Reprinted by Media Marketing, Inc.)

This Is Pro Basketball; Dodd, Mead & Co., 1978 (A Teen-age Book-of-the-Year Selection, New York Public Library)

Sports Superstitions; Coward, McCann, & Geoghegan, 1978 (A Teen-age Book-of-the-Year Selection, New York Public Library)

The Picture Story of Reggie Jackson; Simon & Schuster, 1978

Better Soccer for Boys & Girls; Dodd, Mead & Co., 1977

The Picture Story of Nadia Comaneci; Simon & Schuster, 1977

How Do They Package It?; Westminster Press, 1977

Understanding Hydroponics; Frederick Warne & Co., 1976

This Is Pro Hockey; Dodd, Mead & Co., 1976 (A Teen-age Book-of-the-Year Selection, New York Public Library)

How Do They Find It; Westminster Press, 1976

Better Roller Skating for Boys & Girls; Dodd, Mead & Co., 1976

Home Run!; Dodd, Mead & Co., 1975 (A Recommended Book, Children's Book Council)

Pro Football A to Z; Winchester Press, 1975 (Reprinted by Scribners)

How Does It Get There?; Westminster Press, 1975 (Junior Literary Guild Selection)

Better Gymnastics for Girls; Dodd, Mead & Co., 1975

Understanding Photography; Frederick Warne & Co., 1974 (Reprinted by Simon & Schuster)

Pro Football's Winning Plays; Dodd, Mead & Co., 1974

The Beginner's Guide to Platform Tennis; Coward, McCann & Geoghegan, 1975

The Gamemakers; G.P. Putnam's, 1973 (Sports Illustrated Book Club)

George Sullivan, the author of more than 100 nonfiction books for children, presents himself to new publishers with this fact sheet which he submits with each manuscript.

CHAPTER 12

Finding the Best
Publisher for Your Ideas

One of the biggest problems you face as a nonfiction writer is when to submit your manuscript. Do you want to interest an editor before you have written anything, or wait until you have covered all the material and submit an entire manuscript? Though it varies from author to author and project to project, you are best off doing your research thoroughly before you query an editor. The reasons for this are three: 1) Research can bring a new angle to the way you might write the book; 2) You don't want a long period to elapse between telling the editor that the manuscript is available and actually submitting it, because the editor's enthusiasm can wane; and 3) You don't know until you begin to research your topic if it will hold enough interest for *you* to write an entire book about it.

DO YOUR HOMEWORK

Before you spend a lot of time developing a presentation for your nonfiction book, choose your publisher. The reason for this is obvious to professionals who understand that different publishers have different requirements. If you don't know whom you're writing for, you can cause yourself needless work.

How do you go about choosing a nonfiction publisher?

Begin by going to the library. Although not every library has every new book, you will see the range of titles available from many different publishers there. Make notes of books that impress you with the quality of writing, the production values, and the subject matter. See who's publishing what. Since so many nonfiction books appear in series, you may find one that suits the approach you want to take. Even if a book isn't in a series, you can get an idea of an editor's preferences by studying, publisher by publisher, what has already been produced.

Then ask your librarian if she can lend you the children's announcement issues of *Publishers Weekly, The New York Times*, or *School Library Journal*. These magazines feature the publisher's new lists—the books that they are publishing *now*. The book you admired in your library could be twenty years old, and editorial policies have changed since then. Some lists of book offerings from publishers used to be heavily fiction but are now leaning toward nonfiction. Other publishers who used to publish a lot of nonfiction are now emphasizing fiction. You want to know for sure.

If your librarian can't provide you with these magazines, don't despair. Write to the Children's Book Council, 67 Irving Place, New York, N.Y. 10003. Enclose a stamped self-addressed envelope and request the most recent list of publishers. This is a three-page mimeographed list telling you the name of the editor and the library promotion director for each of the children's publishers. Write to the library promotion director, again enclosing a stamped self-addressed envelope, requesting the latest catalog of juvenile books. Most publishers are happy to comply with this request.

Once you have catalogs in hand, study them carefully. Look for series of books in which your project might fit. Compare the new offerings with the older ones: in which direction is the publisher going? Many editors say that with the increasing cutbacks of library funds, they are publishing less and less nonfiction. This should not discourage you because there is always a demand for a good product, whether nonfiction or fiction. Nonetheless, there are publishers who publish virtually no nonfiction. "Only if it's for the very young and the author can bring to it the passion and interest we find in fiction," says Susan Hirschman, editor-in-chief of Greenwillow Books. You'd think from this that Greenwillow was out of the picture as far as nonfiction goes, but in fact, Greenwillow has published lots of nonfiction, all of it prize-winning. Hirschman is looking for the exceptional, the special, the personal that many publishers are vying for.

One thing you may notice is that many publishers are looking for material for younger and younger readers. Several publishers I talked to feel that the big demand for nonfiction is in the younger age groups, because the teenage market has been saturated.

Little insights from the publishers' catalog will help you choose a publisher. For instance, if a publisher has published books illustrated with photographs, and your book requires photographic treatment, you don't have to worry that the publisher will reject your idea because they don't

FEBRUARY

CLAY PLAY: Learning Games for Children

by Henry Post and Michael McTwigan ———— **First-Time Authors**
illustrated by Diane Martin

———— **Cute Illustration**

Text Approach

These 42 fun-filled learning games for children require just one material: a lump of clay. Each game is presented in large, easy-to-read type, and illustrated with an interpretation of the game. The games are arranged in four sections:
(1) what children can do <u>to</u> clay;
(2) what they can do <u>with</u> clay, exploiting its unique properties;
(3) interaction games—mazes, puzzles and teasers; and
(4) group creative efforts.
An afterword by Mihalyi Csikszentmihalyi of the University of Chicago's Committee on Human Development explains how the games are useful in learning to learn. A guide to buying and caring for clay is included.

**Illustration
Possibilities**

50 line drawings & photographs.
64 pages —— 7 x 9¾   Grades PreS-3   Ages 3-8
Large Format 0-18-136408-1   LC# 72-7277 $4.95j (subject to discount)

The catalog that publishers send to their customers can be a useful guide to authors choosing a publisher. Here the format, the price, the subject, the age group and the selling angle are all laid out for the aspiring author to analyze.

have the facilities to reproduce them. If a publisher has published illustrations by your favorite artist, you know there's a chance that this artist will be available to illustrate your book. If the publisher has a new series in which your idea fits, your chances for publication success are greater than they would be without such a series.

Shop as carefully for a publisher as you would for a doctor. You want to be proud of your association with your publisher, to see your book published well, and to enjoy royalty checks once your book is published. Even more important, you don't want a rejection letter saying that "your book is not right for our list." This can be a devastating experience, since you know your topic and outline are good. You can avoid this kind of rejection by doing a little homework first.

TO QUERY OR NOT TO QUERY?

Some editors prefer a query letter, on the basis of which they hope to determine 1) the author's qualifications, 2) interest in the subject matter, and 3) competition for the book. Editor Edna Barth, prejudiced perhaps by her own second career as a writer of nonfiction, always found query letters useless. "A nonfiction treatment depends on the way the writer handles her subject," Barth maintained. "You can't tell from a query letter how the author treats the intricacies of the subject." Other editors, who review up to two thousand manuscripts each year, appreciate the succinct description that is found in a good query letter. "It's easier to tell from a query letter whether or not a subject is right for our 'Let's Read and Find Out' series," says Marilyn Kriney, the editor at T. Y. Crowell. Once Kriney has determined that the subject is one that will fit in the series, then she considers questions of writing and age level appropriateness.

An effective query letter is short and straightforward. It explains the appeal of the subject matter, the length of the manuscript, the kind of book you envision, and your qualifications for writing the manuscript. A good query can cover these points in two or three short paragraphs. As you write your letter, imagine the editor's need for information and stick to the material that is relevant to submitting the manuscript to the editorial committee for publication. The editor will want to know how your approach differs from existing books on the same subject. She will want to know how your background will enhance the subject matter and the book's readability. She will imagine in her mind's eye how the book will look once it is published. You, the author, can communicate this information to her better than anyone else. But bear in mind that the editor has to go through reams of manuscripts every week and she will appreciate your brevity.

Along with brevity, your query letter should contain some punch. Communicate your enthusiasm for your subject—explain why you have become interested enough in the subject to write a book about it. Share pre-

A Sample Manuscript Page

Top Margin 1¾″

XII-5

Shop as carefully for a publisher as you would for a doctor. You want to be proud of your association with your publisher, to see your book published well, and to enjoy royalty checks once your book is published. Even more important, you don't want a rejection letter saying that "your book is not right for our list." This can be a devastating experience, since you know your topic and outline are good. You can avoid this kind of rejection by doing a little homework first.

Left Margin 1″

To Query or Not to Query?

Some editors prefer a query letter, on the basis of which they hope to determine 1)the author's qualifications, 2)interest in the subject matter, and 3)competition for the book. Editor Edna Barth, prejudiced perhaps by her own second career as a writer of nonfiction, always found query letters useless. "A nonfiction treatment depends on the way the writer handles her subject," Barth maintained. "You can't tell from a query letter how the author treats the intricacies of the subject." Other editors, who review up to two thousand manuscripts each year, appreciate the succinct description that is found in a good query letter. "It's easier to tell from a query letter whether or not a subject is right for our 'Let's Read and Find Out' series," says Marilyn Kriney, the editor at T.Y.

Right Margin 1½″

Bottom Margin 1½″

Manuscripts should be double-spaced. Editors resent manuscripts typed with worn-out ribbons or on a dot-matrix computer printer. The author's name and address should be stamped on the back of each manuscript page in an unobtrusive color (blue is best) and each page should be numbered with both the chapter and page number—the chapter number in roman numerals, the page number in arabic numbers. There's no need for a title page; simply type the title in capital letters at the top of the first page.

liminary opinions from children, teachers, and librarians who have had an advance peek at your manuscript or with whom you have discussed the idea. Those groups are the publisher's ultimate customers, so the editor will be interested in early responses. If you can say, "I read this manuscript to a third-grade class and they were spellbound," you have a strong selling point right there. If you mention that your local children's librarian has bemoaned the absence of a simple introduction to ham radio, you are pointing out a real market need to the editor.

Editors are people, too, and enjoy hearing their books praised. If you can show familiarity with a publisher's line of books, he is going to be more interested in your project than if you don't know anything about what the publisher is doing.

"Don't Call Us, We'll Call You"

Many authors ask if they should call a publisher and discuss the manuscript before they submit it. The answer to that one is a resounding "no." If you call a publisher, it should be only to speak to the editor's secretary. You can ask the editor's name (and be sure to check the spelling!) and inquire how long you will have to wait for an answer to your query. Since the length of time it takes for a publisher to respond can be up to six months, it is often reassuring to hear it from the horse's mouth. Don't insist on speaking to the editor: an editor is a busy person whose time is taken up with meetings, conferences, and editing of manuscripts already on the publication list. So even if you feel a little personal contact would speed your manuscript along, resist the impulse and let your query letter speak for itself.

What if you have a friend who has a friend at a publishing house? Should you submit your manuscript there? Usually the answer is "no" here, too. If you would have chosen that publisher to send your manuscript to in the first place, it does no harm to send in a manuscript with your friend's name on it. Most often, however, the friend's friend at the publishing house will send you a prompt and polite negative because the manuscript doesn't fit into the house's publishing plans. Don't let your professional research into the right publisher get undermined by nerves which make you reluctant to send your manuscript in cold.

The plain truth is, the manuscript speaks for itself. Knowing someone, or worse still, knowing someone who knows someone, isn't going to help you at all. What will help you is a thoughtful query letter.

THE PROPOSAL

Once you get an editor's go-ahead on your query, you're ready to submit a proposal. Sometimes editors will ask to see a complete manuscript if you state in your query that it's available, but most often they want to see a proposal first. A proposal consists of a cover letter, resume, a table of contents or an outline, and a sample chapter.

If you're submitting your proposal in response to an editor's interest, your cover letter can be short and sweet. Mention the date of her letter to you, reiterate any important points about the book, and thank her for her interest. On the other hand, it you're sending your proposal "cold," you need to put a little more work into your cover letter, because it must capture the editor's interest and convince her that this idea is right for her company. Whatever form it takes, however, a cover letter should be no longer than a page.

Here's an example of a letter that covers all bases in a succinct and interesting way.

Dear Editor,

I have written a book about nutrition for the six to nine age group. I have tried this manuscript out on my Sunday School class (ages seven and eight) and the children have responded favorably to my humorous approach. I'm sending the manuscript to you because I have used your books by Judith Seixas (<u>Alcohol and Tobacco</u>) with this same class, and feel that this book fits in well with your easy-to-read line.

I am enclosing my resume, an outline, three sample chapters, and a stamped, self-addressed envelope. I look forward to hearing from you.

Sincerely,

The Resume

Along with the cover letter, send your resume. Your resume should not be the kind you send when you're looking for a job, but a more personal one. Headings should include general information: your home and office addresses and telephone numbers, organizations to which you belong, education, including any writing courses you have taken, and why you are writing for children.

The reason for including a resume is partly to keep your cover letter to one page. The editor wants to know how much you know about your subject—have you taken courses in it, do you belong to organizations devoted to this area of study, are you a teacher or librarian? If you were a painting major in college and are interested in writing a book about art of the Renaissance, the publisher will appreciate your expertise. But suppose you were a painting major in college, and you want to write a book about heat? Here your resume won't help you as much as an explanation in your letter about how a question in physics captured your imagination.

Publishers always welcome manuscripts that stem from real-life questions children ask. If your children inspired your manuscript, your resume will point your editor to the fact that you have three school-age children. If your students sparked the idea for a book, your resume will explain that you have been a classroom teacher. If you have done volunteer work in the local library—as many writers do—your resume should not overlook this important activity. Any work that you've done with children is important to the publisher, because it means you know kids.

Your writing credits should also appear. The most direct contribution a list of your credits can make is to show that you have already been published on this subject. But editors look for subtle points in writing credits: if you have published fiction, she will know that your writing skills are probably good. If you have handled difficult nonfiction subjects, he will know that you have good conceptualizing talents and can handle the new subject you are proposing. If you are a new writer with projects completed that haven't been published, you might want the resume to list your completed projects. The reason for this is that editors are looking for serious writers who are committed to the nonfiction field. If you show promise as a "perennial producer," the editor's interest will be sparked.

When a book is proposed for publication, there is often a section for the editor to fill out in the proposal form on "author's qualifications." You want to establish yourself with information that she can put down in that section, showing expertise in the subject area, knowledge of children and what they like, and writing ability. When the book is published, organizations to which you belong can be used to promote the book. Your previous writing credits can be used on the book's jacket to show your proven writing ability, and special knowledge of the subject will convince the sales staff at the publishing house that you are qualified to write in the nonfiction area you have chosen.

Maybe you don't know anyone on *The New York Times*, but contacts in your area—including those at local newspapers and television stations—can be useful in selling books. If you had an autographing party for your last book at the local bookstore, mention it on your resumé. If you speak to science classes in your neighborhood, mention it. Books are promoted in many ways, and your resume should indicate how you can hustle your book once it's published. Similarly, it's important to list organizations in which you are active, even if it's only the college alumni association or the local scouting group. Word of mouth, beginning with small forays into the media, still sell books better than any advertising campaign.

The Table of Contents

The heart of your submission package is your outline or table of contents. It's especially important for nonfiction books because it gives the editor an overview of the way you're handling your subject, and sets the tone of your presentation. When an editor buys a fiction manuscript, she doesn't pay much attention to the outline, because the author's style makes the book. But in nonfiction it isn't enough to write well—the author must have something to say. The table of contents shows at a glance what that something is.

Structuring your manuscript, which I discussed in Chapter 9, is a magical process, haphazard at best. The ways ideas connect, the way inspiration hits you while you're brushing your teeth, the way one sentence leads to another, are mysterious and idiosyncratic. The outline must be perfectly conceived and perfectly executed. It's like a beautifully tailored garment—not a loose thread, not a crooked seam. And although writing an outline might appear to be routine, it may actually be the most creative part of writing your nonfiction book because there is more work in a single page of outline than there is in pages of any manuscript. Into the outline goes the train of thought that will lead the young reader along. Your special approach to the topic—and there's nothing new under the sun, with most subjects having appeared in book or article form—is the thing that will sell your book to the editor.

Suppose you are writing a book on science projects in the biology field: Will your approach be to divide biology into various subcategories and arrange the projects accordingly? Or will you follow a cookbook approach, listing the projects in random order to appeal to the young browser? Both these approaches are valid, but your editor needs to know which course you will take. Often an editor can suggest from an outline ways to restructure your ideas to fit an age group or interest level. Some writers find that they are able to create a table of contents only after they have completed the research and sometimes the writing as well. Other authors can structure a book easily and find that the hard part for them is the actual writing. But there is no point in proposing a nonfiction book without an outline.

The Outline

You can outline a nonfiction book or article in several ways. Each has its advantages and disadvantages: there is no "right" way to lay out a book. The noun topic outline is the most straightforward. You may have done this kind of outline in school. It's a simple principle: You begin with large headings identified with Roman numerals. If you were writing a book about rabbits, for instance, you might begin with a large heading, *Rabbit Relatives*. Using capital letters to identify the next subheading, you would include the families to which the rabbit is related. Then using Arabic numbers, you would list specific beasts who belong to these families. If there is a tantalizing piece of information you want to include about one of these family members, you would enter that information with a small letter under the Arabic numeral entry. Sticking simply to nouns, you cover the high spots of your story, leaving the sample chapters to show how you will cover individual entries. The noun topic outline works best for writers who want to save the "creative" work for the writing stage. It gives the editor an idea of the ground that you are going to cover without showing exactly how you write.

The "stream-of-consciousness" outline is more detailed than the noun topic outline, and shows more of the flow of your narrative. Arnold Madison is one successful nonfiction writer who uses the stream-of-consciousness outline style. In his proposal for a biography of Carry Nation, he outlined his topic thus:

> Chapter Three: 1865-Dr. Charles Gloyd hired as schoolmaster: room and board at Moore house. Courtship develops with Carry. Father against the courtship because Gloyd drinks. Alcohol and tobacco major sins to Moore. Marriage—1867. Move to Holden, Missouri. Gloyd's medical practice deteriorates as drinking escalates. Carry pregnant and penniless. Marks last visit to Gloyd. "I'll be dead in six months if you leave me." She refuses to stay. Six months later—Gloyd dies.

Whichever approach you take, don't make the mistake of overwriting your outline. The outline is the skeleton of your book and you want to leave yourself freedom to flesh it out in the actual writing process. Writing strictly to an outline is good for a term paper, or even a doctoral dissertation, but it lacks the spontaneity that a good book or article needs to be readable. The outline should be complete enough so that you have a map of where you're going and how you're going to get there. But it should leave enough room for you to develop a voice of your own as you sit down and talk to your reader through your typewriter. This is where the sample chapter comes in.

The Sample Chapter

Writing nonfiction for young people has come a long way since it first developed as a form during the second World War. As author Vicki Cobb, who has written science books for children including *Science Projects You Can Eat* points out: "Originally, the aim of the science writer was to present complex concepts in a clear way that children can understand. Now there is a need for a personal touch, a personality behind the writing. Clarity alone is not enough." If Cobb's success is any indicator, this is the trend in writing

```
OUTLINE for KIDNAPPING: The Persistent Crime

    by Mary Helen Boldrick


I. The History of Kidnapping

   A. Where Kidnapping Was Most Prevalent in Olden Times

   B. What Measures Families Took to Prevent Kidnapping

II. Great Modern American Kidnappings

   A. The Lindbergh Case

   B. The Ransom of Red Chief

   C. Etan Patz

III. How Kidnappings Are Planned

   A. Profile of a Typical Kidnapper

   B. Situations Kidnappers Seek Out

   C. What Kidnappers Want

IV. What Kids Can Do About Kidnapping

   A. When To Trust A Stranger

   B. What To Do When You Are Cornered

   C. Looking After Little Kids: A Guide for Big Brothers

   and Babysitters

V. The Way People Are

   A. Programs for Rehabilitating Kidnappers

   B. Organizations That Help Victims' Families

   C. Survivors: Kidnapped Children Share Their Experiences
```

An effective first outline is consistent and concise. Here two years of research are neatly encapsulated on a single page of balanced topics on a controversial subject.

nonfiction for children: the personal touch. Editors are not looking for ency-clopedic writing which crams the most information into the smallest space, nor are they looking for magazine articles that cover a very small topic in depth. They are looking for book-sized ideas that cover a broad enough range to justify the purchase of a hardcover book, and a writing style—note that word *style*—that is engaging enough to hook the reader and keep him interested. "My vindication," Cobb continues, "was watching a little girl read my book *Lots of Rot*. Her mother told her it was time to go, but the lit-tle girl said, 'I'm not finished.' She stood there turning every page until she finished the book." This is the kind of spellbinding readability that editors look for in nonfiction these days.

Several of the writers I spoke to in preparation for this book com-plained that they loved research so much that they were slow to get started with the actual writing. "I loved the hours at the library, finding new infor-mation and new angles that it took me literally years to get down to the ac-tual writing," confesses Lady Winifred Roll, author of *The Pomegranate and the Rose* and *Mary I*. This is a problem with nonfiction writing, to give up the research and to begin on the exposition. Some writers look forward to the actual writing, but if you dread getting started, you are in good com-pany. Although one sample chapter is all you need to submit to most pub-lishers in order to get an indication of interest in publishing the book, you may not want to submit the first chapter you write. It takes time to develop a voice, an approach, a point of view. Sometimes you have to complete three or four chapters or segments of your book before it emerges as a co-herent whole.

You may want to begin at the beginning, whereas the exciting ma-terial is most likely to fall in the middle of the book, if not at the end. Re-member that your editor is your audience, an expert audience to be sure, but your audience nonetheless. She is looking for the same elements of in-terest that your ultimate reader is, so your sample chapter should be as in-teresting as you can make it.

Although the cover letter, the résumé, and the outline are important, the acid test will be your sample chapter. Labor over it, revise it, try it out on young readers before you submit the chapter to your publisher. Re-search skills are important, but in writing for youngsters the bottom line is your skill at conveying information.

If your book includes original research, and you have found a previ-ously unpublished nugget of information, you may want to highlight this in your sample chapter. Editors are always looking for handles—publishing jargon for that quality that makes a book special. As biographer Esther Douty points out, "From my own experience and that of other writers I know, the sad fact is that the reviewers rarely realize that a juvenile biog-raphy often represents as much scholarly digging as an adult biography. The research for my book on James Forten, for example, took three years."

One way to force reviewers to acknowledge the research you've done for your book is to highlight it in the jacket copy. An editor working with a sample chapter that includes original and new research will be inclined to emphasize it in touting your book.

The question of whether to include more than one sample chapter is a thorny one. If your story covers material of different intensity—for instance, a biography of Julia Ward Howe which includes a fairly quiet childhood and a fairly dramatic adulthood you might want to submit one chapter from each section of the book.

Whether or not you submit more than the sample chapter will depend on the way you like to work. From a purely practical point of view, you don't want to spend time writing a manuscript that isn't right for any publisher's list. Except . . . Except if you have a burning interest in a subject and you want to write the entire book before you try to sell it. Except if you are confident that you are on target with subject and approach. Except if you have researched the subject anyway and the writing comes easily. If you fall into any of these "exceptional" categories, you have the choice of submitting the whole package to a single publisher or submitting one chapter each to several publishers.

MULTIPLE SUBMISSIONS

The question of multiple submission is a hot topic in publishing circles. Whether you should submit to more than one publisher at a time is a decision that you alone can make.

Until about 1980, multiple submissions for children's books were virtually unheard of. Authors endured waits of three months, six months, even a year, to receive no more than a form rejection. For a timely manuscript this was the kiss of death. Authors began to get frustrated, then angry, then outraged. If it takes an average of ten tries to find a publisher for a nonfiction project, and an average of six months to hear from each publisher, you figure that it will take five years to sell one book. A most depressing thought.

It used to be that a writer could interpret a long wait as an indication that his manuscript was being considered seriously, but no more. You can be virtually certain that it's sitting there gathering dust waiting to be noticed by a busy editor. One editor confided to me that her list had grown by 30 percent while her staff had shrunk by 10 percent. I asked her if she maintained a reader to handle the slush pile. I thought it was an eminently sensible question, but she thought it was a great joke. "A reader—a recent college graduate who is willing to work for peanuts for the chance to break into publishing—costs a publishing house about twenty thousand dollars a year, when you consider salary, benefits, office space, and mailing costs. We'd be out of business if we paid for that." Another editor with a more hard-headed approach admitted, "We would rather pay more for agented manuscripts, which we know have been screened, than to spend the staff time going through the slush pile."

So the position of "first reader" is obsolete. Editors make time to look at the slush pile at many houses, but it is a rather haphazard undertaking. Long waits are the rule these days, not the exception they were in the sixties.

The Society of Children's Book Writers (SCBW) decided to examine this situation in 1982. They surveyed publishers and discovered that many editors were aware of the realities and were willing to accept multiple submissions. Naturally, there were a few holdouts who insisted that they be the only ones to see a manuscript, but these were in the minority.

The outstanding finding of the SCBW survey was that so many editors stipulated they be *told* the manuscript was being submitted elsewhere. As an editor, I assumed this was to ensure that the editor act quickly in making a decision in a competitive environment. But as an author, I got a little paranoid: maybe this was a way of saying that editors will pretend to play along and consider multiple submissions, when in fact, they won't consider them seriously. I interviewed twelve editors about this, and they were divided about equally between the ones who really did look at multiple submissions seriously and those who didn't. For some editors, knowing that a manuscript is being considered elsewhere is a spur, for others it's no more than an insult.

Many publishers won't look twice at a photocopied proposal, figuring that you have sent it on to other publishers as well. But most publishers *will* look at originals even if they are sent out to more than one publisher. So if you have time and energy to retype your outline over several times, and you have written enough to have several different chapters to send to several different publishers, then multiple submission may be the road you want to travel.

Many enterprising authors have word processors and submit originals to six or seven publishers at a time. As word processors become more widely available, more standardized and cheaper, most serious writers will become word processor owners. The word processor works just like a type-writer, but it has the capacity to store mountains of material on a small "floppy disk" and to print out any or all of the information on the disk with a printer. It can produce all the "original manuscripts" you need, and there's no way anyone will know.

Should you tell an editor that you are submitting your material simul-taneously, since it's so clear that everybody in the know is doing it and not necessarily saying it? I think not. No editor has ever written to me to tell me that she is considering twenty other manuscripts besides mine, so why should I tell her that I am considering twenty other publishing houses be-sides hers? And, as many an agent has pointed out, publishers submit multiple copies of your book to paperback houses for reprint publication, so why is the idea so abhorrent to them?

There are, of course, cases where multiple submission is rude, crude, and unattractive. Suppose you sold your first manuscript to a sympathetic editor who spent time editing your manuscript, fought for a beautiful jacket, sold it enthusiastically to the sales force and promoted the book (and you, as its promising author) to any reviewer who would listen. The obligation is obvious: any editor who goes out on a limb for you, especially at the beginning of your career, deserves an exclusive look at your next project.

Agreement

made _____ , 19 ___ , between PRENTICE-HALL, INC., hereinafter called the "PUBLISHER," and

_____ hereinafter called the "AUTHOR."

The parties hereto agree as follows:

Grant of Rights

1. The AUTHOR grants to the PUBLISHER and its successors, representatives and assigns, an unpublished work on

_____

with the exclusive right to print, publish and sell the work, under its own name and under various imprints and trade names, during the full term of copyright and all renewals thereof, in the English language throughout the world;

also all rights in said work of digest, abridgment, condensation, selection, anthology, quotation, book club, reprint edition through another publisher, first and second serialization, syndication, advertising, novelty or similar commercial use of the work or material based on the work, translation and foreign language publication, motion picture, dramatic, radio, television, mechanical rendition and/or recording, and any other rights now existing or that may hereafter come into existence, with exclusive authority to dispose of said rights and to authorize the use of the AUTHOR's name and likeness or photograph in connection therewith, in all countries and in all languages.

Copyright

2. The PUBLISHER shall have the exclusive right to take out copyright of the work in the PUBLISHER's name in the United States and in the PUBLISHER's name or in any other name in other countries. The AUTHOR will, upon the PUBLISHER's request, do all acts necessary to effect and protect the copyright and renewals thereof.

Delivery of Manuscript

3. The manuscript, in English, containing approximately _____ words or their equivalent, shall be delivered in triplicate by the AUTHOR to the PUBLISHER in final form acceptable to the PUBLISHER on or before _____ , 19 ___ .

Book Royalties

4. When the manuscript is accepted and when it has been approved for publication by the PUBLISHER and is ready for publication, it will be published at the PUBLISHER's own expense. The PUBLISHER will pay the AUTHOR royalties based on the actual cash received by the PUBLISHER from the sale by it of the published work, said royalties to be computed and shown separately, as follows:

(1) on copies of the regular trade edition in the United States (other than sales falling within (2) through (7) below), 10%.

Read your contract carefully. Too often, authors are so happy to be published that they close their eyes and sign the contract in a swoon. This chapter will help you know what to look for—and look out for—in a publisher's contract.

CHAPTER 13

Contracts—
Before, During, and After

You make contracts every hour of your life, but since they aren't printed in tiny type full of "whereases" and "notwithstandings," they don't have the long-term consequences of a written agreement for an intangible and uncertain creative property. When you tell your son he can ride his motorcycle all day Saturday as long as he stays off the highway, and he promises, the two of you have a contract.

But a publishing contract goes into effect only when both author and publisher have signed it. As you negotiate the terms of your contract with your editor, never lose sight of that final goal of signing and countersigning. It's the signing that establishes the record of who will do what, and how, when things happen. And things do happen—good and bad.

For publishers, to whom a contract is an everyday occurrence, the attitude is somewhat more ho-hum than it is for the author whose work is finally going to see the light of day. But casual attitude notwithstanding, the publisher does want the author to understand how the book is going to be sold; the contract lays the groundwork for these procedures which are just as important to your editor and publisher as they are to you, the author.

Contracts have two important sections: how your manuscript is going to be sold in book form, and how your manuscript is going to be adapted to nonbook media.

Books endure in hardcover editions, in paperback, in specially reinforced library editions, in oversize trade paperbacks, in cheap paper-

Certainly Benjamin's father never gave fame a thought. Mr. Franklin was a Leather Apron man; in other words, he worked with his hands and he had a trade. Carpenters, shoemakers, silversmiths, blacksmiths—all such men were called Leather Aprons because they wore leather aprons when they worked. Mr. Franklin was a soap- and candle-maker. His brothers were Leather Apron men and his sons would be Leather Apron men. That was generally the way it was in those days.

When Benjamin was born, his oldest brother, Samuel, was already a blacksmith. (The oldest son in the Franklin family was always a blacksmith.) Benjamin's brother James would be a printer. Three other brothers would be trained for the candle and soap business. The remaining four brothers died young. Two died as babies and Josiah and Ebenezer were drowned. Josiah ran away from home and was drowned at sea. Sixteen month-old Ebenezer ran away from his mother and was drowned in a tub of his father's soapsuds.

8

Jean Fritz's engaging text for What's the Big Idea, Ben Franklin? *was a success in hardcover and is now a best-selling paperback.*

backs at a very low price for special markets, such as classroom sales, movie tie-ins, or premiums. Books occasionally are excerpted in magazines (first serial rights), in newspapers (second serial rights), in video and audio cassettes (usually sold along with a cheap edition of the book in the same package), in textbooks (a chapter in your book about elephants is included in a junior high school biology text) or in novelty items, like tee shirts, teddy bears, and lunchboxes. The book rights are the heart of your contract, since that's where the juvenile nonfiction writer stands to make the most money. But the other media rights—the subsidiary rights—are also important. The extreme swings in fashion every three years or so make it virtually impossible to predict what will be hot ten years hence: computer games for the home market are nearly extinct, whereas interactive software, often developed from books, has gained a strong foothold in the educational market.

Your publisher knows the sales potential in each of these many markets. His field reps tell him which library systems and bookstore chains are buying what; his library promotion manager knows which systems are revitalizing their libraries; his editors know what the videocassette publisher or the Swedish book club is looking for in the way of new products. Your publisher and his team of experts figure how many of your books they can sell in an ordinary year. These estimates are compiled in a profit and loss statement (P&L for short) which directs your publisher in how much to invest in your book. Since each method of distribution is undertaken by a different company and different agents, the costs vary. The author gets a percentage of the publisher's income *after* the expenses of distributing the book in its many forms are paid off. And that's what a contract generally addresses: how much the author is going to make and how much the publisher is going to make.

THE ADVANCE

Checking out the advance payment before you read the rest of the contract is somewhat like looking at the end of the movie before you see the first hour, but it's what all your friends and associates will be asking you: how much did you make? Any writer knows that the advance payment is just that, money paid by the publisher *in advance* of publication against future sales. You might look at it as a loan which will be paid back by the royalties your book earns as it's sold. A royalty is a percentage of the selling price—about 5 percent of the list price of the book. Authors tend to believe that payment for their work is an affirmation of professional status. This is absolutely true, but an author's work is *not measured* by the size of the advance. Unlike adult books, which generally sell the most copies the first year, children's books get started slowly, then sell over a period of years. A children's author may earn $80,000 in royalties over the course of his book's lifetime, but he will not be given an $80,000 advance as some adult authors are. Advances will start at about $1,000 and rise to about $5,000. Publishers usually base their advance payments on projected first-year sales, and for children's nonfiction these are usually relatively small. In the second year, after the book has been reviewed, book sales often take off. Ask your editor how well she expects your book to sell, how long a period (a year, eighteen months, the first printing, the book's lifetime sales) the advance covers, and what kind of income you can expect in both the best and the worst projections. Armed with this information, you are in a position to consider whether your advance is fair.

Stages of the Advance

The advance for a nonfiction children's book is usually made in four parts:

1. *On signing.* This is an incentive for the author to enter into an agreement with the publisher. Be sure that the signing payment, the money the publisher pays you on the basis of your proposal, is earmarked "nonreturnable." At other stages of the book's development, the publisher has the option and indeed the obligation to refuse your work on the grounds that it is not acceptable, that it isn't what you promised. But at this stage, the publisher is buying the work that you have done on speculation, and effectively is taking the book idea out of circulation, out of the reach of other potential publishers. You deserve to be compensated for this with 10 to 25 percent of the book's total advance. A publisher who refuses this initial nonreturnable payment is probably a crook.

2. *Receipt of the complete and final manuscript.* The complete manuscript needs to be acceptable on several levels, which differ from publisher to publisher but essentially cover what you've said and how you've said it. Be sure that you and your editor have agreed *in writing* what the book should be. It's been my experience as both an editor and a writer, that editors don't have the time to write long careful letters outlining what "mutually acceptable" should be. So when you talk to your editor, take notes. When she sends you a letter, keep it to refer to as you write the letter discussing what you both think the acceptable manuscript should be.

3. *Illustrations.* This payment is for books for older children, where the author gets the full royalty and also takes responsibility for providing the art. Writers for younger children who do their own illustrations also bear the burden of this clause. The art should be reproduction quality (no blurry Polaroids), ready for the printer, and cleared legally (photo permissions are covered in Chapter 10).

4. *Index.* The index is prepared shortly before the book goes to the printer and its preparation is a complex task that must be accomplished at awesome speed, usually three to six weeks, from the page proofs. While many writers find preparing an index tedious and prefer to have the publisher assume the task and charge it against royalties, others find this final step very comforting.

Once you have received the total advance, about three months before publication, do not expect additional money for at least a full calendar year. The advance is meant to cover royalties for the first year of sales. You will not see additional money (unless your publisher is very conservative and underestimated first-year sales) for nearly eighteen months. Poor understanding of this basic publishing arrangement is responsible for much unnecessary suffering and frustration.

Royalties

Many first-time book authors are disappointed by the royalty rate they are offered. The general consensus is that a writer's royalty should start at no lower than 5 percent of the list price of the book. After the first 10,000 copies are sold, most publishers are willing to raise the royalty to 6 or 7 percent. This sliding-scale royalty, beginning at a point where the publisher has recovered his initial investment and begins to make money on your book, makes sense all around, and you are justified in trying to hold out for it. Many writers urge the publisher to escalate the royalty again, to 7 or 8 percent, after 25,000 copies are sold. This is also an eminently fair arrangement, since a children's book that sells over 25,000 copies in hardcover editions these days is counted as a rousing success.

Paperback editions offer somewhat lower royalties, occasionally as little as half the royalty on the hardcover edition. The trick in negotiating a paperback royalty is to spell out a percentage based on the list price of the paperback edition. If it's only 3 or 4 percent, you're still getting a fair shake.

There may be other unpleasant surprises, for author and publisher alike, that can further impede cash flow to the writer:

1. *Publishers sell books on consignment.* This means that the bookseller can return them to the publisher for full reimbursement any time during the book's print life. For this reason, publishers usually hold 15 percent of the author's first-year sales as a "returns allowance." Usually by the second year sales have evened out so the publisher no longer sees the necessity for such an allowance, but don't count on it. Publishers really do need this cash reserve to cover the costs of books that are returned. As Alfred Knopf used to say about book distribution in America, "Gone today; here tomorrow."

2. *High discount royalties.* Many writers look at the clause for regular hardcover sales of their book and calculate the royalty they will receive on this figure. Because hardcover books are sold in small quantities at low discounts, this regular hardcover rate is TWICE the average book royalty rate. High discount book sales through wholesalers and chain stores has made the "regular" royalty the exception, not the rule. If your regular royalty is 8 percent of the book's list price, figure 4 percent as the average royalty for all book sales. The whys and wherefores of high-discount purchasing will be discussed in greater detail in Chapter 16.

3. *Out of stock.* Successful books, called "sleepers" by publishers, are often underestimated, underprinted, and undersold until public opinion creates an overwhelming demand for them. Your book may have accumulated five thousand orders when your publisher only expected three thousand, so he has to go back to the printer and binder to get new books. At Prentice-Hall in the freezing winter of 1979, we published a book called *The Cooling*, explaining how the earth was getting increasingly, dangerously cold. The author made many TV appearances and the demand for this book exceeded our expectations. We called the printer for an emergency reprint. No luck: the subfreezing weather had made it impossible for the printer to run the presses at night, the only time he could have fit us in. Ironically, by the time we printed the additional copies of the books, spring had come and readers wanted something else.

Here's how complicated the out-of-stock situation is:

1) Orders exceed stock and publisher orders reprint.
2) The printer and binder manufacture the reprint.
3) The publisher ships books to customers.
4) Accounts receivable records the shipments.
5) Accounts payable records your royalty.
6) The royalty period closes (sometimes five or six months later).
7) Royalty accounting processes your check (this can be 90 days after the royalty period closes).
8) The royalty check is mailed to you or your agent.

Subsidiary Rights

You won't impress your friends with these contract details as you will with the up-front money, but it is attention to these matters that separates the professional from the bedazzled amateur.

People who are interested in reproducing your work in other forms will contact your publisher to make arrangements, logistical and financial. These other forms of your work are covered in the subsidiary rights section of your contract. Subsidiary rights are the licenses for the publication of the author's material in forms other than the publisher's edition. The publisher grants these licenses for a fee on the author's behalf. This is where the handful of rich authors get rich—through spectacular paperback sales; sales of serial rights to magazines; constant anthology use; foreign editions; filmstrip and movie sales; novelty use.

In most contracts the publisher controls all the subsidiary rights to the book. This means he is responsible for the sales of the book to other licensees, be they publishers, moviemakers, or book clubs. In most cases, the author's share of the subsidiary rights income is 25 percent, with another quarter going to the artist and half going to the publisher.

Anthology rights. Anthology rights include the publication of part or all of the manuscript in elementary school readers, children's literature textbooks, or any other books or magazines. The publisher who reprints your material, abridged, digested, or anthologized, pays a fee to the original publisher of your book. Your copyright appears on the copyright page of the book or magazine in which it appears.

Reprint. This is the republication of your material in its entirety by a publisher *other* than your original publisher. Most often, it pertains to paperback editions, but occasionally it applies to specially marketed hardcover editions. The content is identical to the original edition, but physical appearance may be slightly different (binding, paper, or type size).

Book clubs. Book clubs are as important to the children's book author as they are to adult authors. They reach audiences that publishers do not sell to directly. If Scholastic or Xerox or Troll takes your book on as a selection, it will be sold to children through flyers distributed in the classroom. The Junior Literary Guild sells hardcover editions to school libraries as well as directly to young customers. Book club advances range from $500 to $5,000 on the average; this money is split between the publisher and the author.

First and second serial rights. In contracts, magazine arrangements are usually spelled out under "First Serial" (publication in a periodical prior to publication) and "Second Serial" (publication in a magazine after the book is available to the general public). Historically, first serial rights were valuable—readers eager for the next Fitzgerald novel would snap up the *Saturday Evening Post* for an advance peek. These rights were sold at enormous prices, because people could buy the magazine at a tenth of the cost of a book, and this cut into book sales. These sales were rarely important in children's book publishing, and today first serial rights are considered much less valuable even for adult books. Now they are often sold for very little because it's assumed they offer good publicity. Except for the occasional sensational White House memoir, these rights are not much in demand. second serial rights are of far greater interest to today's picture book writer because a number of periodicals, such as *Cricket*, regularly purchase second serial rights to picture books. This gives the editors of the magazine that will serialize the book the opportunity to evaluate the published book. Again, these rights are sometimes sold for very little, because the publicity value is so great. A conscientious publisher will keep trying assiduously to have a book serialized or featured in magazines, because the exposure and the income benefit both publisher and author.

SUBSIDIARY RIGHTS CHECKLIST

Subsidiary rights have changed drastically in the last twenty years. New technologies present opportunities for writers who study the fine print of this clause carefully.

* Abridgement
* Anthology rights
* Digest rights
* First serialization
* Foreign rights
  —To distribute in English
  —To translate into other languages
* Transcription
  —Records
  —Recordings and accompanying Braille texts
* Reprint rights in cheap editions
  (paperback)
* Reprint rights in special editions
  (often aimed at libraries)

* Cartoon strip
* Radio
* Television
* Videocassette

* Cable television
* Film strip
* Movie

Most publishers are set up to take care of all the copyright information and follow-up; it's your responsibility to provide them with your full name and birth date (to keep them from confusing you with another copyright holder of the same name) when the copyright is registered. Some publishers are so well organized in this area that they will send you a card along with your contract asking for the information that is pertinent to registering a copyright.

Copyright

Anyone who reads is familiar with that fearsome caveat that appears on the copyright page of every book: *All rights reserved. No part of this book may be reproduced, stored in a retrieval system, or transmitted in any form or by any means, electronic, mechanical, photocopying, recording or otherwise without prior written permission of the publisher.*

When your book is published, some version of this notice will appear under your copyright. It protects you and the artist and your publisher from unauthorized editions or reprintings of your work. It also protects you from plagiarism. Obviously you would be lost without copyright protection, so your contract must include provisions for the copyright. But it doesn't matter in whose name the copyright is taken, so long as it is registered with the Library of Congress. Some publishers take the copyright in their own name, just to simplify clerical matters. The contract spells out the arrangement between you and the publisher, and indicates who retains the rights to the story once the book is out of print.

Most publishers aare set up to take care of all the copyright information and follow-up; it's your responsibility to provide them with your full name and birth date (to keep them from confusing you with another copyright holder of the same name) when the copyright is registered. Some publishers are so well organized in this area that they will send you a card along with your contract asking for the information that is pertinent to registering a copyright.

Publisher's Indemnity Clause

Whenever a successful book is published, it's almost axiomatic that someone believes that his or her idea has been pirated. It is astonishing how many lawsuits, threatened and actual, come to the attention of publishers. Though these suits are far more common in adult publishing, the standard indemnity clause, guaranteeing that the work being purchased for the publication is the writer's own and that if the publisher is sued for the infringement of another copyright the author will pay for the damages, is included in children's book contracts. It is practically impossible to talk a publisher out of this clause, so most writers are content to sign their initials to it, knowing full well that it will never affect the course of their book.

Option Clause

An option clause gives your publisher first refusal on your next book project. This is not necessarily such a great thing for you, because your idea might be better suited to another publisher's list, or you might be able to get a better deal somewhere else. Sometimes publishers will delete this clause if you ask them to, but other times you'll have to bargain. If you do sign an option clause, make certain it's as specific as possible: that it includes a cutoff date for the publisher to exercise his option; that the book to which the publisher has first refusal is carefully described; and that it specifies in what form you are to submit this second project.

The option clause can work to the author's advantage as well as to the publisher's, but it should be worded precisely and discussed thoroughly before you sign your name to it.

Approval Clauses

The details of publishing a book are often written into a contract. If you are concerned that it may take ten years for the illustrator the editor has chosen to complete the pictures, you may want to ask that there be a limit to the time the publisher has to publish the book. Most often this is eighteen months after the delivery and approval of the final manuscript. If after those eighteen months the illustrations are not ready, you have the right—but not the obligation—to withdraw the book and take it elsewhere.

Approvals—of the illustrations, of the jacket and jacket flap copy, of the advertising copy—are also occasionally written into contracts. If you have a good working relationship with your editor, such approvals are probably unnecessary, but some writers are more comfortable knowing that those rights are guaranteed in the contract. Especially when a writer has had experience with publishing, so that his input has value, it makes sense to include guarantees of approvals.

Negotiating a Contract

A publishing contract is a business agreement, not a dream come true. Like authors, publishers are usually honest, but not always. What protection does the author have? The basic and best protection is: Read your contract. Contracts don't follow any prescribed order, but there are certain conditions a wise author looks out for. As you read your contract, remember that the publisher *wants* to work with your project. Consider how much work your editor has put into a manuscript's becoming a book *before* the contract is offered. When you are offered a contract, you are in a solid, but not a spectacular, bargaining position. It is understood that you can take the manuscript elsewhere if the publisher does not meet your demands; it is also understood that the publisher can find satisfactory manuscripts from other sources if you are recalcitrant.

Contracts puzzle everyone, even seasoned professionals, so there are many organizations devoted to helping authors know what is a fair contract and what is not so fair. The Authors Guild, 23 W. 43rd St., New York, NY 10036, offers valuble pamphlets and advice on contracts, constantly updated to keep the writer informed about changes taking place in the current marketplace. Your writer friends and local writers' workshops are also invaluable aids in finding out what you should agree to and what you shouldn't.

The following contract checklist gives you an idea of what should be covered in your contract. The more things are spelled out, the less likely there is to be trouble later. How the points are covered is a matter to be discussed between you and your editor, but it's your job to insist that everything *is* covered.

CONTRACT CHECKLIST

One of the most troublesome things about contracts is the important matters that are left out. Be sure that the points below are amplified fully in your contract before you sign it.

* Advance
    —first payment
    —second payment
    —third payment
* Royalties
    —first 10,000 copies
    —second 10,000 copies
    —copies sold thereafter

* Indemnity clause
* Reversion-of-rights clause
* Delivery date
* Publication date
* Approvals
    —text
    —advertising copy
    —illustrations

* Provision for semiannual royalty statements
* Provisions for audit of publisher's books
* Provision that all subsidiary rights not specifically mentioned in contract remain the property of the author
* Grant of rights
    —world rights in English
    —foreign languages
* Provisions for correcting galleys

States. By the 1860s the U.S. was buying eighty-three percent of the annual crop (Spain was only taking six percent) and worrying a lot about the political turmoil in the islands. Many times the United States tried to buy Cuba from Spain, but Spain was not interested in selling. When the war in the 1890s threatened Cuba's sugar industry, many people in the United States wanted to intervene to protect U.S. investments and trade. A mysterious explosion aboard the U.S.S. *Maine* in Havana Harbor was just the excuse needed for the U. S. government to act. The United States declared war on Spain in April 1898.

Spain did not want to go to war with the United States. In August, representatives from Spain went to Washington, D.C. and signed a peace agreement. Part of that agreement called for Cuba's independence. This was formally granted by the Treaty of Paris on December 10, 1898.

The United States occupied Cuba from 1899 to 1901.

A Cuban-American couple awaits the arrival of family members from Mariel Bay, Cuba.   *—U.S. Coast Guard photograph*

While the carefully planned studio shot can give the reader the most information in the shortest space, there's nothing like the spunk of a candid shot.

CHAPTER 14

My Editor, My Friend

The nature of nonfiction influences the nature of the writer's relationship with her editor. Since nonfiction depends so heavily on "slant," the writer and editor work closely in the early stages of the book. In Chapter 12, I talked about the importance of showing your editor your slant as the crux of making a sale. Your editor needs to make a sale, too: to the publishing company for which she works. And the firm in turn wants to sell as many copies of your book as possible, so the editor needs to know from you anything you can give her to sell your slant.

The writer of nonfiction for children has another set of relationships to worry about: the format, or as you hear people saying increasingly, the book "package." The nonfiction book package for children must *look* like a book kids will want to read before it has a chance to *sound* good. We've already established that the writer should think of illustrations, typographical tricks, and headlines as she writes. The editor has them even more clearly in mind as she edits. The writer provides the inspiration, the editor makes the book materialize. As you work with your editor, you will forge a unique relationship. And though you will have close ties to a whole array of professionals in your dealings with the publisher, none will ever be as important as your relationship with your editor.

If you were to look at an editor's resume, you'd see some fairly arcane listings under "Skills" including "P & L responsibility," "editing from ms to limestone covering, are the equivalent of a column's base. Then come 14 floors rising up and up like the shaft of a column.

Greek columns usually feature an ornate capital at the top, and so does the Flatiron Building. Its capital is formed by two upper floors decorated with arches and columns, followed by a final floor with windows that look like the portholes of a ship, and an elaborate cornice.

The gray limestone covering of the Flatiron Building is like that of an Italian palace from the Middle Ages, and the surface is heavily decorated. Looking up at the building from across the street can be like playing "Find What's Hidden in the Picture." At different heights

Comparison of the Flatiron Building and a classical Greek column

one can discover carved flowers, wreaths, the faces of Greek heroes, and the heads of lions. There couldn't be a sharper contrast with the clean, undecorated lines of the Monadnock Block and other Chicago skyscrapers.

Because of its triangular shape and prominent location, the Flatiron Building has attracted the notice of artists, writers, and photographers ever since it was built. Not everyone who saw the building liked it. The English artist Sir Philip Burne-Jones, who visited New   19

In The Skyscraper Book *by James Giblin, a working editor, the text, line drawings, and photographs work together to convey the appearance and engineering of tall buildings. Illustrated by Anthony Kramer, with photographs by David Anderson (Crowell, 1981).*

BB," and "acquisitions." P & L responsibility means that the editor takes profit and loss into account when she signs up your book. In some publishing houses, this means that she gets a bonus if the book is successful and makes a profit, in others, this means that she gets a percentage of the profits. In whatever case, this means that she never hears the end of it if the book doesn't make a profit for the publisher, no matter how terrific the reviews, how good the writing. So the first thing an editor knows is how much things cost. Just like a person balancing the household budget, the editor asks herself constantly, "Is it worth it? Can we afford it? Is this a good investment?"

Editing from ms to BB means that the editor knows how to evaluate a manuscript, edit for content, edit for style, choose illustrations, supervise the preparation of illustrations, and work with the manufacturers who set type, print pictures, and bind books.

Acquisition is the publishing term in America for what the British call commissioning. It means knowing where to find authors (and the people who think anyone can write a book have never been acquisitions editors!), how much to pay them, when to encourage and when to discourage, and how to tie together a book idea with art, typography, and a "selling" jacket. A friend once asked me in desperation what editors *really* do: I reflected on my day at the office for a moment, and replied, "We say no nicely and we say yes fast." That's the heart of editing.

DIVIDING THE DUTIES

We know that boundaries are important because world wars are fought over them. Just as the writer has to struggle against the frustrated publisher in himself, so editors fight against the frustrated writer in themselves. A very successful editor once confided to me that he liked to work with nonfiction writers who couldn't write their way out of a paper bag. I, who enjoy editing nonfiction because it demands such skill in writing, expressed surprise. "It gives *me* a chance to write," the editor grinned. And he meant it. There are editors who love to write, rewrite, suggest book topics, and generally assume the creative work that is the traditional domain of the author. And there are authors (often former editors) who love to intrude on the publisher's turf by demanding a certain illustrator, insisting on a certain retail price, and second-guessing the copy editor.

Actions

EDITOR	AUTHOR
Identifies a market need	Has a great idea for book
Adjusts the idea for age group	Notices three-year-olds love stories about snakes
Presents the book in brief form	Expands the idea to manuscript length
Provides sales histories of similar titles	Knows potential for this book's sales
Knows how to read critically	Knows how to write spontaneously

Concerns

EDITOR:	AUTHOR:
Affordable illustrations	Optimal illustrations
Eye-catching jacket	"Honest" jacket
Fact-checking	Original research
Consistency in writing	Excitement in writing
Meeting pub date	Meeting manuscript deadline

A good editor is a steady bass to the writer's melody. The writer brings the idea to the page and an editor sees its harmony with the other elements of the book: its pictures, its typography, even its trim size. (You wouldn't publish a book about skyscrapers in a matchbook-sized format.)

Like any trained professional, an editor has a grasp of the objective reality of writing as well as a highly developed subjective style. I find that I can often pick editors out at a publishing party because their neutral appearance contrasts so sharply with the fashionably clad agents and the dramatically dressed author who is surrounded with spellbound listeners. But editors are emphatically NOT neutral: they just look neutral. Editors have a star quality, a definiteness that is essential to the editorial job. Everyone who works on a book, from you the writer to the pressman who oversees the book's printing, has to know where the editor is coming from. Writers need to be inventive, creative, inspired; the editor needs to be flexible, analytical, appreciative.

EDITORIAL TYPES

No two editors do everything alike, but there are some standard editorial personalities. One is the cheerleader, the editor who can say "Wow! Great! More!" and, believe it or not, "Boo! Hiss! Yech!" Another is the mentor, the editor who can help a writer through the rough spots, nod knowingly when the writer's on target and show the writer how to grow. The "tough love" editor is the woman who doesn't necessarily return your calls but does let you have your way unless there is a very good reason not to. And there's the empathetic editor, the one who calls you out of the blue and says, "I was worried last night while I was making dinner that you might be having trouble" at exactly the moment you *were* having trouble.

In these days of publishing musical chairs, there is no guarantee that the editor who buys your manuscript will be the editor who works on it. And in that atmosphere of uncertainty, it would be foolish to try to select an editor as you would select a spouse. The relationship isn't that personal that you need to have absolute compatibility, though it's nice when it happens that way. I have worked with two editors who to my mind encompass perfection, each in his own way. One never calls me unless it's a dire necessity; the other calls to chat. One is respectful of my writing and has never suggested a change; the other urges me to revise, try a new tack, add a new chapter, throw out the introduction. One skimmed the manuscript on his way home without so much as a pencil in his hand, the other fills the pages I've written with as many comments in blue ink as there is black typewriting. They are both terrific editors. Writers know—or they come to find—that the right author/publisher relationship for one project is not the right one for another project. My noninterventionist editor is right for projects that I want to be exactly my way; my involved editor has seen me through several book projects, each more ambitious than the next.

Many writers also find that a close relationship with an editor can be beneficial at certain stages of a writer's career, while less helpful at others. George Ancona, the photographer-author of *Wheels*, worked with Ann Durrell at Dutton on his first book. When this first book took off, Ancona began collaborating with other writers as the photographer for their projects, including Barbara Lalicki to Lothrop, Lee and Shepard. As he works with other writers Ancona has found new vistas but he will always publish the books he writes with Dutton.

A complication of the editor/author relationship is what to do when your editor moves to another publisher. Some authors, like Mitsumasa Anno, move to the new publisher. Others, like Anne Rockwell, do books with both the new editor at the old publisher, and the old editor with the new publisher. Still others like Demi, whose editor Margot Lundell moved from Random House to Golden Press, stop working for both the editor and the publisher. Demi is now very happy being published by Putnam Publishing.

Editorial Intervention

Certainly some editor/author combinations are more effective than others. Does your project require tender loving care or total freedom? I've found out the hard way that a perfect manuscript can be mangled by an editor who diligently changes everything in front of her. When I was a brand-new editor, I was being considered for a senior spot at Prentice-Hall. After endless interviews, the editor-in-chief, Kate Ernst, gave me a manuscript to evaluate. As luck would have it, the weekend I had set aside to evaluate and edit this sample manuscript, my niece Amy Reeves was born. In the excitement and busyness of this great event, even reading the manuscript that would get me the job of my dreams was not possible. There was no time and there certainly wasn't either quiet or solitude. Monday I dragged myself to work and Kate called to say the decision was to be made on the position that morning. Never mind a written evaluation—what did I think of the manuscript? I felt faint, for I hadn't looked at it. I didn't know what it was about, I didn't know where I'd make brilliant suggestions for revision. But I wanted that job so much I could taste it. I lied.

"It's a terrific manuscript," I babbled nervously. "I wouldn't change a word of it." As awful as it was to lie, I didn't want anybody to think that I put my personal life first ever, under any circumstances. I expected the world to end and it didn't seem like that bad a possibility.

Instead Kate said, "Great! The job is yours. I knew you were a good editor." She's joking, I thought. But she went on to explain. "That is the manuscript for a book that's being published next week. It's already received the Boston Globe/Horn Book award as the Best Book of the Year. They read it in the manuscript, the same one you have. And what we want in an editor is someone who knows a good thing when she sees it." I cried for three hours after I hung up the phone and I learned once and for all that while all manuscripts can benefit from being read carefully, not all manuscripts can be improved by an earnest editor. The most successful book I've ever published was rewritten extensively over a ten-month period, but the second most successful was published without changing so much as a comma.

EDITORIAL VISION

A good editor then, is part accountant, part art director, part historian, part movie star, part literary agent, part psychiatrist, part magician, and part car pool mommy. An editor's work includes evaluating an author as an investment, acquiring his manuscript, and arranging a merger with an illustrator that will be greater than the sum of its parts. Just as the merger of Merrill, Lynch, Pierce, Fenner and Smith created an institution in the field of stocks and bonds, so the mergers of Muriel and Tom Feelings (authors of *Jambo Means Hello*), Millicent Selsam and Jerome Wexler (*The Amazing Dandelion*), Guilio Maestro and Marvin Terban (*In a Pickle*), and Joanna Cole and Jim and Ann Monteith (*A Dog's Body*) have become institutions in the children's book field.

An editor has a sense of what a book can be. Inspired by that vision, the editor sets about pulling in the diverse talents—from copyeditor to printer—to make the author's idea into the editor's vision of a physical book. As Donna Brooks, of E. P. Dutton says, "There are no editors without authors. We editors count on you authors for the new ideas, the inspired concepts, that we can help make into a reality for young readers."

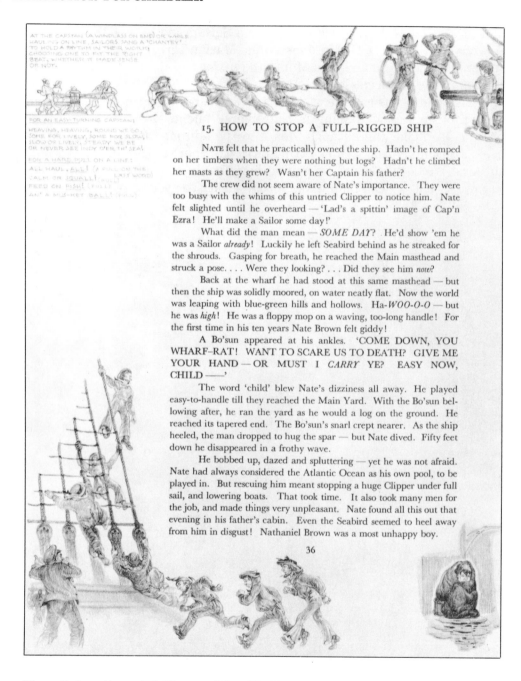

15. HOW TO STOP A FULL-RIGGED SHIP

NATE felt that he practically owned the ship. Hadn't he romped on her timbers when they were nothing but logs? Hadn't he climbed her masts as they grew? Wasn't her Captain his father?

The crew did not seem aware of Nate's importance. They were too busy with the whims of this untried Clipper to notice him. Nate felt slighted until he overheard — 'Lad's a spittin' image of Cap'n Ezra! He'll make a Sailor some day!'

What did the man mean — *SOME DAY*? He'd show 'em he was a Sailor *already*! Luckily he left Seabird behind as he streaked for the shrouds. Gasping for breath, he reached the Main masthead and struck a pose. . . . Were they looking? . . . Did they see him *now*?

Back at the wharf he had stood at this same masthead — but then the ship was solidly moored, on water neatly flat. Now the world was leaping with blue-green hills and hollows. Ha-*WOO-O-O* — but he was *high*! He was a floppy mop on a waving, too-long handle! For the first time in his ten years Nate Brown felt giddy!

A Bo'sun appeared at his ankles. 'COME DOWN, YOU WHARF-RAT! WANT TO SCARE US TO DEATH? GIVE ME YOUR HAND — OR MUST I *CARRY* YE? EASY NOW, CHILD ——'

The word 'child' blew Nate's dizziness all away. He played easy-to-handle till they reached the Main Yard. With the Bo'sun bellowing after, he ran the yard as he would a log on the ground. He reached its tapered end. The Bo'sun's snarl crept nearer. As the ship heeled, the man dropped to hug the spar — but Nate dived. Fifty feet down he disappeared in a frothy wave.

He bobbed up, dazed and spluttering — yet he was not afraid. Nate had always considered the Atlantic Ocean as his own pool, to be played in. But rescuing him meant stopping a huge Clipper under full sail, and lowering boats. That took time. It also took many men for the job, and made things very unpleasant. Nate found all this out that evening in his father's cabin. Even the Seabird seemed to heel away from him in disgust! Nathaniel Brown was a most unhappy boy.

36

The collaboration of Holling and Lucille Holling on black and white illustrations for Seabird *(Houghton-Mifflin, 1948 renewed 1975) reveals telling details.*

CHAPTER 15

How Your Book Is Produced

A book is like a baby," quips veteran editor Chaucy Bennetts. "It takes nine months to make a book out of a manuscript." During this nine months, the author who thinks his work is done because his manuscript is complete is in for a few surprises. Although your stint at the typewriter is over, there is still a great deal to do. Let's take a look at the many steps it takes to produce a book.

THE MANUSCRIPT

When your manuscript is accepted for publication, you may have many chapters yet to finish. Your contract stipulates the due date for the entire manuscript. Most publishers' contracts spell out a grace period of anywhere from one month to three months between the delivery date stated in the contract and the last possible moment a manuscript can be delivered. After this last possible moment, the publisher is entitled to ask for the advance back and can institute legal action against the author for failing to live up to his end of the contract. Although you have probably heard stories about manuscripts that were delivered years after their due date, these are the exception. The temptation to put off writing until the last minute can be great, but the author who is thinking of the next book is careful to abide by deadlines. Editors are responsible for scheduling books, and if a book slips off this schedule because of an author's procrastination, the editor is not likely to forget it. The professional author is mindful of deadlines, and proceeds in a spirit of cooperation.

The condition of your manuscript when you deliver it is also important. A manuscript should be neatly typed, double-spaced, with wide margins. The editor needs room to make comments, both specific ones within sentences (hence the double spacing) and general comments that fit into the margins. If you are not a crack typist, it's worth the money to have your manuscript typed professionally. Most publishers require a duplicate manuscript, and many publishers stipulate in the contract that you keep a third copy of the manuscript in your files. The reason for this third copy is that manuscripts do get lost. In a publishing company where hundreds of books are published each season, it's easy enough for pages or even an entire manuscript to be mislaid. It doesn't happen often, but it does happen.

The reason for sending two manuscripts to your publisher is that while the editor is going over your manuscript, the production department has already started the process of making your manuscript into a book. Though it varies from house to house, the sequence is usually this. The two manuscripts arrive at the publishing house. The editor takes the original and begins to edit it. The production manager takes the second manuscript and sends it to a designer.

BY DESIGN

The designer who chooses the type for your book is mindful of many things—especially the age level of your audience. For picture books, a large type is most often chosen. For easy readers, a large type is used with wide leading between the lines. This large spacing makes the lines more distinct and easier for young eyes to follow. (A first grader's eyes, believe it or not, are not yet fully developed.) The older age groups use type faces that are a little larger than those used for adult books. In books for eight- to twelve-year-olds, an adult-looking appearance is important, because the young reader doesn't want a book that looks babyish. In the 10 to 14 and the teenage groups, the look of the book is almost indistinguishable from a well-designed adult book. The type face may be a little larger, and there are probably more illustrations, but the book does not look "juvenile."

The designer next considers the book's subject matter. A book about pirates might be printed in an old-fashioned face like Caslon or Palatino, while a book about a rock star might be set in a sans serif face like Helvetica. (See the typography chart on pages 170-171 for examples.) Serifs are little flourishes at the base of each letter, and whether a type is "serif" or "sans serif" is the basic distinction in type faces.

A sans serif face may look like the printing children learn in school, and for this reason, many teachers prefer it. But the serif faces provide an invisible line along which the young reader's eyes can easily focus, and for this reason, it too has a following among teachers. It's largely a matter of taste, but there are reasons, both practical and esthetic, to select one type face over another. The designer is well acquainted with the latest type styles and the old stand-bys, and brings to your manuscript experience and expertise about the ways a book can look.

The designer also considers the illustrations, and what typeface will look right with photos, diagrams, or illustrations, or a combination of all three. Nonfiction books, because they are often profusely illustrated, are a type designer's dream. The chapter heads and subheads, the page numbers, (called folios), and other design elements are all carefully considered to make your book look as good as possible.

When the designer has made the page design as complete as she can, she submits it to the typesetter, or compositor, for a "cast-off" and estimate. The compositor, who sets the type for the book, counts the characters in several lines of your manuscript, multiplies this by the number of lines on each page and then by the number of pages in the manuscript. He figures out, using the typeface the designer has selected, how many pages the book will be. This is called a "cast-off." Then he estimates how much it will cost the publisher to have the manuscript set into type. This is called the estimate.

Most publishers send the manuscript with the designer's markings to several compositors. Each compositor sends in his bid for the job (the estimate) and a set of sample pages. The publisher considers questions of price and quality and decides which compositor will set your book. If you ask your editor for a set of sample pages, she will most likely send them to you. The sample shows, in three to five representative pages, what your manuscript will look like once it is set in type.

Writers are sometimes disappointed in the designer's work. It is impossible to say whether the designer's solutions to the problems of your book—the way the captions contrast with the text type, the size of the folios, the placement of headlines—are the best possible. Her taste may be different from yours. When you see the sample pages, try to appreciate them for what they are, and put your own taste aside. Sometimes the author is thrilled with the work of the designer. If your book looks just the way you would like it to, be sure to let your editor know. The designer, however expert, is human too, and will appreciate your praise.

EDITORIAL PROCEDURE

While the sample pages are being set, the editor is editing your manuscript. The first step in evaluating a nonfiction manuscript is to send it to an expert. The expert reader is usually an academic with a specialized knowledge of the field you are writing about. His input is important in making sure that the information you are including in your book is the most up-

Ragged right, ragged left—Unjustifed type that is allowed to run to various line lengths

Roman—A type in which all the letters are upright.

Sans serif—A typeface without serifs

Serif—The short strokes that project from the ends of the main body strokes of a typeface

Typeface—A specific design for a type alphabet

Type family—All the styles and sizes of a given type

Word spacing—The spacing between words in a line

Uppercase letters (u.c. or c.)—The capital letters or caps

x-height—The height of the lowercase x in a given typeface

Three commonly used faces shown in various sizes.

Baskerville	Times Roman	Univers
9/10 Once upon a time once upon a time once upon a time once upon a time once upon a time once upon a time once upon	9/10 Once upon a time once upon a time once upon a time once upon a time once upon a time once upon a time once upon a time once upon	9/10 Once upon a time on ce upon a time once upon a time once up on a time once upon a time once upon a time once upon a t
10/11 Once upon a time once upon a time once upon a time once upon a time once upon a time	10/11 Once upon a time on ce upon a time once upon a time once up on a time once upon a time once upon a	10/11 Once upon a time once upon a time once upon a time once upon a time once upon a time
11/12 Once upon a time once upon a time once upon a time once upon a time once upon a time once upon a time	11/12 Once upon a time o nce upon a time on ce upon a time onc e upon a time once upon a time once u pon a time once up	11/12 Once upon a time once upon a time once upon a time once upon a time once upon a time once upon a time

A showing of 18 pt. Souvenir Roman (the face used for this book).

abcdefghijklmnopqrstuvwxyz1234567890
ABCDEFGHIJKLMNOPQRSTUVWXYZ$

Trade
Gothic

Garamond

Century

**Cooper
Black**

Univers

Korinna

Gill Sans

Helvetica

Tiffany

Times Roman

Futura

The Author's Guide to

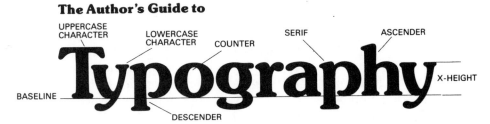

The words are yours and type is the medium used to convey these words to the reader. The right typeface can enhance your concepts and embellish the appearance of your book. It is the job of the designer to make those choices that would most effectively convey your meaning. To give you a sense of what the designer deals with, the following is a general description of the most used typographic terms:

Melior

Ascender—The part of a lowercase letter above the x-height

Baseline—The line on which the characters appear to stand

Optima

Characters—Individual letters, figures and punctuation marks

Counter—The enclosed or hollow part of a letter

Palatino

Descender—The part of a lowercase letter that falls below the baseline

Serif
Gothic

Em—A printer's unit of width measurement which is equal to the body size of the type in question. An 8-point em is 8 points; a 14-point em is 14 points, etc. It takes its name from the widest letter in any typeface: M.

Bodoni

Font—A complete alphabet: one typeface in one size

Italic—A type in which the forms slant to the right

Caslon

Justify—To set a line to a desired measure

Leading—The spacing between lines (measured in points)

Letterspacing—The space between the letters in a word

Bauhaus
Demi

Lowercase letters (l.c.)—The small letters

Pica—A unit used to measure the length of a line of type. One pica (0.166″) consists of 12 points and six picas (72 pt.) equal one inch

Benquiat

Point—Used to measure the typesize—from the top of the ascender to the bottom of the descender plus space above and below to prevent the lines of type from touching. The point (0.1383″) is the basic unit of

Baskerville

printer's measurement.

Caledonia

to-date. However, there are drawbacks to the expert reader's opinions.

The expert is usually so immersed in his field that he has chosen one camp or another within that field. You, as the author, cannot be expected to advocate one position over another in a brief introductory book. If the expert agrees with the conclusions you have reached, fine. But what if his approach to the subject is different? The controversies that rage in academia are myriad, and it's possible that you will become embroiled in a reader's report that criticizes your text.

At Prentice-Hall, we published an overview of dance in Africa by former dancer and Africa expert Lee Warren. Finding an expert to review the manuscript was no easy task. Finally, we found an anthropologist who specialized in ethnic dance. She expressed an expert's short-sighted horror that all of the dance of Africa could be covered in a single volume. With the ferocity one might expect from a doctoral dissertation, the expert tore apart Warren's sensible interpretations and generalizations. As the editor of the project, I was devastated. I worried that the coverage was too superficial, and that if the author were to follow all the inclusions the expert advised, we would have an unreadable reference work. The author and I went over the expert's report line by line, incorporating all corrections of fact, but without sacrificing the basic introductory quality of the text. It was a hard lesson for both of us, but it pointed out that the children's nonfiction writer is introducing a subject, and in the interests of providing a valid first impression, the book may come under attack from scholars. Warren stood her ground, standing up for her original research and her writing style, and together author and editor made the best of a critical reader's report. The book was well reviewed, so well reviewed that we asked Warren to do a sequel, this time on African theatre. The expert reviewer chosen for this book had nothing but praise for the project. Warren's style hadn't changed: It was just the luck of the draw.

A happier experience with an expert reader was finding a pomologist (someone who specializes in apples) to read Alvin and Virginia Silverstein's *Apples: All About Them*. The expert commented on the manuscript, correcting errors of fact and clarifying places where two sources conflicted. He then mentioned that even he had learned something about apple folklore from the manuscript. So you can never tell if the expert reader is going to be appreciative or critical. The important thing to remember is that you are an expert, too: an expert at writing for children. Listen carefully to what the reader says about your manuscript but don't be cowed by it.

With the expert's report in hand, the editor goes over your manuscript, and hones it down to the perfect model of economy and readability. When she has finished, she submits the manuscript to you with queries for additional information, sources for dubious information (experts often offer opinionated advice, so that if you can provide a source for your information, it will stand despite her objections), and suggestions for tightening up the writing. Usually this is accompanied by an editorial letter which covers the main points your editor wants to discuss or change.

This is a ticklish moment for the author, just as the first look at the expert reader's report is. You have worked hard on your manuscript and it breaks your heart to see the chapter that you thought so inspired re-arranged by an editor. Before you lose patience, though, consider what reasons she gives for the revisions she's suggested. An editor is an expert too, with exposure to many books, and it's a rare editor who makes suggestions for revisions without good reason. It's important that you respond to every query the editor brings up, even if you feel the answer is obvious. Revisions require work from everybody, and the editor's job is to make your book clear, correct, and complete.

In the final analysis, though, remember that you are the author and that it's your book. You know the subject better than your editor, and you know writing for children better than the expert reader. If you feel that the editor is proposing changes that would make the book different, not better, speak up. If your arguments are closely reasoned and your response to the editor's suggestion is sensible, the editor is more than willing to listen.

FROM COPYEDITING TO TYPESETTING TO DUMMY

After you return the manuscript to the editor, she will send it for copyediting. The copy editor checks the facts, corrects the spelling and punctuation, and generally makes certain that the reader can believe everything he reads in your book. While some editors actually copyedit the manuscript they have worked on themselves, most feel that fresh eyes are important. Copy editors can be members of the editorial staff, but most often they are freelancers, working out of their homes. Whichever is the case with your book, your editor will be the liaison between you and the copy editor. The copyedited manuscript is returned to you with perhaps a few more queries, and once you have approved it, it's ready to be typeset.

After the sample pages and the copyedited manuscript are approved, galleys are set. Galleys are long, narrow sheets of newsprint with the text printed continuously on the sheets. (They are called galleys after ship's galleys, which are also long and narrow.) You will have a chance to read your galleys and make corrections on them. But beware! Every line you change is costly to the publisher, who may pass those costs on to *you*, so you won't want to make changes from the original manuscript that aren't absolutely necessary. Sometimes such changes are necessary, though, and you will want to add some recent research, or an irresistible quote that just arrived. If the printer has made an error, make the change back to match your original. Some authors identify this sort of change with PE (printer's error) and a small circle. This is a sign to the editor that you don't pay for it—the printer does. Your changes are called AA's (for author's alterations).

HOW TO MAKE A BOOK

Content and copyediting

Castoff, sample type

Design

Typesetting and proofreading

Keying in art

Dummy (page proofs)

Sample art

Roughs

Comps

Camera copy

Paste-up

Repro proof—finished art

Indexing

Finished art

Printing

Trim, fold

Gather

Jacketing

Shipping

Going to Press

The corrected galleys are given to the designer who cuts them up to make a page dummy, allowing room for illustrations, page numbers, running heads (the abbreviated titles that may appear with the page numbers) and headlines. The dummy is then returned to the typesetter who makes up page proofs. If you ask to see page proofs, your editor will most likely cooperate. If there have been heavy changes in the galleys, it's probably a good idea to request to see the page proofs. If it's just curiosity that prompts you to ask to see them, your editor may say "no," but ask anyway.

One important test in the page proofs is called "slugging." The proofreader at the publishing house will do this for you, but you might want to double-check and do it yourself. It involves checking to make sure that the last line of each page is followed by the correct first line on the following page, in case the printer has dropped a line or transposed paragraphs in the process of making up pages.

The final stage of the camera copy preparation is the making up of page proofs into reproduction proofs. These are sharply reproduced proofs on shiny paper, with black and white contrast that will be picked up by the camera to give the sharpest reproduction on the printed page. It's unlikely that the editor will show you reproduction proofs or "repros," as they are called in the trade, because they are expensive and the slightest smudge undoes their value. The designer then marks your photographs or illustrations to size, placing a photocopy of a negative of the illustration in place in the camera copy. These "mechanicals"—perfectly placed pages, ready to be photographed by the camera—are then sent to the printer where they are stripped in large sheets to be filmed to make the printing plates. Since printing plates—sensitized plastic—are used over and over again, the negatives are saved and used when your book is reprinted.

Prints of the film from which the printing plates are made are sent to your editor. These ozalids, or "blues," (so-called because of their blue color) are used to make sure that the sequence is correct, that no illustrations are upside down, and that there is no broken type. Usually the editor returns the blues a day after she receives them, so there is usually no way for the author to see them.

Then your book is put on the press. The huge sheets—sometimes four feet by six feet, as in a sheet-fed press, or twenty square feet, as in a web press—come barreling off at a fantastic speed. It is an exciting process to watch, and you should ask your editor just once if you can tag along to the printer's to see your book come off the press—the smells, the sounds, and the sights are for many of us the most exciting part of publishing.

Your book is then bound. Publishers use a sturdy cardboard called "binder's board" to create the "case" for a book. The binder's board is divided into three pieces: the front, the back, and the spine. It is then covered with cloth, or more often for children's books, a sturdy man-made material (one that is waterproof, biteproof, and fingerprint-proof) which is either stamped or printed. If it is stamped, the spine carries your name, the book's title, and the publisher's name. The front of the book might carry a small decorative spot illustration that is stamped on the cover. If the book cover is printed, the spine will contain the same information, but a more lavish illustration may appear on the front. At the back of your book, the ISBN (International Standard Book Number) is printed.

The Book Jacket

The jacket is prepared separately from the rest of the book, because it's usually needed long before the book is printed. The jacket is the publisher's primary sales tool, and often the jacket is finished soon after the manuscript is complete. Jackets are carefully printed, usually in color, on heavy coated stock to ensure bright and crisp reproduction. Once the jacket is printed, it is covered with a plastic laminate which protects it from scuffing and scratching as it is handled. You would be surprised to know how often a book is picked up, packed, unpacked and put down in the course of its life as it goes from the bindery to the warehouse to the wholesaler to the retailer to the customer.

If there are aspects of your book that make you unhappy when you see it in final form, you are in good company. Every book is in some way a disappointment. It could have been perfect, if only. . . . Sometimes the flaws are minor, like glue seeping out of the top and bottom of the binding, sometimes they're major, like a photo in the wrong place. Whatever the mistake, don't fly off the handle, because the damage is done. Write a furious letter to your editor, and then ceremoniously burn it. Write another letter to your editor, coolly and politely requesting that the error be remedied on the reprint.

The original hardcover edition of your book may well be the first of many editions—in trade paperback, rack-sized paperback, special library edition—and each edition goes through the same painstaking sequence of printing and binding. It's fun to see the many forms your book can take as it is published at different times for different audiences.

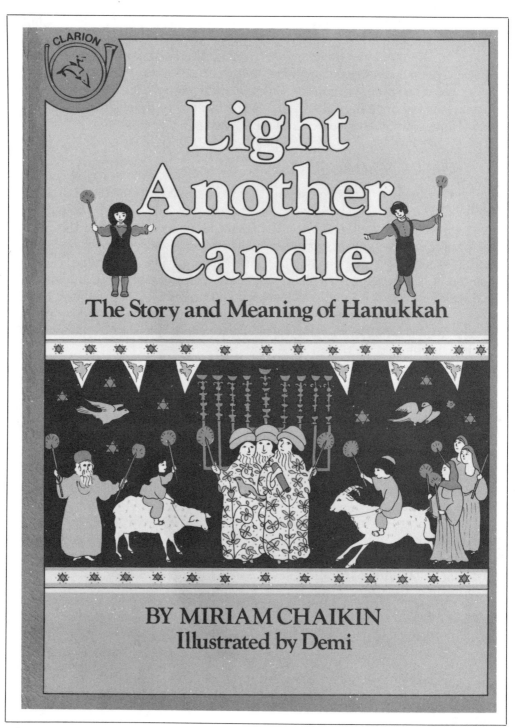

Paperback front cover plates usually have more whammy than hardcover book jackets, as shown by the cover of Light Another Candle: The Story and Meaning of Hanukkah *by Miriam Chaikin, illustrations by Demi (Clarion, 1981).*

CHAPTER 16

The Marketing Mindset

Remember how birthday parties used to be? You spent a whole month's allowance on a truck for your very best friend Beth, a truck with a hydraulic lift. Then you wrapped it yourself, and spent an hour getting dressed, but when you got to the party there were seventeen other first-graders just like you in fancy clothes carrying pretty presents. You who thought yourself so special were just one of the crowd. But you survived.

And as you survived this, so you will succeed in your publisher's marketing machine, a juggernaut designed to turn your book into a "product," you into a "name brand," your potential readers into "demographics," the book's title into "retail pull," your book's audience into "a target." Whew! But it happens every day and most authors, like most six-year-old birthday party guests, live to tell about it. I did, and here's the scoop:

The editorial department buys a manuscript and creates a book with some help from you, the author. When the book is ready, it is turned over to the marketing department for "distribution to the trade." That's what marketing people say, honest.

There is no magic to selling books. It takes a lot of work on the part of the editor, the salesman, the library promotion expert, the publicity person—and most important, you, the author. You know your book better than anyone else so you can think of ways to promote your book that won't occur to the other experts involved.

But I'm a writer, you protest. Why should I be concerned with selling my book? The answer is that many books are published, but publication itself is no guarantee of success. Many books get lost in the shuffle—this is easier to understand when you realize that three thousand children's books are published each year. Not every one can be a rip-roaring best seller. Because of the diversity of titles published, you have to scramble to get yours promoted. But on the bright side, listen to Jean Mercier, book reviewer for children's books at *Publishers Weekly:* "Whatever people say about juvenile publishing, the fact remains that more hardcover books are being sold than ever before. Children's books are certainly not a dying breed."

WHAT YOU CAN DO

Understanding the processes by which books are marketed is the first step in ensuring success for the book you have worked on for so long. When your book is put under contract, the editor prepares an information sheet telling about you and your book. This sheet, prepared at the *first* stages of publication, is the basis for future promotion efforts. In some publishing houses, this sheet is called "The Editor Says," in others, a "Release Memo" or "About the Book."

The Editor Says sheet includes information about the book: the subject it covers, what the competition is, what the author's qualifications are, and ways in which the book can be sold. The editor will do a much better job on this sheet with your help. So don't be shy: start off with a positive attitude, and watch the momentum build.

You will want to share your ideas for promoting with your editor at this early stage, before the information sheet is released. Enthusiasm is contagious, and enthusiasm from your editor will win you points with the sales staff as well. This is important because an interesting phenomenon happens at most publishing houses: one or two books are chosen for "special treatment." These books—and it's usually the books with the enthusiastic authors—are adopted as favorites from the beginning. From the president of the company to the mailroom clerk, personnel in publishing houses take an interest in some books long before they become books. This interest is based on the "The Editor Says" sheet and early reports on the manuscript. You want this kind of enthusiasm to be devoted to your book, and one way you can generate it is to tout your book from contract on.

293 Selling Days Until Pub Date

As soon as you sign the contract, start thinking of ways to sell your book. Consider your work objectively, and figure out who might be interested in it. Write down all your ideas, bearing in mind that modesty is your worst enemy at this point in the process.

Imagine that you are asked to speak to a class about your book: What can you say? Who would be interested? Write down the answers to these questions and include the answers in a letter to your editor. For instance, if you have written a book about an endangered species, suggest the editor get in touch with wildlife preservation groups to see if they will promote the book for you. If you have written a biography of a New England patriot, suggest local bookstores in the area where he lived as a possible outlet for sales. If you have written a book of science projects, talk to the science teacher at your local schools. Find out from him what periodicals he reads, what organizations he belongs to. This is valuable information for promotion of your book.

A secret to keeping enthusiasm for a project alive that many authors forget is keeping in touch with their editor as the book progresses from the editor's desk to the production department, the promotion department, and the sales department. You don't want to be a pest and call your editor every other day, but it doesn't hurt to write. Don't expect an answer to every letter: editors are busy people who have long lost the leisurely touch that distinguished Maxwell Perkins and the great editors of the twenties. Today's editor is a minipublisher concerned with the details of reading manuscripts, preparing interoffice memoranda, answering the constantly ringing phone, and making sure, through an interminable series of meetings, that the best possible sales effort is being made to sell the books they've published. So an editor may be too busy to answer your letter but not too busy to read it. Spontaneous ideas presented in a letter can create new ideas. Suppose you have written a book about the history of ice cream and it suddenly occurs to you that a party with an ice cream freezer would be just the thing to promote your book at the local bookstore. Your editor may think this is too messy an undertaking, but if you put the ice cream freezer on the sidewalk outside the store, maybe it could work . . . Your editor may find some of your ideas far-fetched, but they are grist for the mill. Crazy ideas can be modified into something viable, but no ideas at all will ensure that your book will get lost in the shuffle.

In gathering information for your editor, try to be as inventive as you are with your own writing. The Editor Says sheet includes information about the book: look for interesting things from the book that haven't appeared elsewhere. List these facts on a sheet called "Did You Know?" Consider the places where you did research. Was it at a museum that has a bookstore attached to it? Chances are, the bookstore would be interested in carrying your book. If you do your research at a university, try the student bookstore. If you have traveled to do research, consider the bookshops in the areas you visited. These may be long shots, but suggesting an idea may trigger other ideas.

WHO NEEDS WHAT WHEN
How a Book Is Promoted

WHO	WHAT	WHEN	WHY
Bookstores	Catalog Book jacket Printed proofs of sample pages	3 months before pub	Order initially for store; decide what to promote
Libraries	Catalog Library of Congress's Cataloging-in-Publication Data (CIP)	Pub date	Schedule for evaluation meeting; notice for possible awards consideration
Wholesale Book Distributors	ABI Forms Catalog Print run	3 months before pub	Initial order
Schools	Finished book Three reviews	3 months after pub	Evaluate book *and* reviews for inclusion in collection or curriculum
Reviewers	Galleys Jacket Catalog	4 months before pub	Include for review and schedule for publication
Newspaper Editors	Glossy of author Press release	1 month before pub	Arrange interview; hold for slot in paper
Book Fair Organizers	Poster Book jacket Catalog	Pub date	Must know book is available for shipping
Magazine Interviewers	Press releases about book and author Candid photos	2 months before pub	In-depth interview; usually held until sale of book warrants inclusion
Television Shows	Press release Publicist's evaluation of author "presence"	Pub date	Fast interview with one reference to book's content or "talk show" approach where authorship is used as jumping off point for longer discussion

MARKETING MECHANICS

Anyone who maintains that you can't judge a book by its cover is not in publishing. Charles Scribner used to admonish his editors never to allow a book to be published unless its title could be read from the Fifth Avenue bus as it lurched past the shop window in which it was displayed. Assuming that the windows of both the shop and the bus are clean, the viewer's contacts are in place, his gaze fastened on the right side of the street and his wits not diverted by the half-naked roller-skater zipping by on the sidewalk, this is a good starting point.

The attention a book gets must come early and be strong. A good title can get your book looked at, and, if you're lucky, read. While your book is just one of a long list to your publisher, it is your special baby. *You* are the one who can provide an inspiring title for your book.

After the editor has prepared the Editor Says sheet, the marketing department takes over. They prepare all the advertising and sales materials for your book, and usually have control over the title, as well. You can help marketing prepare advertising for your book just as you helped your editor prepare the Editor Says sheet by providing ideas for the title and jacket.

The Title

Titles have visual cachet as well as literal meaning. A collection of letters called *Dear Emily* is going to look different from that very same collection under the title *In and Around Amherst: The Selected Correspondence of Emily Dickinson, 1850-1884*. Long titles can be catchy, as *Real Vermonters Don't Milk Goats*, or deadly, as *Roman Society in the Last Century of the Western Empire*, both very good books. Short titles can stick, as *Big Pig*, or elude, as *That Quail, Robert* (which I have heard referred to as *Bob the Pheasant*). From the physical point of view, the title is a trade-off between making your intent and scope perfectly clear (as long titles can) or allowing room for the illuminating additions of an illustration, the author's name, or even a short banner featuring a blurb ("The only book you'll ever need to read about the geology of the minor Hawaiian islands!")

A nonfiction title has many demands on it: it must tell its subject matter, and it should also have some life and interest of its own. In 1971, author Seymour Simon wrote a book called *Chemistry in the Kitchen*. A year later, Vicki Cobb, a master of great titles, wrote a book called *Science Experiments You Can Eat*. Both were attractive, well-researched books which received good reviews. Ten years later, Cobb's book, with its inspired title, is in print as both a hardcover and a paperback. Simon's book is out of print. Cobb, the mother of two sons, maintains it's only fair: "After all, Seymour," she told him jokingly at a party, "which one of us has spent her life in the kitchen?" Cobb's book was such a rousing success that seven years later she

SEEDS Pop·Stick·Glide

TEXT BY Patricia Lauber PHOTOGRAPHS BY Jerome Wexler

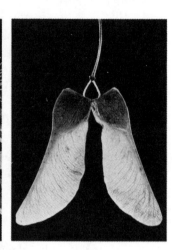

The front plate of the jacket is the single most important element of your book. The front plate of Seeds: Pop, Stick, Glide *by Patricia Lauber, photos by Jerome Wexler (Crown Young Books, 1981) anticipates the book's total design.*

wrote a sequel, *More Science Experiments You Can Eat.*

"Cute" for its own sake doesn't work with nonfiction titles, although I think for fiction titles cuteness might have an advantage. The first component of a good title is that it convey what is inside the book. Seymour Simon missed out on *Chemistry in the Kitchen,* but struck gold with *The Paper Airplane Book* and *How to Be a Space Scientist.* Simon's approach is basically straightforward, and it usually works.

Another key to a good title is a sound underlying concept. If your book is well organized and offers an interesting point of view, the title may simply present itself. Judi Freidman's *The Biting Book* shows how different animals use their teeth. This nofiction book has some of the same charm as Else Minarik's *No Fighting, No Biting,* a storybook for the same age group.

There's an art to titles, and although publishers, specifically the marketing department, usually have the final say on what a book is called, the author does have input. For instance, when I proposed Manfred Riedel's excellent manuscript about statistics, calling it *A Kid's Guide to Statistics*, I was hoping the sales staff would remember his earlier successful book *A Kid's Guide to the Economy* and accept the title for its serious interest. No go. I conferred with the author and he suggested, half kiddingly, *Winning with Numbers*, with *A Kid's Guide to Statistics* as a subtitle. I re-proposed the book, and on the basis of the new title alone, I was able to get him an advance that was 30 percent greater.

We have now reached what may be the sorest point between author and publisher: deciding on a final title. Editors *do* listen to author's suggestions for titles. Publishers *do* listen to editors' suggestions for titles. Agents *do* succeed in obtaining contractual approval of titles for their clients. But unfortunately, there are cases when the publisher decides on a title that the author simply hates. You can avoid this by communicating your title ideas to the editor and marketing manager in a friendly way, *before* the title has been chosen. You might point out how your choice serves the audience by conveying the book's content, as well as your approach, in an interesting way. Be open to suggestion (inflexible authors are not very popular) but establish yourself as knowledgeable and concerned with the sales aspects of the title. The marketing department will appreciate your professionalism and you'll find them to be more cooperative than if you play the prima donna author who must have his or her own way.

The Jacket

After the title has been decided, marketing goes to work on the jacket. Jackets are usually printed long before the book itself is, and are shown to key accounts by the salesmen months before the book is available in order to generate advance sales. Sometimes the copy for the jacket is prepared even before the manuscript is ready. Since you are the only one who knows what will be in the book, you can help the marketing department prepare copy for your book.

There are some important things to know about "flap copy," as the jacket copy is called by marketing people. The flap copy at the front of the book describes the book's contents, but it is a come-on, not a summary. One of the best ways to write flap copy is to pose questions that the book will answer. For instance, if you are writing a book about animal appetites, you might start off by asking "What does it mean to 'eat like bird'? What does it mean to 'eat like a horse'?" These are teasers that will draw your reader into your book.

What you *don't* want to do is give the book away. You don't want to display your conclusions before the reader has had a chance to read up on the background you provide in your book. Suppose you have written a book about the discovery of photosynthesis. Keep the reader guessing about who finally discovered the process and how it actually works. The flap copy

These little numbers at the bottom right on the front flap of the book jacket show that the book is targeted at 8- to 12-year-olds.

$7.95

EATING THE VEGETARIAN WAY

GOOD FOOD FROM THE EARTH

by Lila Perl

illustrated with photographs

Americans are among the world's most voracious consumers of steaks, hamburgers, and hot dogs. Yet awareness of the world food crisis and worry about the fats and chemicals in the meats they eat is encouraging a growing number to turn toward vegetarianism. Now comes a revealing report on some of the reasons behind this remarkable change.

Following a discussion of the origins of vegetarianism, Lila Perl shows how rich societies that feed grain to cattle hog a disproportionate share of the world's food resources. She also investigates the heavy use of hormones and antibiotics by livestock breeders, which has convinced many that meat is dangerous to human health. After an explanation of complementary plant proteins, the author demonstrates how different foods can be combined to provide a nourishing, natural, and more healthful diet. A selection of vegetarian recipes that use wholesome, unprocessed ingredients and are high in protein closes the book.

Lively and informative, *Eating the Vegetarian Way* shows how everyone —whether vegetarian or not—can benefit more from the good foods of the earth.

Morrow Junior Books

ISBN 0-688-22248-X
ISBN 0-688-32248-4 (lib. bdg.)   008-0012

is an introduction to the contents of the book: it is meant to pique the reader's interest, not satisfy his curiosity.

The back flap copy is about you, the author. Writing flap copy for juvenile nonfiction books is different from writing flap copy for fiction books, or adult books. You want to establish yourself as an expert in the field you are writing about. Explain how long and where you researched the book, but don't overlook the fact that you are writing for young readers. They are interested in what you like to do, why you wrote about the subject in the book, and where you live—whether it's a city apartment house, a ranch, or the suburbs. It's important to list your credentials to capture the attention of adult buyers—who want to get their money's worth by having an expert on the subject—but you don't want to lose the children who are interested in you as a person. Good back flap copy combines the personal touch with professional credentials.

Established authors often have it written into their contracts that they have approval of the jacket copy. Although it is difficult to have this provision included in your contract, you can achieve the same effect by letting the marketing department know that you will be of help to them in writing jacket copy. Write a short essay about your book—the points it covers, the new research it includes, the scope of your discussion—the way you would like to have the front flap read. Send it either to your editor or to the marketing director and suggest this as a good starting place. Let them know that you are interested in looking at what they finally decide to include, and you'll be surprised at the level of cooperation you receive.

The jacket is the most important selling tool of your book. Sales managers today are very aware of the concept of packaging, and this extends to books. The package of your book begins with the jacket. In addition to consulting your editor about the copy that appears, try to get involved in the actual artwork for your jacket. An old print for a historical biography, an exciting shot for a science book, a photograph that is especially appealing for a book about animals—these are things that you can supply to your editor with the suggestion that they would make a good jacket. Authors and editors often don't agree on jackets. The editor may want your book to fit into a series, and then you are stuck with the "series" look. But even then you can suggest an interesting illustration.

HOW YOUR BOOK IS SOLD

What we writers want is to be read, and even re-read. But publishing is a form of commerce, so first you have to get your book into the hands of a library, a bookstore, or a wholesaler. This means that the librarian, the bookstore buyer, and the wholesaler must order it. If you understand how books are ordered, you will see how important your title is to the success of your book.

What marketing managers in publishing have to do to get your book distributed requires the patience of Job and the wisdom of Solomon. Children's books are sold in a special, and especially complicated, way. Since many children's books are bought with public money—through school and public libraries, some day care centers and community centers—the publisher has to make sure that your book is not only noncontroversial but also relevant to each of these government-funded book markets. Sales to classrooms and directly to students through book fairs pose a special problem: Parents have a way of finding the oddest things objectionable. "Why," an outraged schoolteacher in Texas wrote to the publisher of *The Diary of Anne Frank*, "does a child in Texas in 1985 need to know about a child in Holland in 1945?"

The idea that many authors have—that a book that is good is good for everyone—is not part of a book marketer's reality. So the marketer targets his markets in the school and public library areas, to make his offerings both relevant and irresistible. He understands that a book about subways will be more appealing in Boston than in Sioux City; that a book on Tglingit customs will do better in Spokane than in Tallahassee. He matches the book with a market, much as a teacher matches the child to a reading group.

Sales Techniques

A typical sales call involves a sales rep and a book buyer. The rep makes an appointment with the buyer or librarian, and her duty to him is not to waste any time. A sales rep knows what her accounts can sell, and she builds up a working relationship with her customers by highlighting titles of special interest to a store or library and skipping lightly over those titles she knows the account won't be interested in.

Estimates vary, but let's say it costs the publisher about $150 to call on a single bookstore. This covers the rep's salary, travel costs, and sales materials. For this reason, publisher's sales representatives may carry many lines, many titles. Some of these reps are on a salary, employed by the publishing house, while others work on a commission basis, making a percentage on each book they sell.

Books are sold in advance of publication, so the selling tool is the catalog. It would be nice if the salesman could carry around samples of each title that she sells, but this is not physically possible. Each book weighs about a pound, and multiplied by a publisher's seasonal offering of titles, this could easily be three hundred pounds of books! So the catalog is the primary source of information. A typical catalog page includes the title in large type, a sample illustration or jacket art, a short paragraph describing the book, a biographical note about the author and maybe the artist, the designated age group, the price, the standard book number (called the ISBN), the size of the book, and the number of pages.

BY THE SAME AUTHOR

Paddle-to-the-Sea

The New York Times says:
'Here is geography presented with freshness and originality and imagination. Younger children respond to the idea of the small canoe making its long voyage to the sea, older readers are delighted with the fine sweep of country the book shows them.'

Elementary English Review says:
'The story is realistic — there is no whimsy nor fantasy, and the pictures are magnificent. Excellent from every angle.'

The Horn Book says:
'This is geography of the best kind, made vivid by the power of imagination.'

The New York Herald Tribune says:
'Striking at first sight, compelling attention to the last, this is more than a brightly colored picture-book. It carries a cargo of information and moves with a purpose. The little traveler will . . . teach many children many things.'

Parents Magazine says:
'A spectacular and useful book which is sure to fascinate children.'

A typical ten-year-old reader says:
'I like "Paddle-to-the-Sea" because it could have happened very easily. The pictures I thought were wonderful.'

The back panel advertisement of Tree in the Trail *by Holling Clancy Holling (Houghton Mifflin, 1941) for the author's other book reveals the breadth of his appeal to children's book audiences.*

The back jacket flap of The Joy of Chickens *by Dennis Nolan (Prentice-Hall, 1980) establishes the author as an expert and a personality.*

About the Author/Artist

Dennis Nolan is a fourth generation San Franciscan. He has lived in California all his life. As a young boy, he moved to Burlingame with his family. He attended the college of San Mateo and received a Master's degree from San Jose State College. Trained as a painter, Mr. Nolan has held several one-man gallery shows and contributed to many group exhibitions.

Mr. Nolan has been a free-lance illustrator for a number of years, residing in Redwood City on the San Francisco Peninsula with his wife Susan and son Andrew. It was here that neighbors encouraged his interest in gardening and farming, which led to the purchase of his first flock of chickens. Research for this project sent him to poultry shows, fanciers, breeders, and the Avian Science Department of the University of California at Davis. The reproductions in this book are the same size as the original paintings, which were executed on 100% rag board with transparent watercolor paints.

Mr. Nolan still maintains a flock of chickens, painting daily to the sounds of their contented clucking.

Prentice-Hall, Inc.
Englewood Cliffs, New Jersey
Printed in U.S.A./1980

It is from this small amount of information that the bookseller makes his decision whether or not to buy the book. And, increasingly, this is the book's only chance to end up on bookstore shelves. Six months after publication, a book—even a children's book—is old. It's not likely that a bookstore will order a book that is more than a year old, unless the author is local, the book is given "classic" status, or is reissued as a paperback.

The Five Main Channels for Distributing Children's Books

1. *The public library*, traditionally the publisher's biggest market, and while this still holds for hardcover books for older children, it is less true for books for younger children and is untrue for paperbacks.
2. *The school library.* This is the biggest market for juvenile nonfiction, since the library in the school serves as the source for homework assignments, and library and research skills are part of the curriculum.
3. *Book clubs and book fairs.* Here books are sold directly to the child with some help from parents and teachers in selecting titles. These books are usually paperback (two dollars is a standard book club/book fair price) and chosen with the broadest interest in mind. Thus, regional and special interests get short shrift, while books on more general topics, such as endangered species or different kinds of weather, sell well here.
4. *Retail stores.* There are a number of children's bookstores, like Trespassers William in Albuquerque, the Cheshire Cat in Washington, D.C. and The Owl and the Pussycat in Lexington, Kentucky. These stores cater to local customers, many of whom have long relationships with the stores. They are important opinion leaders in establishing the reputations of books and authors. The total number of books they sell is not calculated to warm a sales accountant's heart, but editors and publishers recognize that the specialty store is an important belwether for new books.
5. *Wholesalers and jobbers.* These giants customers buy books in quantity. They supply the first four categories of customers with books in less than half the time and at about 10 percent more in cost than the most efficient publisher can. Wholesalers can be specialists, as is the Book Nook in Newton, Massachusetts, the most important wholesaler of children's books; or they can serve many customers, as does Baker and Taylor, with its offices in New Jersey and Utah.

What makes wholesalers different is that publishers give them a high discount to encourage their buying many books. A jobber with a large children's book clientele might buy two or three hundred copies of a new nonfiction book *before* it is published. They keep it in stock as word of mouth gets around and the reviews start coming in. If a teacher, librarian, or retailer sees a notice of the book in the paper on Tuesday, a call to a wholesaler might get her a copy by Friday. In this age of media assault, where too often once a book's published, it's forgotten, the wholesaler serves an invaluable function.

You'll notice, if you've been to a shopping mall lately, that I haven't mentioned the big bookselling chains as part of the juvenile nonfiction distribution network. Though this can change, and we all hope it will, Waldenbooks, and B. Dalton's, and the smaller chains do far better with paperbacks and picture books than they do with the well-written children's books on a nonfiction subject. Their customers for children's books are looking for gifts and vacation reading, not additions to the children's libraries. Because, like any store, they depend on high turnover, they seek media tie-ins, like novelizations of movies and spinoffs of licensed toy characters. They have not yet discovered the slow and steady income that is to be had from selling nonfiction. But as picture books turn more often to nonfiction for subject matter, as they have recently in Mitsumasa Anno's and David Macaulay's books, and as teenagers get fed up with escape fiction and turn to the connection with the real world that nonfiction offers, this trend will certainly change.

Each method of juvenile nonfiction book distribution has its costs and benefits.

TYPE	COSTS	BENEFITS
LIBRARY	Long wait for reviews	Display and promotion once purchased
	Payment slowed by bureaucratic requirements	Full royalty to author
SCHOOL	Reviews often quirky	Books actually read for school assignments; reading encouraged by both teacher and school librarian
	Regional prejudice can knock out an otherwise fine book	Books pitched to kids in classroom as well as library
	Slow payment	Full royalty
BOOK FAIR	High discount to jobber	High volume, but low royalty
	Fine market for local-interest book	Book fair jobbers scattered across country;

Type	Costs	Benefits
		intensive promotion to reach every single one of them
Book Store	Child owns book and takes corresponding interest in reading it over and over	Individual reading only Not circulated, not replaced
Book Club	Fantastic national distribution	Low, low payment to author; often one-time flat fee of 25¢ or less
	Heavy promotion, so people who don't buy it at least have heard of it.	Clubs will shun your books in the future if sales don't justify their heavy advertising and promo costs
Wholesaler	High volume	Pitiful discount; author receives ½ the standard royalty here
	Availability	Returns may diminish your royalty check years later when you least expect it

THE IMPORTANCE OF REVIEWS

"My husband says I would make a terrible reporter," Jean Mercier, the children's book reviewer for *Publishers Weekly*, laughs. "I have strong opinions, and I don't keep them to myself." And that is why Mercier is such a successful reviewer—she reacts to books with a consistent and charming subjectivity. Like Zena Sutherland of the Center for Children's Books, or Trev Jones of *School Library Journal*, Mercier states her criteria, acknowledges the needs of her special audience, and has developed a style of writing in her reviews that makes her readers feel at home.

Writers often look at reviewers as the insensitive enemy, not bothering to appreciate the subtleties of the work they have done. This is especially true of nonfiction reviews, where a reviewer may disagree with a set of facts or the interpretation of them, attacking a well-written, well-researched book because it looks at a subject differently than the reviewer might.

While it is true that reviewers, who sift through thousands of books and review hundreds of them, can't pay the close attention to an author's work that the author herself might, they offer a context for the potential purchaser that neither the author nor the publisher provides. You can control negative assessments of your work to some extent by researching the competition carefully, and by insisting that your publisher have the manuscript reviewed by two experts (using only one is dangerous, since opinion runs high in nonfiction; two expert readers, carefully selected, can give advice you and your editor can balance out). Another way to disarm reviewers is to include a firm stand in your writing that reminds the reader that this is how you, the author, feel about a subject you've studied carefully.

But there are surprises. Ten years ago, four biographies of Gertrude Stein appeared simultaneously, to the surprise of editors and authors alike. Any anniversary, be it Bach's birthday or the appearance of Halley's Comet, is a sure occasion for publishing a book about it. When several books come out at the same time on the same subject, you can be sure that you are going to be compared, often on grounds that seem absurd to you. But no matter—the attention a review, however unfavorable, brings to a book is better than nothing. A well-known and prolific author recently complained to me that she hadn't gotten any hate mail: "All my writer friends get these nutty letters telling them how wrong they are, and I feel a little left out that nobody has ever bothered to write one to me!" A passionate response to a book arouses passionate interest; it's a true test of a writer's writing power. A child who wants facts, nothing but the facts, as Mr. Gradgrind insists in Dickens's *Hard Times*, can find them in the encyclopedia. A nonfiction book is a far more personal and deeper exploration, and the author is responsible for tone, form, and style as well as for content.

Reviewers regulate these elusive qualities. The stated editorial policies of *The Horn Book*, *Publishers Weekly* and *School Library Journal* are protected carefully by their editors, even when a host of reviewers contribute evaluations of individual books. Each of these established publications has a special angle, a special audience. *The Horn Book* reviews of nonfiction are adventurous, individual, and as concerned with literary merit as are the fiction reviews. *Publishers Weekly* reviews new writers and, as the editor says, "the very good books" and "the very bad books." *School Library Journal* is concerned with the appropriateness of format, reading level, and content in broad terms, since its readership is enormous. *ALA Booklist*, serving the small library, confines its reviews to books it can recommend, and offers the librarian who wants to purchase the book good reasons why it belongs in the library's collections.

MARKETING'S SECRET LANGUAGE:
A GLOSSARY OF BUZZWORDS

TOC: The Table Of Contents of a book, giving the book sales rep and his customer the opportunity to get the "feel" of the book at a glance.

SLANT, ALSO KNOWN AS ANGLE: The author's perspective on her subject. *All About Words* has an encyclopedic slant, whereas *Where Words were Born* has a historical angle. When your editor identifies the slant for the marketing department, he is mindful of both your style and content.

LIST: Your book and the thirty-seven other books published in the same season (Spring, Fall) in the same year. The reps carry these titles to customers over a three- or four-month period. Brand-new titles are on the *front list*, whereas books from previous seasons are on the *backlist*. Most juvenile nonfiction shows up in the publisher's *midlist*, meaning that the books there have steady but not spectacular sales potential. Midlist books, while they don't appear initially as blockbusters or lead titles, make good backlist books. That means that your rep expects to sell them at a steady rate over a five- to ten-year period.

REP: The publisher's sales representative. The marketing department organizes a sales conference for each selling season, often in a glamorous resort in the Bahamas or the Catskill Mountains. The sales representatives from all over the country gather there to hear about new books, which they then carry to the field—the bookstores, libraries, or wholesalers who want to hear about new books they can purchase. A rep is usually either a bright young college graduate who wants to experience the grassroots world of publishing, or a seasoned pro who has strong relationships with his book customers. Young people bring enthusiasm; the older people bring experience: both are essential ingredients in getting customers to buy your book.

SALES FORECAST: How well the publisher believes your book will sell over a given period of time. Sales forecasts are no more than educated guesses, but they determine how many copies are printed, what the selling price will be, the promotional support assigned to the book, and the quota the rep is expected to sell. A book that exceeds its forecast is a sleeper; one that falls short is a bomb. For this reason, the author should encourage his editor to make a conservative estimate of the book's potential.

BOUND GALLEYS: When the manuscript for your book is in page proof, sets are bound in soft covers for distribution to interested customers. For instance, *The Man Who Was Don Quixote* by Raphael Busoni, which went on to win the Newbery Award, was sent to 200 reviewers in bound galleys four months before the book was published.

The Cheshire Cat Chronicle

May, 1986

Calendar of May and June Events

Sat. May 17 - ARNOLD LOBEL - Chalk talk and autographing - 11:00 a.m. (Ages 3+)

Sat. May 31 - JAMES HOWE - Book discussion and autographing - 2:00 p.m. (Ages 8-12)

Sat. June 7 - LOCAL AUTHORS' FESTIVAL - 3:30-5:30 - See note below. (All ages)

Local Authors' Festival

The Washington area is blessed with a large number of distinguished authors and illustrators of children's books. We have invited authors and illustrators of recently published books to visit the store on *Saturday, June 7,* to talk informally about their work and to autograph their books. Please note the times they are scheduled to appear for this festive occasion.

From 3:30 to 4:30

Brent Ashabranner and **Paul Conklin** - *The Children of the Maya*
A sensitive portrayal of the plight of a group of refugees from Guatemala who have settled in a small town in Florida. Ages 11+

Mary Downing Hahn - *Jellyfish Season*
Hard times force Kathleen's family to move in with relatives and cope with the difficulties that arise. Ages 10-12

Anne Lindbergh - *Hunky-Dory Dairy*
Zannah and her mother chance upon a magic dairy in Georgetown inhabited by people from the 19th century. Ages 9-12

Phyllis Naylor - *The Keeper*
Nick's normal, funny, adolescent life at school contrasts with tensions at home where he and his mother grapple with his father's growing mental illness. Ages 13+

Nancy Patz - *Gina Farina & the Prince of Mintz*
A spoiled prince is no match for quick-witted, strong-willed Gina in this lavishly illustrated picture book. Ages 5-8

Colby Rodowsky - *Julie's Daughter*
A teenager and her mother who had abandoned her as an infant make their peace as they unite to care for a testy old woman artist. Ages 13+

Linda Shute - Illustrator of *Katy's First Haircut*
After she is mistaken for a boy, a first-grader has second thoughts about having had her long, bothersome hair cut off. Ages 3-6

From 4:30 to 5:30

Jan Adkins - *Workboats*
All sorts of water craft swing into action when a fisherman is missing off the coast. The text and detailed drawings abound with information about working boats. Ages 9-12

Barbara Johnson Adams - *The Picture Life of Bill Cosby*
This biography of the comic entertainer is written for children just beyond the beginning reading level. Ages 7-10

Karen Gundersheimer - *Colors to Know* and *Shapes to Show*
Pre-schoolers will have fun learning their colors and basic shapes from these two books scaled for very small hands. Ages 2-4

Marguerite Murray - *A Peaceable Warrior*
A family vacation in the West Virginia mountains turns into a hunt for a dangerous man called Copperhead. Ages 10-12

group of curious, energetic nursery school children as they help build play equipment in memory of a beloved teacher. Ages 4-6

Candice Ransom - *Blackbird Keep*
Holly finds romance and solves the mystery of a long-lost brooch while spending the summer with relatives. Ages 12+

Peggy Thomson - *Auks, Rocks, & the Odd Dinosaur*
The author gives a lively, informative look behind the scenes at some twenty objects on display at the Smithsonian's Museum of Natural History. Ages 10+

New Books

I Can; I Hear; I See; and *I Touch* by Helen Oxenbury 2.95 *each* Ages 1-2½
With limited text, four new board books by Helen Oxenbury feature her round-headed wispy-haired toddlers engaging in familiar activities.

Jamaica's Find by Juanita Havill Ill. by Anne Sibley O'Brien 12.95 Ages 4-7
Playing by herself in the park, Jamaica finds a red hat and a well-worn cuddly toy dog. Although she turns in the hat at the Lost and Found Office, she takes the stuffed pet back to her home where her mother starts her thinking about the dog's real owner. O'Brien's engaging pictures add a special liveliness to a very human story.

oodnight Hug; The Playground; Spring and Summer Days by Harold Roth 0 each Ages 1-3
lor photographs and simple complete sens give these four board books an appealing y.

illage of Round and Square Houses by Ann Grifalconi 14.95 Ages 5-8
At the foot of the Naka Mountain in West Africa lies a village in which women live in round houses and men live in square houses. One night Gran'ma Tika tells her small granddaughter the story of the custom's mythic origin. Grifalconi's vivid oil-crayon illustrations and poetic storytelling create a memorable book.

Best Friends by Steven Kellogg 12.95 Ages 4-7
Kathy is left behind during summer vacation as Louise goes off to Pine Cone Peak promising to miss her every day. Instead the postcard reports, "This place is terrific." Instantly a best friend turns worst friend with the anger and anguish such a change brings. The ending suggests that even if life is not always fair, special friends still ease the bumps along the way. Kellogg's winsome illustrations highlight the amusement and poignancy of his story.

The Magic Horse Retold and illustrated by Sally Scott 11.75 Ages 5-9
An evil wizard angrily sends Prince Kamar al-Akmar aloft on a magic flying horse carved out of ebony. After he discovers how to land, the prince meets and falls in love with a beautiful princess, but he must outwit the wizard and then a sultan before gaining her hand. Scott has illustrated her adaptation of a story from "The Arabian Nights" with elegant paintings in the style of Persian miniatures.

Book promotion begins at home. Local stores, whether their specialty is books or something else, are a good starting place for the launching of a book. This brochure from a bookstore shows the kind of publicity local stores can provide.

CHAPTER 17

How to Promote Like a Pro

For a very short six weeks, your book is the center of attention. The catalog arrives in your mail and in the mail of thousands of others, announcing your book. The kids buy you roses, your editor sends you a telegram, the writers' workshop features you as a speaker and the local paper interviews you. Wow! When your mother warned you thirty years ago, "It's too good to last," she may have had a book's publication in mind. Unless you work hard at this crucial period, you're headed for disappointment.

Before anyone reads your book, they see the cover, the advertising copy, and maybe an interview in the local paper. You want to convert passing interest into enduring interest, and you don't have much time. Here's a short list of some emergency measures:

1. The cover is the advertisement for the book as well as its package. Ask your editor for a black and white photostat of the cover, then make three hundred copies of it. Send it out indiscriminately to the gas company with your check, along with Christmas cards, birth announcements, and thank-you notes.
2. While the general reader will need only the enticement of your book's cover to get interested, a professional will need more technical information. The librarian or teacher in your community will appreciate a photocopy of the catalog announcement with its ordering informa-

Long ago,
in distant, ancient Greece, there was a man
named Diogenes who dressed like a beggar and
lived in the streets. Yet he became known
as one of the greatest philosophers of his time.

This is how it happened.

Diogenes: The Story of the Greek Philosopher *by Aliki (Prentice-Hall, 1963), shows how typography can be used creatively to open a story.*

tion, length, age classification, and physical specifications. Write a personal note along with the copy. An advantage of a catalog copy announcement is that the copywriter has already sung your book's praises, so you can be becomingly modest.

3. Before you are interviewed by the local penny saver, the church newsletter, or the college alumni magazine, send out a press release covering the background of the book. This frees you and the interviewer to talk about far-flung topics and at the same time inspires professional respect for you. Many publishers are happy to supply letterhead and helpful advice to authors with some leads into media. And publishers are not concerned that the audience is small: they seek quality, not quantity. What drives publicists nuts is the writer who thinks *The New Yorker* and the London *Sunday Times* will want to run a front-page photo feature on his book. More realistic goals will endear you to publishers who see the small notice in the *St. Louis Cookbook Guild Quarterly* as entree to a new market.

4. Prepare a fact sheet about yourself, with photo, educational and professional credentials, publication history, and the title of your new book. Send this out when local groups and schools ask you to speak. Start thinking professionally and you'll be treated professionally.

5. Write letters (don't make a phone call without sending a letter first: be a pro, not a pest) to radio stations, television programs originating in your area, magazines specializing in your subject area, and experts in your field advising them of the publication of your new book. If you aren't on a corresponding basis with these people, a card announcement will do nicely.

6. Write your publisher's sales rep a note with suggestions of places where you are known and the book might be sold. I once talked my corner grocer into carrying my book for six days, and he sold three copies—three copies that would never have been sold without his help.

Barbara Marcus, the marketing director of Scholastic Books, says "A good idea is a good idea. Even," she laughs, "if it comes from an author." Don't be shy about advancing suggestions to your publisher's minions. "Nine out of ten suggestions will never make it," Marcus says. "But the tenth one can make the difference between success and obsolescence." Aside from my general advice about shouting the news of publication from the rooftops, you want to design your own ploys for publicity, peculiar to you, your book, your location, your occupation, and your publisher. If you understand what your publisher is doing to reach your potential audience, you can better plan your own strategy for success.

TOOTING YOUR OWN HORN

Jumping into the fray that surrounds your book's publication can give you the edge that you need to keep your book in print. An ounce of enthusiasm initially is worth a pound of enthusiasm years after the book's publication. By establishing relationships with the publicist and the sales representative and doing the thankless follow-up work of arranging appearances and interviews, you establish yourself as a person who works hard, not a prima donna author. Since the vast majority of publishing people have never written a book, they aren't entirely aware that writing is work. If you show that you are willing to help them do the job they've been hired to do for you and your book, and display a cooperative spirit, your book can only benefit. When Charles Spain Verral wrote his biography of Robert Goddard, the father of the atom bomb, the editor promoted it as a science biography of national interest. But Verral's research had taken him to Los Alamos where he had interviewed Goddard's widow. Verral got a note praising the book from Mrs. Goddard, which he photocopied to send to the New Mexico sales rep. When the book threatened to go out of print twenty years later, that sales rep, Dwight Myers, screamed and carried on as though his favorite child was being sacrificed. The book's still in print. And Dwight Myers is still selling it.

Every amateur believes once his book is published, it's around for eternity. Every professional knows that nothing could be further from the truth. But the professional isn't discouraged by this reality: he sees it instead as a challenge. And anybody who can sell a manuscript to a publisher can sell a book to a reader. It takes persistence, it takes chutzpah, it takes brains, and most of all it takes a powerful sense of humor.

Mike Thaler, the author of seventeen successful humor books for children, dazzles the marketing professionals on his publisher's staff with his zany ideas for promotion. For instance, he was able to get a plug for his picture book, *Lemon Seed*, on a late-night FM radio news show because the same imaginative persistence that goes into writing his books goes into promoting them.

Avoiding the Backlist Blues

After the initial launch of a title, publishers get preoccupied with the list coming up. After a season in the sun, your book is relegated to the backlist, described earlier. The backlist can resemble Nirvanah, Limbo, or the furthest reaches of Hell, depending on how you, the writer, take advantage of your book's availability.

A "backlist book" has been reviewed, has been sold by the sales representative, has been purchased by bookstores and libraries. It's not news anymore. For the writers who don't quite understand why their publisher

credit: Beverly Hall

Daniel Cohen

Daniel Cohen was born in Chicago, Illinois on March 12, 1936. He attended the Chicago public schools and the University of Illinois School of Journalism.

After graduation he went to work for <u>Science Digest</u> magazine. He remained with the magazine for nearly ten years, the last three as Managing Editor. During that time the magazine moved its editorial offices from Chicago to New York City, and Mr. Cohen moved with them.

He published his first book, MYTHS OF THE SPACE AGE, in 1967. In 1969 he left the relative security of editorial work and went into full time freelance writing. Since that time he has written over 75 books for adults and children. Many of his books have dealt with aspects of the weird or supernatural such as monsters, ghosts and UFO's. He discusses these subjects on radio and television and recently appeared on the CBS-TV special "Everything You Wanted to Know About Monsters But Were Afraid." Daniel Cohen has also been a guest lecturer at college campuses throughout the United States and Canada.

He has been a keynote dinner speaker on high interest/low vocabulary writing at a preconference meeting of the American Library Association. He delivered a paper on Creatures from UFO's at the International Symposium on Creatures of Legendary at the University of Nebraska. Because his Hi/Lo books have been so popular, he has been asked more and more often to talk to elementary and junior high school students and appear at school book fairs. He also participates in a growing phenomenon known as the conference telephone call,

Dodd Mead & Company, Inc.   79 Madison Avenue
(212) 685-6464   New York, N.Y. 10016

where librarians and teachers arrange a time for students to interview favorite authors by phone.

"I'm doing a number of phone conversations," Daniel Cohen said recently. "The students are interested in UFO's and monsters and they sometimes ask questions like: How did you get into writing? What happens if a book is rejected?"

Daniel Cohen works on several projects at one time. He has recently completed a book about the "mysterious airship". It concerns one of the strangest and least known episodes in American history, for back in 1896 and 1897 thousands of people all across the U.S. reported seeing an airship -- that was six years before the Wright brothers made their successful flight at Kitty Hawk. He is at work on an encyclopedia of the world's monsters, and a book on dinosaurs. Mr. Cohen's articles have appeared in publications as diverse as <u>The Nation</u>, <u>Omni</u>, <u>Popular Mechanics</u>, and <u>The Parapsychology Review</u>. He is a Fellow of the Committee for the Scientific Investigation of Claims of the Paranormal.

Mr. Cohen lives in Port Jervis, New York with his wife, who is also a writer, their daughter who is thirteen and a collection of cats and dogs.

Books by Daniel Cohen
Published by Dodd, Mead & Company, Inc.

High Interest/Low Vocabulary Series:

    CREATURES FROM UFO'S
    THE GREATEST MONSTERS IN THE WORLD
    MISSING! Stories of Strange Disappearances
    REAL GHOSTS
    SUPERMONSTERS
    THE WORLD'S MOST FAMOUS GHOSTS
    FAMOUS CURSES
    MONSTERS YOU NEVER HEARD OF
    SCIENCE FICTION'S GREATEST MONSTERS
    GHOSTLY TERRORS

Other Titles for Children, Young Adults,
and Adults:

    IN SEARCH OF GHOSTS
    THE MAGIC ART OF FORESEEING THE FUTURE
    MEDITATION: What It Can Do For You

    MYSTERIOUS DISAPPEARANCES
    TALKING WITH THE ANIMALS

    THE FAR SIDE OF CONSCIOUSNESS
    MASTERS OF THE OCCULT
    A MODERN LOOK AT MONSTERS
    MYSTERIOUS PLACES
    VOODOO, DEVILS, AND THE NEW INVISIBLE WORLD
    DEALING WITH THE DEVIL

    A CLOSE LOOK AT CLOSE ENCOUNTERS
    THE GREAT AIRSHIP MYSTERY

Dodd Mead & Company, Inc.   79 Madison Avenue
(212) 685-6464   New York, N.Y. 10016

This four-page flyer about author Dan Cohen is sent by his publisher to teachers and librarians who are interested in his books. In addition to biographical information the flyer includes a photograph and a list of books the librarians and teachers can order.

hasn't gotten their book for fourth graders on the problems of strip mining onto the best-seller list, the five or so years that their book is in print but not publicized can be hellish. The frustration at being neither rich nor famous can quell creativity, undermine confidence, and even drive them to drink. For writers who realize that people won't necessarily rush out to buy such a title, the frustration is simple confusion. They don't expect miracles from their publishers, but they don't really know how to work miracles themselves. They think there may be some people who really are interested in talking to kids about strip mining, if they could only find a way to bring the book to their attention.

Writers who revel in having a backlist book or two in their published repertoire are writers who know that a book is an interesting starting place for building a reputation as a writer. For them, having a book that's available but not exactly the talk of the town gets the entrepreneurial impulses beating. Before your book was published, in the quiet excitement of getting your editor enthusiastic about your project, you had some ideas. At the time they seemed far-fetched because your book wasn't a reality yet. Now that your book *is* a reality look back over those dreamy suggestions. Did someone send the Audubon Society a copy of your book about bluebirds? You write the publisher and discover, yes they did send a copy to the national office, which felt the subject was too local and the book too expensive for them.

But you live in northern Connecticut where bluebirds abound every spring, so you call the local chapter. A book? Well, they don't sell many books, but perhaps you'd like to give a lecture. You're not a great speaker, you counter, but you have some wonderful slides that served as the illustrations for the book. So it would be primarily a slide show. Oh? A slide show. That might interest children. The Audubon Society has a program in the schools, so perhaps you'd like to consider that. Some of its members are teachers, and if they like the presentation, there's no telling. . . . Sure enough, two years later, you find yourself sighing to your husband at breakfast that you have to give that damned bluebird slide show to two classes today and it's raining. And he reminds you without so much as putting down the sports page that your editor put the book in paperback because of the success of your classroom slide shows. Moral: The spin-offs to these "far-fetched" ideas can spell a long (and lucrative) life for your book.

"E" is for Expert

How can you match your book to its audience after the publication fanfare is over? It's easy: you're not a celebrity anymore, you're an expert.

If you think your book on hydroponics is never going to move off the bookstore shelf until you appear in *People* magazine with your Pekingese, your third husband, and your agent in your hot tub, you needn't worry. Promoting yourself to the world of young readers is just as splashy, but not

WALKING DRAGLINE

Walking draglines are used to dig out the ore in open-pit mines. Some of these super excavators weigh over 3 million pounds.

At the end of a 300-foot boom swings a giant bucket. The bucket on the left can scoop up to 85 cubic yards in one bite.

A walking dragline working in a phosphate mine ▶

12

In clear text and fascinating photographs, George Ancona, author-photographer of Monster Movers *(E. P. Dutton, 1983), describes the operations of sixteen mechanical giants.*

that risqué.

Unlike celebrities in the general culture, the juvenile nonfiction writer gets to know his audience as individuals, not just demographics. By appearing in classrooms, school auditoriums, at book fairs and after-school programs, the self-promoting author actually sees his readers, hears their voices, and as the years go by sees his influence on them as they become definite personalities.

The first ingredient—and really the only essential one for the nonfiction self-promoter—is faith in himself. This faith breaks down into four distinct parts: (1) faith in his ability to get interested in something he's writing about, even when his friends and family tease him about his obsessiveness, (2) faith in children, so that he feels he is doing something important, not easy, by writing specifically for children, (3) faith in his ability to present a subject that engages and holds the child's attention, with the writing and research skills that it requires, and (4) faith in his appeal to others. This last is an elusive quality, and learned only through trial and error. It is fatally easy to admit that you know only an iota of what there is to understand about Uranus, but what children want and need is authority, expertise, and a living, breathing example in their favorite authors. A novelist can get away with a squeaky voice and nervous twitches, but a nonfiction writer has no such luxury.

Building self-confidence to promote yourself starts with your own life. Aliki, the prolific author of many biographies and science books for children, is a native of Philadelphia. Although she has spent her adult life in New York, Florence, and London, she still keeps her loyalty to her hometown. She retains ties to the Philadelphia Free Public Library, which promotes her books as "hometown girl creates masterpiece," and the Drexel University Library Science School which has honored her continued commitment to children's nonfiction. Aliki is proud to be from Philadelphia, and she encourages Philadelphia to be proud of her. It makes everyone feel good to be members of the same Mutual Admiration Society.

But not everybody comes from a book town like Philadelphia. Muriel Batherman, who uses her skills as a graphic designer and writer to create winning picture books, promotes her books in Morristown, New Jersay, a place she just happens to live because her engineer-husband works nearby. To the children of Morristown, Batherman is an institution, because she has been writing books and telling children about them for fifteen years, which to seven-year-olds is two lifetimes, at least.

Dennis Nolan, who thinks of himself as a painter first and a writer second, has always written picture books for young children. Imagine his surprise when he became the most sought-after author in the literacy programs for adults in San Jose, California, where he teaches art on the college level. The books that were inspired by Nolan's own son when he was young—*Alphabrutes*, *Monster Bubbles*, and *Big Pig*—were winners with men who were returning to school in their thirties and forties to learn how to read. Nolan's humorous graphics were hip and funny and outrageous, so these adult men weren't embarrassed to read them, as they had been with sweeter stories about duckies and bunnies. In fact, one man, an ex-convict, confided to Nolan that his wife thought one of the monsters in *Monster Bubbles* (a counting book) looked just like him.

Vicki Cobb started writing as a way to combine her experience in science, journalism, and teaching while she raised two sons. After nearly twenty years of steady output, she was established as a sort of celebrity among science teachers. Her publisher began a direct-mail campaign showing these science teacher-fans how Cobb's thirty books could be integrated into the upper elementary science curriculum. The campaign was a hit, but the teachers wanted more: they wanted Cobb herself. By this time, Cobb's children were independent enough for her to travel and she takes what she calls her "dog and pony show" to schools all over the country. And since she sees this as professional work, not just promotion, she insists upon being paid as a consultant. This makes her status stronger so that both Cobb and the teachers know that her marvelous lectures to school children on science subjects are in fact serious business, not just publicity puffing.

Dan Cohen is another science writer who came to children's books from *Science News*, a serious journal for adults. Prolific and enthusiastic, he springs to life on the printed page. His readers wrote to him, suggested that he unravel the great mysteries of the supernatural for them. And so about ten years ago, Cohen became a self-educated expert on the supernatural, operating from a tiny city in western New York State with a fine interlibrary loan program. And after five years of writing about monsters, ghosts, and poltergeists, Cohen became a real celebrity, featured on CBS television. Not because he was a children's book author, but because he knows more about the supernatural than anyone else. Cohen's ability to get interested himself, and to interest others, created a winning television personality. And the TV exposure has done wonders for his book sales.

Authors are amused that young children are interested in the same things their parents are: money, age, friends, and fame. "Are you famous?" children ask veteran picture book writer Tomie de Paola. And de Paola assures them that he is, and tells them all about it. Having thus won their trust, de Paola asks them some cheeky questions back. "What do you like to see in pictures?" he asks. "If you could read a book about anything, what would that anything be?" And from this, de Paola has collected a treasure house of secret ingredients for books, which include child-inspired tomes on popcorn, quicksand, and pet sheep.

A Star Is Made

In previous chapters, I emphasized the importance of the team spirit in getting your book written and published. In this chapter, I am emphasizing another aspect of being an author. It is part of the complex choreography of writing for any age to be able to work in isolation, to create a book, then to work with others to get it published well, and then to slip into star status to let the world in on a very large secret: your book. From my many years in publishing, I know this is important because the "star quality" is more prominent in nonfiction authors than it is in fiction writers. Pauline Watson, the author of *Cricket's Cookery*, started out as a singer, and when she sings "Oh, My Darling Sugar Cookies" to the tune of "Clementine" to turn people's attention to her book, you can see those early years weren't wasted. Lee Warren, who writes for teenagers, was a dancer, and she presents her lectures on African arts with aplomb. Betsy Hearn is an expert on children's reading, and was a folk singer before she went to library school. When she talks about children's favorite books—including some she's written herself—you can spot that stage presence.

Knowing yourself enables you to wear the many hats of a nonfiction writer for children. If you are nervous about how your audience is going to receive you and your book, you may introduce doubt where doubt is neither necessary nor useful. But if you allow a little vanity either by reading your writing aloud to yourself, or prancing a few minutes before the mirror, you will find that you are your book's best advertisement, and the book is the best advertisement for you.

PART FOUR

Your Career as a Nonfiction Author

*I'm afraid my life is totally wrapped up in
books. Most of the people I see are in the business in one way or another, but you don't plan
your life this way. It sort of creeps up on you,
and suddenly there you are.
—George Sullivan, author of
more than thirty-five
books for children*

A simple postcard announcing the publication of your book can be sent without embarrassment to potential customers. Author Bernice Selden designed this card to let acquaintances and colleagues know what she was up to without obligating them to buy the book.

CHAPTER 18

Now You're a Published Author!

Newcomers often ask me how writers find out that they're officially going to be in print. The answers to that question are as numerous as there are editors. Some editors confide off the record over lunch. Others pick up the phone as soon as the president's signature has dried on the approval form. Others write letters that are suitable for framing. Once an editor called me at 10 P.M. on Christmas Eve to tell me that my book had been accepted—she was still at work!

Just as idiosyncratic as the editor's delivery of the good news is the author's reactions to it. "Is that all?" a novelist friend of mine said to his editor when she joyfully informed him that his book on the physics of bicycling had been accepted. "Gotta hang up," a first-time author said to me before I could fill her in on the details. "I'm going to be sick." "I'm late for the PTA meeting. We'll talk about it tomorrow," another author said when I called to accept his book. (I was happy to comply. Being late for PTA meetings can really ruin a reputation.) One telegrammed from Florence, where she was vacationing: "Is this a joke?" We cabled back that it most certainly was not. She went to the open-air market and spent the advance she'd been promised on handblown Italian glass, which arrived at her home in Baltimore, shortly after her book was published, in thousands of shattered pieces. She didn't mind—she was still euphoric.

Keep Your Feet on the Ground

Editors, by nature more sociable than their writer cohorts, enjoy the unique and surprised response. But after the initial shock, editors appreciate writers who take the *responsibility* of being published writers. The worst thing an editor can hear, and editors hear it often, is the author's declaration that he's going to quit his job, sell his business, let his license lapse and set himself up as a full-time writer. Editors hate hearing this becaue it's unrealistic. If the poor editor can't talk the author out of it—and it's suicidal to quit on the basis of a single sale—then the writer will blame the editor and badmouth her for the rest of his broke and broken life.

The second worst thing an editor can hear is, "Oh, you liked it! I have eight other manuscripts I'll send you by Express Mail." An editor buys a manuscript for many reasons, the excellence of your manuscript being only one of them. She wants to publish the one that's sitting on her cluttered desk at the moment, and AFTER you've had a chance to work together, consider others.

The third response that editors hear at times and never want to hear again is the overbearing writer's intrusion into territory customarily assigned to the editor and publisher. "It has to be in paperback so that everyone in the world can afford to buy it." "I have a great idea for the jacket, you must use it!" "I want it published at Christmas time so I can give it for presents!" This type of obnoxious remark shows no understanding of the complexities of an editor's life. Your editor has really worked to put your book under contract. She has sat through meetings, endured discussions, fought low sales estimates, argued that your advance should be larger, dreamed about how great your book can be, tried to get the print run large enough so that its price won't be exorbitantly high. She should be applauded for her bravery, and lauded for her ability to spot your talent. Suggestions from the author, in most cases, will be given proper consideration by the publisher's staff. *Demands* by the author, on the other hand, generally do little more than raise its collective hackles. Hard as it is, you really do have to put aside your own worries that your manuscript is slipping out of control to help your editor publish the best book possible.

Because that's what editors want to do. The sweetest thing an editor can hear from an author is, "Now I'm going to get out the manuscript, look it over, and see if there's anything I can do to improve it." It shows a spirit of cooperation, but it also reminds the editor why she's in this crazy business: the most wonderful of editorial experiences is the way an editor's enthusiasm can shore up an author's confidence. An editor can fill you with a sense of your own abilities that will really get you going. That's what the editor/author alliance is all about. When it happens to you, you'll know it.

. . . But Let Your Hair Down a Little

Publication means admission to the ranks of the professional writer, and the cool, cooperative behavior I've prescribed above is not delivered just to make the editor's life easier; it's to make your writing life easier. But don't be a perfectionist. Professional behavior is not a twenty-four-hour undertaking. It's what you do at the office. Dentists forget to floss, accountants can't always make out their bank statements, plumbers' toilets back up, and psychiatrists do scream at their mothers. So you can let your hair down a little after you've set the tone of your collaboration with your editor. You don't want to create impossible expectations, but you do want to entertain possibilities. Here's how real writers do the latter while avoiding the former:

1. Wait until your mother-in-law's on her way out the door before you mention your sale: "Oh, I almost forgot to tell you . . ."

Being cool about your success makes you seem all the more awesome. There are many standard putdowns of the new author, and if you act too happy, you increase your chances of being the butt of comments that range from, "I have an idea for a children's book myself" (suggesting that it took you a couple of hours to knock this one off) to "Owls? Who in the world needs to read another book about owls? Why don't you write about Goya? You know, we were in Spain last spring . . ."

2. Let your husband take three rolls of pictures of you for the author's picture on the book jacket.

Most publishers shy away from author photos taken by amateurs. But if you tell that to your husband, who likes the way you look and wants the world to recognize you, it's only going to cause hard feelings. If you explain that the editor wants lots of shots to choose from, he'll have the opportunity to exercise *his* creativity and imagination, which is threatened at the moment by your success. (This does not mean he's jealous. In fact, he's very proud, just feeling a little insecure.)

A good author picture is usually a close-up, so that the reader gets to know your face. If it's a full-figure shot, take care not to cut off legs, heads, left arms. Kids are more appreciative of action photos than adults are, so if you want a shot of you fixing your motorcycle, flying a kite, or reading to your grandchild, go ahead. Editors are particularly appreciative when the action photo has something to do with the book you've written. You and your dog for your dog-training book, you in the library on the jacket of *How to Write a Term Paper*, you eating ice cream for that cookbook of sweet snacks for summer.

3. Practice your autograph.

This one is fun. It's a solitary activity, a quiet activity, and a portable activity. Maybe this is the moment for you to buy an antique fountain pen. Or start using purple ink. Or writing with your left hand. You can study the signatures on the Declaration of Independence, or in that paperback on graphology to get new ideas about styles in signatures. Some publishers actually stamp the author's signature on the front case of the book cover (not jacket). A good signature might inspire them to do this for you.

4. Read *Writers at Work* and see if it reads differently now that you're one of them.

A book contract, like a college degree or a marriage certificate, is "just a piece of paper." And that piece of paper can change the way you look at yourself and the world looks at you. Reading about other writers writing gets you thinking, "Hmmm. Maybe I should do that," or "Imagine! He wastes all that time on the first draft!" You are now part of the great community of writers that readers actually pay money to read, and it's fun to submerge yourself in it. It's also a reminder, reading about other writers, that you're not the first person this has ever happened to. And, yes, that's sometimes hard to believe.

5. Call your nephew's English teacher in Chicago, the one whose biography of Shakespeare was published three years ago, and ask her what it looks like in retrospect: her answers will be interesting.

Sharing your good news with a person who's been through it is often helpful and uplifting. Helpful because more experienced writers can advise and prepare you for pitfalls your editor doesn't have the time and inclination to mention. And uplifting because published authors remember just what a thrill that first sale was. Oddly, I've never heard of envy entering into these conversations between old-timers and newcomers. The shared pleasure is universal.

6. Look over your unsold manuscripts and put yourself in your editor's shoes. What did the one you sold have that these don't?

When you look at the manuscripts you've written but haven't sold (yet!) from the vantage of a published writer, you'll find that you have the confidence to be critical of yourself. You will find that some scripts simply need to be retyped and sent to prospective publishers while others need to be revised, rethought, rewritten. And you'll see that sometimes a piece of writing, like the performance of a song, can best be forgotten. There is nothing so liberating as *throwing away* a terrible script. It's like throwing out the failed soufflé or the jeans that are more patches than pants. You don't need a bad manuscript in your files, and realizing that every word you write is not sacrosanct puts you in the ranks of real pros.

7. Go to the library and bone up on the trade gossip in *Publishers Weekly, The New York Times Book Review, The Washington Post Book World,* and *The New Yorker.*

Publishing is, in some aspects, a glamour industry. Your family and friends will now expect you to be an expert not only on the subject of your book, on children, and on writing, but also on publishing in general. They will expect you to magically assimilate the world of million-dollar advances and fabulous libel suits, even though they have nothing to do with the hard work you are doing to write nonfiction books for children. And even if you're not an expert on publishing, you'll have fun in the library boning up on the latest trends and personalities. It's a game, but it's a great game, and you're now a varsity player.

The subtle changes that you are feeling in yourself now that you have been accepted on a publisher's list are respected by publishing people and non-publishing people alike. You have authority, sophistication, and expertise—all of which you had when you started writing—but now it is official. You will find that this is both a reward for the hard work you've done, but also a spur for taking on new challenges. As every published writer can tell you, one acceptance makes a thousand rejections worth the effort.

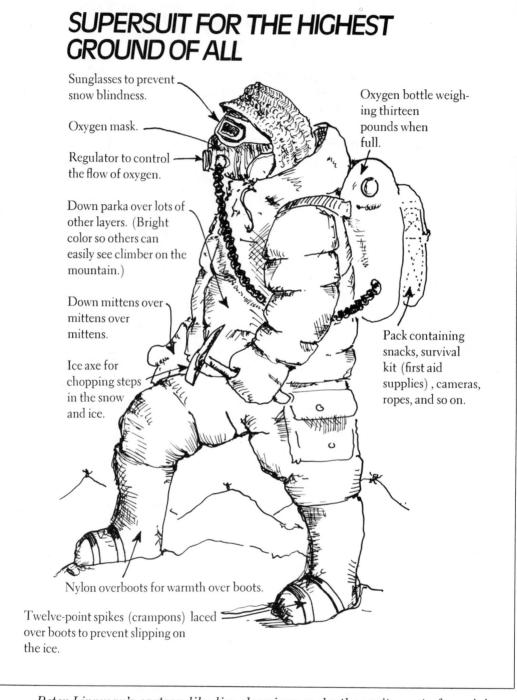

SUPERSUIT FOR THE HIGHEST GROUND OF ALL

Sunglasses to prevent snow blindness.

Oxygen mask.

Regulator to control the flow of oxygen.

Down parka over lots of other layers. (Bright color so others can easily see climber on the mountain.)

Down mittens over mittens over mittens.

Ice axe for chopping steps in the snow and ice.

Oxygen bottle weighing thirteen pounds when full.

Pack containing snacks, survival kit (first aid supplies), cameras, ropes, and so on.

Nylon overboots for warmth over boots.

Twelve-point spikes (crampons) laced over boots to prevent slipping on the ice.

Peter Lippman's cartoon-like line drawings evoke the excitement of surviving in severe environmental conditions for Vicki Cobb's book Supersuits *(J. B. Lippincott, 1975).*

CHAPTER 19

Agents and Other Allies

As in other aspects of life, the writer with an agent is convinced that it would all be much easier without him. And the writer without an agent is convinced that an agent would solve all her problems. New writers believe that an agent can sell an unsalable manuscript; first-sale writers are convinced an agent can get them more money, better promotion, a better contract; established writers figure an agent can introduce them to new markets and a wider audience; entrenched authors believe, after all that experience, that an agent can help get good old books back in print and hold now-defunct publishers to their contracts.

The writer's life is fraught with problems as his career advances, and an agent can help, no question. But writers switch agents as often as they switch publishers. Agents are not fairy godmothers. They are market researchers, salesmen, cheerleaders, accountants, and paralegals (sometimes legals, too, in the case of lawyer-agents). Some agents are effective watchdogs for contracts; others put more emphasis on sales and will sign anything as long as it means a cash advance for the writer.

THE ABC'S OF AGENTS

The literary agent is not an officially defined professional, though there are similarities in literary agents' talents and background. By personality, a literary agent is not shy. She can call an editor she's never met and suggest they meet for lunch. Or she can call an editor who's turned down her last twenty projects and suggest that at last she has the right one for the editor. A literary agent is also highly organized. Keeping track of correspondence, checks, manuscripts, and phone messages is the heart of her occupation, and she certainly knows how to keep from being snowed under, a talent that is shared neither by the editors who buy from her nor the authors who are her clients.

Aside from these two aspects of personality—chutzpah and organization—agents are various in their credentials. Some, like Patricia Ayres, actually hold editorial posts in publishing and work as agents on the side. Others, like Carol Mann, were editors before they became agents. And some, like Janet Chenery, were agents between editorial jobs. Mark Levine was a lawyer; Blanche Massey was a French teacher; Shelly Fogelman was an editor's husband and a lawyer before he switched to being a lawyer specializing in literary properties. And Elizabeth Pomada came from the marketing side of publishing.

The writer and the agent have an even longer, stronger association than the writer and the editor. Publishers go out of business, revamp their publication programs, fire and hire editors with a wave of the hand, and change staff more often than any other business besides restaurants. The agent, ideally, stands by the author through long stretches, even through whole careers. How does an agent match up with a writer?

Jeanne Betancourt met her agent Charlotte Sheedy at a party. Now Sheedy suggests projects, urges Betancourt to try new directions, and watches her royalty statements like a hawk. But it was the chance conversation that made these two women aware of each other and the possibility that they could work together.

Demi met her first agent, Julian Bach, through a school connection of her father's. "If you get an agent," her father told her, "I'll buy you a paper cutter"—something Demi dearly needed. Her father, a Boston businessman, knew there was no point in buying his artist/daughter a papercutter if there wasn't going to be money to buy paper to cut. The way to get money was to get contracts, he reasoned, and the way to get contracts was to have an agent representing you to publishers. Fifty-two books later, Demi switched agents to Marilyn Marlowe, a specialist in children's books with a great knowledge of the problems of the illustrated book. Demi found Marilyn through friends in the children's book field.

Editors are a fine source of agent recommendations. When packager Roberta Miller went back to working for a publisher, she recommended Carol Mann to her author Tom Allen. She didn't know Mann except by reputation, so it was a good recommendation. Not every editor knows every agent, but a lot of editors know the reputations of a lot of agents. When Daniel Manus Pinkwater got overwhelmed with the clerical details of having twenty books in print, he asked the five editors he had active working relationships with to recommend an agent. The one name that appeared on every list was Dorothy Markinko. She and Pinkwater got together and worked together for many years.

THE TIE THAT BINDS

The author's relationship with the agent is often informal, even haphazard. Arvid Knudsen, who works as both an agent and a packager, represents authors on projects they take on during their "downtime." This might be a series book, a ghostwriting job, a section of a textbook. Sometimes the author will request that his name be omitted from the book thus published, while other authors see such projects as exposure in a new market (workbooks, readers, toy tie-ins, licensed characters) enhancing the author's prestige. In this case, the author's name is featured prominently.

The contract with the publisher for a given project is usually the only written instrument that binds the agent and the author together. The contract between the author and the publisher usually states in a separate clause that "all monies due under the terms of this agreement will be discharged through Annie Agent of the Literate Literary Agency, 4123 Fifth Avenue, as the sole recipient. Any deviation from this agreement must be approved in writing by both the agent and the author."

The rest of the time the author and the agent work together on the basis of a handshake or a letter which is not any more binding than your letter to the gas company complaining about the error in your last bill. It does show that both parties acknowledge a mutual responsibility, but it is not a legal document.

FINDING AN AGENT

Finding an agent is a tough business, even with a few books under your belt. The writer-agent relationship has all the pleasures and tensions of any partnership. If the agent hasn't been able to sell the writer's last three manuscripts, he naturally tends to explain it as a failure on the writer's part. The writer, of course, wonders if the agent is doing a conscientious job. The pressures of survival for both agent and writer can create explosive situations. And sometimes agents and writers part company on less than friendly terms. The informality of the original agreement between writer and agent keeps the matter out of court.

Many writers are frustrated by their editor's reluctance to take sides in writer-agent disputes but editors often have close relationships with agents, as they do with writers. Most publishing houses have a strict policy of neutrality when inevitable differences of opinion arise.

Choosing the right agent is one of the most constructive steps you can take in your writing career, and choosing a wrong agent can be disastrous. Since you will be working long and closely with your agent, it's a good idea to interview him before you commission him to sell your book. If you can't meet him in person, ask him to set aside a half-hour to talk to you on the telephone. Find out who his other clients are. Ask him about recent sales. Talk to him about writers you admire, and books you have enjoyed. Discuss which publishers he likes to work with. If you don't like the answers he's giving you, let him know. Listen to what he says, and look between the lines. Your agent is the person you will turn to when your book goes out of print, when Walt Disney Studios makes a six-figure offer for the movie rights, when a pirated edition of your book turns up at a book fair. You have to trust him, and it helps if you like him, too.

Agenting is a business, and as you look for an agent, you should bear this in mind. Unable to read all the manuscripts that come across their desks, enterprising agents have invented the "reading fee." Sometimes this is money well spent, but be sure you know what you are paying for when an agent offers to review your work for a price.

For children's nonfiction manuscripts, the reading fee usually ranges from $100 to $300. If you want an opinion from a person who doesn't know you, this service can be useful. But bear in mind that most big literary agencies that offer this service have a special reading staff. The people on this staff are usually not the agents who sell manuscripts. They are teachers or writers or journalists making a little extra money on the side. They might know less about children's book writing than you do.

Some agents who offer a reading service will consider representing you if the reader's judgment of your manuscript is positive. If they are able to sell the manuscript—and it does happen—they will deduct the reading fee from the standard agent's percentage of your advance. This is certainly a fair arrangement, protecting your time and the agent's. Be sure, though, that it is spelled out in writing before you go ahead with such a deal.

The "personalized letters" from some of the larger agencies can swell your ego, but only until you discover you've been had. If you receive a letter implying you have potential and suggesting that the agent read your manuscript for a fee, write back:

Dear Mr. Agent:

Thank you for your letter about my manuscript, *The True Story of Paul Revere*. I would like to work with you in revising and marketing it, on the condition that you will deduct the reading fee from my advance as part of your agent's commission, once the manuscript is sold. If this arrangement is satisfactory to you, please let me know.

I think it's fair for an agent to charge a reading fee, for a thoughtful reading of a manuscript requires skill and attention. But there's no point in having your manuscript read by someone who may have no intention of selling it, unless you have decided beforehand that this is what you want. For this kind of reading, you are probably better off with a writing school, a workshop, or a course in children's literature.

On the Subject of Money . . .

It's important that you lay out your relationship with your agent from the beginning. Specify what you expect from him and be sure that compensation agreements are put in writing. Publishers pay agents, who then pay authors. Though traditionally the agent's cut has been 10 percent of all monies paid to the author, the costs of doing business in the increasingly specialized atmosphere of book publishing have raised agents' fees to as high as 25 percent of the author's income. The nature of the project and its timing are the factors in determining how much the agent has earned.

Even after you have made dollar arrangements with the agent, you will also want to make scheduling arrangements with him for your payments. Book contracts specify a date by which author's royalties are to be paid to his agent. The agent has to wait for the check from the publisher to clear, deduct his percentage, then prepare and mail a new check. This operation can take as long as a month or as little as three days, depending on the mails, the banks, and the agent's efficiency. So if you're counting on the publisher's royalties to pay the mortgage, having an agent may be a luxury you can't afford. While it is generally true that agents can get more money for their authors, it's usually quite a lot less than the percentage that they take from the author's income. Generally, an agent can squeeze an extra 3 to 5 percent from a publisher, but when it shows up on the author's bank statement, it's diminished again by 10 to 25 percent. From a monetary point of view, it really isn't worth it.

The Supportive Agent

An agent is a valuable ally for certain kinds of writers. George Sullivan, whose published books number close to two hundred titles, finds his agent an invaluable record-keeper. Anne Rockwell, whose books focus on the very young, finds her agent is expert at locating different editors who do the same kinds of books. Tomie de Paola, whose output in contrast is diverse, finds that his agent is terrific at placing his properties with the publisher who can promote them best. Dan Cohen, whose longtime agent handles a variety of best-selling authors and Hollywood screenwriters, finds that his agent's brusque no-nonsense treatment of editors is effective at the contract stage, with the agent playing the role of bad cop to Cohen's good cop.

But many forms of support that are traditionally ascribed to agents can in fact be supplied by other people. Franz Brandenberg came to New York to be a literary agent for his wife Aliki as well as other writers. Aliki had a special hold on his time, and as the years passed, Brandenberg sold his successful literary agency to manage Aliki's business affairs full time. The side benefit, for both members of this couple, is that he had time to encourage Aliki's work as well as manage her income, and he's become a successful published writer as well!

Many writers hope an agent will be able to guide and encourage their careers in constructive directions. Very few agents have the time or inclination to do this, but Uri Shulevitz found this kind of direction in Susan Carr Hirschman, one of his editors. Hirschman has directed him to become not only a Caldecott Medalist twice, but also to a second career advising and teaching other writers, through lecturing, teaching, and writing instructional textbooks.

Charles Spain Verral met his wife Jean more than fifty years ago at Street & Smith Publishers, where she was an editor and he was an aspiring writer. He finds that she is the one who can spot the salable idea, who has the training and instinct to suggest the small change that makes all the difference. Verral has a literary agent as well, but if the agent doesn't like his proposals, he doesn't revise them to suit the agent. He submits them directly to the publisher, and often places them himself.

Agents, then, conform to about the same general profile as editors do. Some agents are strong in sales, others are good at follow-up, still others are sympathetic supporters of the writer's craft, but to make a list of skills and duties would be impossible.

One thing that many writers with agents mention as a plus is the separation that an agent allows. An agent has an office Elsewhere, far from the writer's ivory tower. The agent does the dogwork, leaving the writer free to pursue more creative directions. But for a beginning writer to find an agent is difficult, far more difficult than finding a publisher or even a sympathetic editor who doesn't buy but does comment.

Is an Agent for You?

The literary agent is most valuable to the *established* writer who does not want to sully his relationship with his editor with arguments over royalty rates or foreign-rights splits. An agent can help a writer who is making a substantial income from his writing with tax advice, ammunition against writer's block, and new contacts. These are services that a promising *new* writer doesn't need yet. And the one service an agent cannot provide is selling an unsalable manuscript.

Selling a manuscript is only a tiny part—though an essential one—of an agent's job. The agent is primarily concerned with selling the manuscript on the terms most favorable to the author, and this is possible only when he has a proven sales and review record to work with. Only when a publisher has expressed interest in buying the manuscript does the agent's real work start.

Ironically, as a new writer you have a better chance of selling your book *without* an agent. Your contract for that first book may not end up in the Authors Guild Hall of Fame for its generous terms and large advance, but it gets your foot in the door! Agents are interested in setting precedents for future contracts, and it is just possible that an agent's professional standards for an acceptable contract won't—and can't—be met by a publisher on a first book by an unknown author. With the second book, you'll have learned from experience, and can represent yourself more forcefully.

If you do your homework, and ask for help from the Authors Guild, the Society of Children's Book Writers, and local writers' groups, you will be able to handle your own contract negotiations for the first few books. After you have proven to yourself and the world that you are seriously interested in this form, then it is time to think about finding an agent.

BE YOUR OWN AGENT

In the early stages of your career, you probably won't need an agent. But you can set up your own agency, with yourself as the client. Here's how:

Set aside a small desk, with a Rolodex, a file cabinet, a typewriter, and a telephone. Nothing is to be done at this desk except the work an agent would do. The Rolodex will be your list of professional contacts: other writers, publications of professional interest, schools and conferences you've appeared at, and publishers you'd like to work with. The typewriter is for writing business and query letters; it is *not* for knocking out manuscripts. The file cabinet (it can be a desktop file or a simple under-the-desk two-drawer number) is for storing royalty statements, rejection letters, and contracts. The telephone (and an answering machine can be a plus here) is a separate line for publishing calls only. Such an office can be set up for less than $300 if you are ingenious and don't insist on a vintage rolltop or an electric typewriter. Your "office" will serve three important purposes:

1. It will make it clear to your family and friends that you are serious, not just about writing but about publishing.
2. You will have creative freedom to write, and yet when you sit at this agent's desk you will be a salesman pitching your hot client—YOU.
3. The IRS will love it. They may even come to your home to look at it. (The IRS is somewhat uncertain about what constitutes a professional writer. In order to establish criteria for your individual case, they may make a house call. They called on writer Myron Levoy three years ago because he had deducted not only the space for his desk but

also the square footage that had been the family rec room before the children left home. He convinced the IRS to allow the deduction, showing them the worn path across the linoleum where he paced while he was thinking about how to revise what he'd written!)

Another task agents perform is to keep the author abreast of the competition. Most agents average about 100 clients, and they have a good overview of who buys what from whom. You can get the inside track by reading the trade journals, writers' newsletters, and the newspapers. And by being your own agent you'll be sure of one important thing: that you are your agent's favorite author!

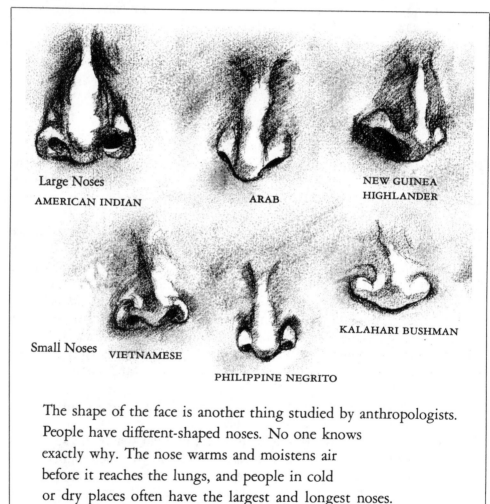

Large Noses
AMERICAN INDIAN

ARAB

NEW GUINEA HIGHLANDER

Small Noses VIETNAMESE

PHILIPPINE NEGRITO

KALAHARI BUSHMAN

The shape of the face is another thing studied by anthropologists. People have different-shaped noses. No one knows exactly why. The nose warms and moistens air before it reaches the lungs, and people in cold or dry places often have the largest and longest noses.

In Why People Are Different Colors *by Julian May (Holiday House, 1971), Symeon Shimin's drawings bring out the marvelous variety in mankind.*

CHAPTER 20

Building Your Career

Nonfiction writing for children is still a new enough discipline so that enterprising writers can work in various ways to make it their own. For Seymour Simon, a science teacher, it offered first an adjunct to his teaching, then a full-time career. For Miriam Schlein, it was an opportunity to use her editorial skills first while she raised her children, then, after many years of success, an opportunity to tie in book subjects with her interests and travels. For Franklyn Branley, director of the Hayden Planetarium, it has provided an absorbing and challenging task for his retirement. For Vicki Cobb, a former science teacher and television writer raising two boys in the suburbs, it's a chance to work when she can to write what she wants. Whichever of these people you identify with, you can see no cut-and-dried formula exists for a successful and satisfying career as a nonfiction writer for children.

A nonfiction writer for children can survive in several ways. The most logical for most is to work in an allied field—teaching, parenting, publishing, advertising, or public relations. Others find that working in a totally removed area—being a butcher, a baker, or candlestick maker—presents stimulation to write through contrast. Still others devote themselves to full-time writing for children, studying the newspaper, following television programming, and perhaps working in the community on a volunteer basis to promote literacy and books as a way of committing themselves fully to this rewarding profession.

WHAT KIND OF WRITER ARE YOU?

You need to look at your life and your aspirations to discover which route is for you. Writers do suffer burn-out, but the nonfiction writer has the advantage of going back to research when the writing gets tough, and turning to writing when other work is overwhelming. Even with this advantage, a steady diet of nonfiction writing can become tedious, and occasionally impossible. Some nonfiction writers set up five-year plans for themselves, with some years devoted to writing and time set aside for other pursuits. A nonfiction writer has some highly salable skills that can be utilized for temporary jobs, such as writing technical manuals, working as a newspaper editor, developing press releases for politicians and companies, or teaching a course on the basis of a book they have written. These people see their primary occupation as a nonfiction writer for children, but they recognize that jumping back into the world for a few months or a few years enriches their writing and gives them new perspectives.

The nonfiction writer working in an allied profession as a primary job is likely to be a little more sociable and a little less confident than the full-time nonfiction writer. A steady job in a situation where a writer enjoys the stimulation of other people day in and day out (like a classroom or a television studio) is a good solution for you if you like the security of a work-week routine and a steady paycheck. Many writers find that the more-than-full-time job of looking after the children and taking care of the house fits in nicely with writing—if one has the energy and the discipline to write while the kids are setting fire to the garage or listening to Van Halen at full volume.

The nonfiction writer who is the most private, and often the most productive, is the one whose job has nothing to do with his writing. Manual labor is especially attractive, since it gives the body a good workout while allowing the writer thinking time. Even full-time writers recognize this ideal combination, stopping to mop the floor, weed the garden, or rearrange the kitchen cabinets when writing leaves the brain weary and the body bored.

Underlying the decision of which of these three courses is best for you are the eternal questions of time and money. If you are short on either of these precious commodities, your writing will suffer. If you are writing to make a living, you may find yourself writing things you'd rather not write about. You may damage a perfectly cordial relationship with an editor or an agent by screaming about a delayed check, because you can't buy groceries for the kids. You may be so edgy about finishing a job to collect the fee that you do less than your best work, a fact you'd like to forget, but your editor never will. On the other hand, committing yourself to making a living as a writer may be just the ticket for the prolific writer who has disguised himself as a procrastinator. Necessity is the mother of invention, and you

Many of the offices on the second level were rented by businessmen who kept similar offices in other cities, including Rome. These men bought much of the produce from the fields around the city and shipped it to markets all over the empire.

In City *(Houghton Mifflin, 1974), writer-illustrator David Macaulay creates the imaginary city of Verbonia to show just how superbly the Romans built cities. This drawing depicts the market place.*

may find yourself able to write letters to editors you've never met, or harass your agent with a compelling urgency, just because you need to pay off your American Express bill.

For a writer, time is more important than money. Money can help you buy time, but you can't be a writer unless you have the time to be a writer. T. S. Eliot and Franz Kafka were brilliant at making time, even though they had many other commitments. Writing takes two kinds of time: thinking time, which is best found in places like bus stops and laundry rooms, and writing time, which should be quiet, private, and attached to a work surface, whether it's at a computer or on a commuter train with briefcase on lap, pencil in hand. Some people find time more manageable if they don't have a great deal of it for writing: they get it while they can. These creative creatures do better knowing that they will write for five hours every Thursday night, except when Christmas Eve falls on a Thursday.

Others do better if they have all the time in the world. They don't write well unless they feel like writing, and they never know when the muse is going to stop by. These people need more time, and, deprived of it, are paralyzed. They're willing to eat TV dinners, pay their grandson to mow the lawn, and forgo their mink coats to have enough time to think, to research, to write. There's no superior way to manage your writing time, but it is imperative that you be absolutely honest with yourself about how much time you need, and how much you're willing to give up in the way of hockey games, going shopping, or other activities in order to write.

Bouquets and Brickbats

Anyone who entertains the notion that a nonfiction writer's life is routine should disapprise himself of the idea as quickly as possible. The writer's life is fraught with perils, some inspiring, some hilarious, and some simply annoying. The surprises that lie in wait for you seem as fictitious as the books you write are factual.

Take fan mail. The fiction writer, having gone through the agonies of creation, sits back and enjoys the fan mail. "I just loved your book," the reader writes. "I especially liked the part where the computer talks to the answering machine and the answering machine can't talk back!" Not so the nonfiction writer-expert. Gathering the mail is a mixed blessing. "I liked your book, *The Kitty Cat Cookbook*, but I have a problem. My cat won't eat the Meow Salad that appears on page 53. Can you tell me some way to make him eat it? My mom says that if my cat doesn't stop eating her philodendron, I can't keep him."

And then there are the critics. "I thought the diagram on how to lay out a pattern for a bathrobe was very confusing. Why didn't you show that the cloth had to be folded in half? I tried to make it, and it came out all wrong. Is there anything I can do to fix it?" Although the diagrams were done by an artist you have never seen, and you told your editor that you wanted to check the diagrams before they were printed (a tight production schedule didn't allow it) you are stuck writing to the young seamstress, telling her how to salvage her bathrobe.

But it really isn't that bad. You will get letters asking you if you will please write another book about snakes; you will get letters asking you if you will write a book about pandas because your book about giraffes was so good. And you will be asked if you will give a lecture on any of the subjects that you've covered as well as lectures about being a writer. Strangers will call you to ask questions about a subject you wrote about ten years ago; your family will turn to you to settle arguments about the difference between clouds in the eastern sky, because, after all, you wrote a book about it.

When I was a young editor, I asked Chaucy Bennetts, a former actress who was working as a children's editor, how she felt about sitting at a desk as compared to being on the stage. "Oh I love it," she beamed. "I'm always learning something new! Look at this—a book on skateboarding, a book on dinosaurs, a book about eels . . . things I didn't even know there was anything to know about." But after the stage, wasn't it terribly dull? I ventured.

"It's the same thing, dear. You have the stage in the book itself, the performance in the way the author presents the facts, and the illustrations are the scenery. And of course you have the best audience in the world—kids." This little lunchtime interchange fascinated me, who saved my pitiful editorial salary to see Broadway shows. I realized *I* was in show biz.

Keeping Up Your Image

The roar of the crowd lures writers for young people as certainly as it does actors. One experiences the enthusiasm of children, and just as often, adults looking for a simple introduction to a subject they don't know a thing about. In fan mail, in the applause at the end of a speech, in the reviews of books, and in the lines in the bookstore when you're autographing a new title, you are a star, and you have to weigh each project as carefully as an actor considers a role. Is the subject consistent with your image?

This true story of the evolution of a nonfiction writer shows the surprising twists this decision can take:

Sue Burchard, the librarian at the Trinity Lower School in New York, writes sports biographies for children in the easy-to-read format. The children she works with as a librarian think it's neat that she has written books they want to read, and the royalties for her books pay for what she jokingly calls her "librarian habit." As S. L. Burchard, she has written fifteen illustrated biographies for children aged 6 to 9. Burchard follows the sports scene closely, and writes for the same age group, in the same format,

Signs...

In Signs *(Thomas Y. Crowell, 1983), Ron and Nancy Goor present more than fifty familiar signs in settings that help convey their meanings.*

in book after book. When she first started writing sports biographies twenty years ago she collaborated with her husband, Marshall Burchard. They were divorced, and the question of who would continue the sports series came up. It was decided that Marshall would continue to write for the 8 to 12 age group that the Burchards had established themselves in. When Barbara Lucas, their editor, moved from Putnam to Harcourt, Brace, she suggested that Sue come along with her, and write for slightly younger children. Since Sue's job had been to edit the texts down to the middle-age level, while Marshall provided the angle and the research, she welcomed the suggestion and has continued to publish many successful biographies. Burchard feels that her books compete with both magazines and fiction about sports. "As the sports stars become more and more public figures, the story of their lives becomes as full and interesting as any novel. And with photographs of their private lives becoming easier to obtain, there is an immediacy that the slick celebrity magazines once had a monopoly on." Burchard checks to see that protective families and aggressive lawyers are willing to cooperate before she starts writing a book. She enjoys the challenge of writing simply, and delights her family, students, and friends with her total familiarity with what's happening on the football field and tennis court.

Another writer who ended up in an unexpected spot is Charles Spain Verral. As an editor himself, he works for Reader's Digest Books, writes a sports column for the newspaper *youngperson*, and—at the age of eighty—feels deprived if he doesn't get in a couple of games of tennis every week. Verral's books on the early development of aviation led him to write related books, including a biography of Robert Goddard and one of the first books for children on jets. He admits that "writing short" is the hardest kind of writing, especially when he is called upon to explain complicated concepts such as aerodynamics or atomic theory. His ability to visualize illustrations to clarify his fact-packed text, stems from early training as an artist and professional experience as an art director. Verral is a man of many interests, and when he finds himself getting interested in a subject, whether science or sports, he sits down at his typewriter and tries to capture that kick on the page. Sometimes, this means working until the wee hours of the morning.

A resident of New York's Greenwich Village, Verral infuriated the neighbors with his middle-of-the-night bouts with a new project. It wasn't that the pleasant click, click, click of the typewriter annoyed anyone, it was that the neighbor's dog began to bark when he saw Verral staying up past his bedtime. Verral received an anonymous note one day, complaining that he was keeping the whole block awake. Since the enthusiastic writer knew he wouldn't be able to change his work habits, and didn't know who had sent the note, he used a writer's imagination to remedy the situation: he typed a note, which he then copied forty times, and put it in the mailbox of everyone within hearing distance. The note said: "I know who you are." The complaints stopped. And Verral still works as hard as the deadlines demand, even if it means keeping unorthodox hours.

SHOULD YOU USE A PSEUDONYM?

An author's name becomes as valuable as any brand name, as readers search out "another book by . . ." Although the biggest single selling points for nonfiction are the scope of the subject and the slant of the author, the discerning reader learns fast enough that a book by Lucy Kavaler or Barbara Seuling is bound to be interesting. This leads the author to wonder if she should use a pseudonym. It's often a good idea, but not always.

I can remember the days—and it was only fifteen years ago!—when leading trade publishers would not publish serious nonfiction under a woman's name. A lot of the initials you've encountered in your reading life stand for Catherine, not Charles; Helen, not Howard. While this bias is no longer officially enforced—too many women have produced too many good books under their real names to allow this to be so—there are some die-hards out there who feel that women can't really write a book on Pele or soldering circuits or wrestling bears. And just to make things really complicated, there are other sexist censors who think that men shouldn't be writing about Chris Evert Lloyd or designing dresses or babysitting. On principle, a writer should be allowed to write about whatever interests him; but from a marketing point of view, a writer might want to enhance the chances of being published and being published well, by slipping into a pseudonym here and there.

The most liberated of children's book editors, Barbara Lucas recognized that sexism is less apparent but just as rampant after the women's movement as it had been before the movement got off the ground. In order to maximize the chances of Sue Burchard's series of sports biographies winning acceptance with boys as well as girls, she suggested that Sue use her initials. Burchard's success probably rests on her up-to-date knowledge of what interests children and her painstaking research, but even the little boys who know her from the library where she works are more comfortable being seen on the bus with a book by S. H. Burchard because (just in case you haven't talked to any eight-year-old boys lately) girls are just not with it as far as sports go.

This prejudice extends beyond all boundaries of sex, race, color, geography, religion, and nationality. For instance, many people are surprised to discover that John Goodall or Mitsumasa Anno don't live in Boston or Los Angeles—they are citizens of foreign countries. If you are lucky enough to be named William Least Heat Moon, a native's view of America is going to sell better than if you are named John Elliott Freeman, even though you may have the same racial heritage. Authors are, for the moment at least, celebrities, and just as "Marilyn Monroe" was a catchier name than "Norma

Jean Baker" for a movie star in the fifties, so it might be that the illusion you want to create for your book is enhanced by a flashier name than the one you were born with.

This is not a license to misrepresent yourself. You can hedge by using initials, or an anagram of your name, or a combination of your husband's and your sister-in-law's names, but you can't call yourself "Red Smith, Jr." or "Edward Gibbon III" just to sell a manuscript on baseball or medieval history. If you want to enhance your chances of selling a manuscript and your name is inappropriate to the subject matter, be sure to check *Books in Print* for the last ten years to make sure you aren't leaning on another author's established reputation.

There's another reason to use a pseudonym, and that's not because your name is inappropriate, but because it's unwieldy. If your name is Cynthia Preel-Borek Corso, it may be difficult for people to recall the spelling or the sequence. Since you don't want to hurt your husband's feelings, or your father's or your mother's, you can shorten it to C. P. B. Corso, which is catchy and includes everything folks have to know to recognize you.

And then there are those of us whose names are so common that they don't have any distinction. I dragged out my hated middle initials to distinguish me from the noted children's book editor, Ellen Roberts. Too many times I had been at receptions or meetings where I'd be announced by name, and as people met me their faces would fall: I was not the lovely lady they knew from Doubleday—in fact, I hadn't even been born at the time of her tenure. If you are among those of us named Barbara Williams, David Jones, Kathleen McCarthy, or Howard Smith, some adjustment is called for, perhaps something as drastic as a pseudonym.

The most felicitous reason for using a pseudonym is to avoid glutting the market with books with your name on them. Reviewers raise a skeptical eyebrow when they see five books published by the same author in six months, but the truth of the matter is that you may have spent twelve years working on those five books, and by a fluke, sold them at the same time. It does happen. Corrine Gerson, a prolific writer of books for children and articles, spent the ten years her children were young writing. She sent out manuscript after manuscript to publisher after publisher for a decade with no response—until the happy year of 1982 when she sold four of them to four different publishers, just in time to pay her daughter's law school tuition!

The last use of pseudonyms is by the professional writer who feels she might have gotten stale, and wants to see if her work will be plucked from the slush pile on its own merits, or whether it's really because she named her first son for her agent who is having an affair with the publisher's nephew. The reviewer who called her last offering "eloquent" might find the new book "ambitious, but flawed" because he thinks he's dealing with a newcomer. As subversive as this may seem to those starting out, it's really helpful for the writer who is trying to develop a new style, or to perfect an old one, to see how her work does on its own.

BECOMING A "CATCHER-IN-THE-RYE"

It's hard to believe that there really are advantages to being in a field where you won't necessarily see your name on the best-seller list—nonfiction for children often sells very well, but not in the short period that makes for best-seller status—or appear on every single national morning news program.

But that's okay. You may not be a hit at cocktail parties, or the guest on a prime time television show, but you will be able to form the opinions of children. Any person who can keep in touch with his own childhood to the extent that he can talk to children knows that the experience is enriching to him as well as his reader.

In writing this book, I came to question many things that I had taken for granted as a writer, editor, and teacher. Why, for instance, should anyone write nonfiction for children when encyclopedias present so much information so well? There are hundreds of editions of encyclopedias which describe history, science, biography, sports, and crafts in short, readable, well-researched articles. My own coming of age happened in the third grade when I graduated from the *World Book* to the eleventh edition of the *Britannica.*

Yet I remember books, not encyclopedia articles. Holling C. Holling, Genevieve Foster, Eva Knox Evans, Mae and Ira Freeman: these writers were teachers, giving me a sense of world that no encyclopedia article could communicate. The shapes, the colors, the words, the individuality of each of these books stays with me long after I have forgotten what the highest mountain in Switzerland is, or what year John Adams died. I remember shutting a book on a picture of a Portuguese man-o-war: surely the most deadly creature I could ever imagine. I remember the opening line of *All About Atoms*, published by Random House in 1954: "If Abraham Lincoln were alive today, he would be very surprised. He would be astounded by cars, radios, telephones, and televisions. He would be surprised to see electric lights and central heating." This single thought gave me, an insular nine-year-old, a new perspective on history, a valuable insight into the era in which I lived. It would have taken me years to come to this conclusion on my own, but there it was, a small gift from a man I did not know, mine to savor in the privacy of two hard covers.

To me, this exemplifies the best in juvenile nonfiction: the adult sharing his perspective with the child reader in direct, unpatronizing prose. This author knew his readers were familiar with Abraham Lincoln, and he utilized the reader's previous knowledge to take her one step further. "I wish more writers for children knew children," says S. H. Burchard, the author of twenty-five sports books, and a school librarian. Her complaint is justified: thousands of books cover subjects that editors and writers deem of interest to children, but rare is the author who *talks* to children through nonfiction writing.

Author Millicent Selsam, with over a hundred books to her credit, has been a teacher and a mother. Her advanced degrees notwithstanding, she knows how to write for children. "When a child asks an adult a question," she maintains, "the adult can make two fatal errors: to say too much, or to say too little." On the one hand, you don't want to turn a child off by burying his enthusiasm under a mountain of information. On the other hand, you want to say something, a little bit, in the hope that he will ask other questions. Leading the child through the process of inquiry is the nonfiction writer's challenge and responsibility.

Economist Gary Becker calls children "durable goods"; historian Steven Mintz calls family life "a prison of expectations"; novelist P. D. James calls childhood "the only sentence we all have to serve." Behind the pessimistic diction you will see an underlying optimism: children, like all people, are durable, capable of experiencing the good and bad, and surviving. We adults are survivors of the childhood experience, an experience we share with everyone else. Writers for children are people who care enough about kids to want to share the real world with them. They do a particular kind of sharing, through writing and reading.

As a writer of children's nonfiction, you have the flexibility to try new forms of writing—for instance, to spin off a novel from your research into quarks, or simply to modify your established style, writing a picture book after you've concentrated on middle-graders.

Flexibility and choice are the two advantages writers mention most often as their reason for coming to and staying in this exciting but little-known field. "I'm a looker and a learner and a catcher-in-the-rye," says Jan Adkins, author of twelve nonfiction books for children. Is there a better way to live?

Appendix of Awards

THE CALDECOTT MEDAL, awarded by the Association for Library Service to Children, is given for the "most distinguished American picture book for children." It was the first award to recognize excellence in illustration. Typical nonfiction winners include Ingri and Parin D'Aulaire's *Abraham Lincoln* (Doubleday, 1940) and Dorothy Lathrop's *Animals of the Bible* (Stokes).

THE BOSTON GLOBE-HORN BOOK AWARDS, given by the Boston Globe Newspaper Company and The Horn Book, Inc. established an award in 1976 for the best nonfiction for children. Typical winners are Peter Dickinson's *Chance, Luck and Destiny* (Little, Brown/Atlantic Monthly Press) and Alfred Tamarin and Shirley Glubok's *Voyaging to Cathay: Americans in the China Trade* (Viking).

AIGA BEST BOOKS are given annually by the American Institute of Graphic Arts for design and quality manufacturing. Typical nonfiction winners are *Handtalk* by Remy Charlip (Parents) and *Anno's Alphabet* by Mitsumasa Anno. (Harper and Row)

THE NEW YORK TIMES TEN BEST ILLUSTRATED BOOKS OF THE YEAR are chosen annually by *The New York Times* during Children's Book Week in November. A board of experts, chosen by the Children's Book Review Editor selects titles for excellence and appropriateness of illustration. Nonfiction winners are few and far between, but author/artist Guy Billout has been honored three times for his *Stone and Steel, Spider and Squid,* and *By Camel or by Car* (Prentice-Hall).

WESTERN WRITERS OF AMERICA AWARDS included a category of juvenile nonfiction from 1967 to 1975. The awards were established in 1953 by the Western Writers of America, Inc. to encourage better writing on Western subjects. Typical winners include Marian T. Place's *Retreat to Bear Paw* (Four Winds) and Jules Loh's *Lords of the Earth* (Crowell/Collier).

THE JOHN NEWBERY MEDAL, awarded annually by the Association of Library Service to Children, is given for the most distinguished piece of literature published for children in the preceding year. Rare is the nonfiction winner of this prize, but James Daugherty's *Daniel Boone,* Elizabeth Yates's *Amos Fortune, Free Man* (Aladdin) and David Macaulay's *Cathedral* (Houghton-Mifflin) have been selected as winners or runners-up.

THE CHILDREN'S READING ROUND TABLE in Chicago offers an annual award for an outstanding contribution to children's literature. Winners have included nonfiction advocate and reviewer Zena Sutherland of the University of Chicago, Dorothy Hass, editor of many outstanding nonfiction books for children, and S. Carl Hirsch, author of *Stilts* (Viking).

THE DOROTHY CANFIELD FISHER AWARD is given annually by the Vermont Department of Libraries and the Vermont Congress of Parents and Teachers. The titles are selected by the state's children. Picture books are not eligible. Though fiction is most often the winner, Mildred Mastin Pace's *Old Bones, the Wonder Horse* (McGraw) and Walt Morey's *Kavik the Wolf Dog* (Dutton) are nonfiction winners.

THE GARDEN STATE CHILDREN'S BOOK AWARDS were established in 1977 by the New Jersey Library Association. Nonfiction winners include Jill Krementz's *A Very Young Dancer* (Knopf) and Millicent Selsam's *How Kittens Grow* (Scholastic). The nonfiction award is for grades two to five.

THE GOLDEN KITE AWARD is given by the Society of Children's Book Writers to stimulate the creation of good books for children. There is a separate nonfiction category, in which such books as *How I Became a Writer* by Phyllis Reynolds Naylor (Atheneum) and Robert McClung's *Peeper, The First Voice of Spring* (Morrow) are typical winners.

THE NEW YORK ACADEMY OF SCIENCES encourages the publishing of high-quality science books by offering two awards—one for older children and one for younger children—each year. Aliki's *Corn is Maize* (Crowell) is a typical winner in the younger age group; Herman Schneider's *Laser Light* (McGraw) is a typical winner in the older category.

THE CATHOLIC LIBRARY ASSOCIATION offers the Regina Medal to a writer or illustrator whose life's work has been in the chidren's field. May McNeer and Lynd Ward, authors of *John Wesley* (Abingdon) and Tomie de-Paola, author of *The Quicksand Book* and *The Popcorn Book*, (Holiday) are in the range of winners.

THE CHARLES AND BERTIE SCHWARTZ AWARD is given by the Jewish Book Council for a children's book published on a Jewish theme during the previous year. Nonfiction winners include Regina Tor's *Discovering Israel* (Random House) and Charlie May Simon's *Martin Buber: Wisdom in Our Time* (Dutton).

THE SOUTHERN CALIFORNIA COUNCIL ON LITERATURE FOR CHILDREN AND YOUNG PEOPLE AWARDS gives a prize to a Southern California resident whose contribution to children's literature is noteworthy. Jean Rouverol was awarded a prize for her outstanding contribution to nonfiction for her book, *Juarez: A Son of the People* (Macmillan) and Terry Dunnahoo was awarded a prize for *Before the Supreme Court: The Story of Belva Ann Lockwood* (Houghton).

THE CHILDREN'S BOOK GUILD of Washington, D.C. has awarded prizes for outstanding nonfiction writers for the body of their work. Recipients have included Jean Fritz, Tana Hoban, and Millicent Selsam. The award is given during Children's Book Week.

Annotated Bibliography

WRITERS WORTH READING

As anyone who has witnessed the loyalty of children to Richard Scarry, Beverly Cleary, or Judy Blume can attest, the name of the author is as important as the name of the book. Surprisingly, perhaps, this applies to nonfiction even more than it does to novels or picture books. Here follows an extremely selective list of nonfiction writers who have contributed to children's literature over many decades, featuring those books that are still available.

Preschool and Kindergarten: Ages 2 to 5

Donald Crews. *Freight Train.* 1978. The specialized cars of a train are shown in various landscapes at various hours.

Harbor. 1982. The tugs, tankers, and ferryboats of a big city harbor are brought to life in lively crowded pictures.

School Bus. 1984. Again emphasizing the time sequence, this time in the activity of a bus, Crews portrays its journey across town and back again.

Carousel. 1982. Whirling motion and the variety of animals on a merry-go-round are captured here with a minimum of text.

Bicycle Race. 1985. The world from twelve two-wheelers, with the suspense of competition and the whir of landscape, shown in a bicycle competition.

Parade. 1983. A parade down main street is described before, during, and after.

Ten Black Dots. 1968. This rhyming counting book, with its crisp depictions of everyday objects, is a good example of simplicity assuring a long life for a picture book.

Tana Hoban. *Push, Pull, Empty, Full.* Macmillan, 1976. Uncluttered photographs show opposite pairs on facing pages of this spare picture book.

A, B, See! Greenwillow, 1982. Everyday objects children can name are grouped according to the letter of the alphabet which begins their names.

Big Ones, Little Ones. Greenwillow, 1976. Baby animals are shown side by side with mature animals in this unusual collection of black-and-white photographs.

Dig, Drill, Empty, Fill. Greenwillow, 1975. Heavy machinery in big city settings shows, through illustration with a simple verb for a caption, the basic functions of these mechanical monsters.

I Read Signs. Greenwillow, 1983.

I Read Symbols. Greenwillow, 1983. Using the same format, photographer Hoban shows signs and symbols in settings familiar to children.

Is It Red? Is It Yellow? Is It Blue? Greenwillow, 1978. This wordless colorful picture book, meant to be read by a child under adult supervision, offers beguiling opportunities to identify basic colors.

I Walk and Read. Greenwillow, 1983. Color photographs show children on the street exercising their reading skills deciphering signs which the reader of the book can read too.

More Than One. Greenwillow, 1981. A new turn for Hoban, this book explores the many nouns we use for groups of things, emphasizing word choice with clear photos as a springboard.

Is It Larger, Is It Smaller? Greenwillow, 1985. The standard size of the book page and the isolation of the double-page spread are used by the author to show relative size.

Is It Rough? Is It Smooth? Is It Shiny? Greenwillow, 1985. Color photographs show the nuances of texture—from pennies to tree trunks—and give the young "reader" of the wordless text a chance to come up with his own adjectives.

Grades 1 to 3: Ages 6 to 9—The Easy Reader

Aliki. *Corn Is Maize: The Gift of the Indians.* Crowell, 1976. The discovery of corn is illuminated by the uses of corn today.

My Visit to the Dinosaurs. 1969.

Digging Up Dinosaurs. 1981. More than a decade separates the creation of these two complementary descriptions of how scientists have reconstructed facts about dinosaurs, and how museums present these facts to the public.

Fossils Tell of Long Ago. 1972. This double history—first the natural history of the fossil, then the scientific history of fossil analysis—shows the strengths of Aliki's understanding of the techniques of science.

My Hands.

My Five Senses. Crowell, 1962.

Aliki's keen analysis of the hands (on the one hand!) and the senses on the other, bring scientific rigor within the grasp of the beginning reader in a combination of text, charts, and illustrations.

Wild and Woolly Mammoths. Crowell, 1977. Aliki's talent for showing what we know about the ancient mammoths, and how we came to know it, is evident in this examination of prehistoric beasts.

Millicent Selsam. *Egg to Chick.* Harper and Row, 1970. Twenty-one days—from laying to hatching—is just the right time span for this 64-page combination of text and pictures covering the development of an embryo.

The Amazing Dandelion. William Morrow, 1977. A plant many children know firsthand is the model for basic botanical concepts, reinforced here with bold close-up photographs.

Hidden Animals. Harper and Row, 1969. A hide-and-go-seek thriller for the young naturalist, explaining how to locate animals in their natural camouflage.

Catnip. William Morrow, 1976. As a plant, a medicine, a drug, catnip exercises its spell on young botanists in this honed-down introduction to plant development.

David Macaulay. *Castle.* Houghton Mifflin, 1977. Central to medieval life and intriguing for its historical romance, the castle is constructed and used in this thoroughly illustrated book.

Cathedral: The Story of Its Construction. Houghton Mifflin, 1973. The long project of building a cathedral, from cutting down thousands of trees to erecting the spire, is the subject of this narrative sketchbook.

City: A Story of Roman Planning and Construction. Houghton Mifflin, 1974. Ancient history, known for evoking great yawns, is captured here in the organization of Roman cities.

Mill. Houghton Mifflin, 1983. Here Macaulay addresses the rise of modern industry in a quasi-fictional evocation of an English milltown 150 years ago.

Pyramid. Houghton Mifflin, 1975. The mystery of the pyramids is unveiled in this carefully detailed study of a pyramid's construction.

Underground. Houghton Mifflin, 1976. Underneath an intersection, down a present-day rabbit hole, Macaulay shows us the underpinnings of a modern city.

Grades 4 to 6: Ages 8 to 12

Melvin Berger (with **Gilda Berger**). *The Whole World of Hands*. Houghton Mifflin, 1982. The uses, the development, and the psychology of hands, including participatory experiments.

Melvin Berger. Scientists at Work Series. Crowell.
Animal Hospital, 1973.
Consumer Protection Labs, 1975.
Disease Detectives.
Exploring the Mind and Brain, 1983.
Medical Center Lab, 1976.
Oceanography Lab, 1973.
Police Lab, 1976.
Sports Medicine, 1982.

A decade-long labor of love, this series for teenagers includes you-are-there photographs for career-minded kids, as well as scientific methods employed by public health professionals.

The New Earth Book: Our Changing Planet. Crowell, 1980. Experiments in earth science encourage interest in the ways in which the earth was formed and the effect of pollution on its further development.

The Funny Side of Science (with J. B. Handelsman). Crowell, 1973. Laughing all the way to the laboratory at anecdotes, jokes, and cartoons, the young reader finds a painless entree into the world of science in this concept book.

Bernard Wolf. *Anna's Silent World*. Lippincott, 1977 (also available in a Spanish language edition). The everyday life of a congenitally deaf child is captured in the year she learns to sign and communicate with those around her.

Connie's New Eyes. Lippincott, 1976. A blind young woman beginning her teaching career learns to live and work with a seeing-eye dog in a photo documentary that is immediate and informative.

Don't Feel Sorry for Paul. Lippincott, 1974 (also available in a Spanish language edition). A boy born with malformed limbs learns to cope with a horse, the classroom, a birthday party, and the clinic where his special problems are addressed in this two-week diary illustrated with photographs.

In This Proud Land: The Story of a Mexican-American Family. Lippincott, 1978. A Texas family of itinerant laborers learns a new way of living without letting go entirely of the old traditions; candid photographs and a sympathetic text.

Aronsky, Jim. *Deer at the Brook*. Lothrop, 1986. A naturalist who writes and draws captures the glimpses of two fawns at the watering hole, in paintings with captions that will inspire young teens to keep their own nature diaries.

Drawing from Nature. Lothrop, 1982.

Drawing Life in Motion. Lothrop, 1984. Aronsky's original idea is that young teenagers can learn from a book not only how an artist renders, but also how an artist *sees*.

Flies in the Water, Fish in the Air. A Personal Introduction to Fly Fishing. Lothrop, 1986. Izaak Walton for contemporary teenagers, this guide not only instructs, but like Aronsky's art guides, inspires.

Secrets of a Wildlife Watcher. Lothrop, 1983. One hundred carefully segmented wildlife experiences—from sleeping to flying—are delineated here, both as examples of nature reporting and as selections from the author-artist's work.

Young Adult/Teenage; Grades 7-12, Ages 12 to 16

Robert H. Curtis, M.D. *Triumph Over Pain.* McKay, 1971. The dramatic history of anesthesiology, including scientific and historical information in a smoothly readable text.

Questions and Answers about Alcoholism. Prentice-Hall, 1977. The questions teenagers really ask about the short- and long-term effects of alcohol on their bodies, their minds, and their lives.

On ESP. Prentice-Hall, 1975. An introduction to the new science of parapsychology, with interviews to create a sense of immediacy about this exciting, and occasionally irresponsible, frontier of research.

Medical Talk for Beginners. Messner, 1973. A reference book and a "building block" introduction to the language of doctors, geared to the interests and limits of teenagers.

Mind and Mood: Understanding and Controlling Your Emotions. Scribner's, 1986. The complexities of the body, mind, and behavior of teenagers is explored and reinforced with clinical examples.

Sara Gilbert. *By Yourself.* Lothrop, 1983. For the latchkey child or the independent teenager, a guide to the problems and pleasures of being alone: safety, entertainment, eating, and emergencies.

How to Take Tests. William Morrow, 1983. Practical and psychological tips for doing your best in a tense situation.

How to Live with a Single Parent. Lothrop, 1982. A resource guide as well as a sympathetic read, this book includes reasons for taking action and ways to find help in doing so.

Trouble at Home. Lothrop, 1981. Death, illness, troublesome brothers and sisters, and divorce are brought into perspective for the teenager, with informed advice about when to take matters into your own hands, and when outside help is needed.

What Happens in Therapy. Lothrop, 1983. The author describes five kinds of adolescent therapy, when it's appropriate, what it's like and where to find it, all in a hundred crisply written pages.

BOOKS ABOUT CHILDREN AND BOOKS

Bader, Barbara. *The Children's Picture Book: From Noah's Ark to the Beast Within.* Macmillan, 1976.
This history of American children's picture book publishing includes two informative chapters on the development of the illustrated science book after World War II.

Carr, Jo. *Beyond Fact.* American Library Association, 1980.
A ground-breaking collection of articles by an array of children's book professionals delineating what is wrong with contemporary nonfiction for children, and what is right with it.

Commire, Anne. (editor) *Something about the Author.* Gale Research, 1966-present.
Annotated autobiographical sketches by authors and artists themselves, this multi-volume collection includes insights, bibliographies, addresses, and agents.

Duff, Annis. *Bequest of Wings: A Family's Pleasure with Books,* Viking, 1949.
The former editor of Viking Junior Books shares her family reading experiences from the

editor's viewpoint. Although dated, it gives the writer for children a full picture of the way books are shared in the American family.

Egoff, Sheila. *Only Connect: Readings in Children's Literature.* Oxford, 1973.
An overview of children's publishing in the English language, this collection of expert essays helps ground the writer in the traditions and conventions of children's books.

Gillespie, John. *Best Books for Children.* Bowker (annual).
A listing of recommended books, arranged by subject matter, used extensively by teachers and librarians in building their collections. Identifies issues and attitudes for the aspiring writer.

Hearne, Betsy, and Marilyn Kaye. *Celebrating Children's Books: Essays in Children's Literature in Honor of Zena Sutherland.*
Essays exploring why writers for children write what they write, librarians choose what they choose, and children read what they read.

Hearne, Betsy. *Choosing Books for Children.* Dell, 1982.
An expert but opinionated survey of the world of children's books as seen by Hearne, a writer, librarian, and mother. Includes an excellent short chapter on nonfiction.

Larrick, Nancy. *A Teacher's Guide to Children's Reading.* Merrill, 1960.
An excellent introduction to the ways teachers use books in the classroom to encourage reading, to encourage learning.

A Parent's Guide to Children's Reading (Fourth edition). Bantam, 1975.
Illustrated with pictures and excerpts from books for children, this book addresses the way leisure reading can enhance a child's intellectual and social development.

Robinson, Evelyn Rose. *Readings about Children's Literature.* McKay, 1966.
A library science professor addresses problems of selection of children's books in articles by educators, librarians, and authors. The coverage of nonfiction reading is idiosyncratic and consistently interesting.

Sutherland, Zena. *The Best in Children's Books.* University of Chicago, 1970, 1975, 1980.
Selected reviews from the Center for Children's Books at the University of Chicago, this collection reveals Sutherland's long commitment to thorough and fair evaluations, especially of nonfiction material.

Index

Other Books of Interest

General Writing Books

Beginning Writer's Answer Book, edited by Polking and Bloss $14.95
Getting the Words Right: How to Revise, Edit and Rewrite, by Theodore A. Rees Cheney $13.95
How to Become a Bestselling Author, by Stan Corwin $14.95
How to Get Started in Writing, by Peggy Teeters (paper) $8.95
How to Write a Book Proposal, by Michael Larsen $9.95
How to Write While You Sleep, by Elizabeth Ross $12.95
If I Can Write, You Can Write, by Charlie Shedd $12.95
International Writers' & Artists' Yearbook (paper) $12.95
Law & the Writer, edited by Polking & Meranus (paper) $10.95
Knowing Where to Look: The Ultimate Guide to Research, by Lois Horowitz $16.95
Make Every Word Count, by Gary Provost (paper) $7.95
Pinckert's Practical Grammar, by Robert C. Pinckert $12.95
Teach Yourself to Write, by Evelyn Stenbock (paper) $9.95
The 29 Most Common Writing Mistakes & How to Avoid Them, by Judy Delton $9.95
Writer's Block & How to Use It, by Victoria Nelson $12.95
Writer's Guide to Research, by Lois Horowitz $9.95
Writer's Market, edited by Becky Williams $21.95
Writer's Resource Guide, edited by Bernadine Clark $16.95
Writing for the Joy of It, by Leonard Knott $11.95
Writing From the Inside Out, by Charlotte Edwards (paper) $9.95

Magazine/News Writing

Basic Magazine Writing, by Barbara Kevles $16.95
How to Sell Every Magazine Article You Write, by Lisa Collier Cool $14.95
How to Write & Sell the 8 Easiest Article Types, by Helene Schellenberg Barnhart $14.95
Writing Nonfiction that Sells, by Samm Sinclair Baker $14.95

Fiction Writing

Creating Short Fiction, by Damon Knight (paper) $8.95
Fiction Writer's Help Book, by Maxine Rock $12.95
Fiction Writer's Market, edited by Jean Fredette $18.95
Handbook of Short Story Writing, by Dickson and Smythe (paper) $8.95
How to Write & Sell Your First Novel, by Oscar Collier with Frances Spatz Leighton $14.95
How to Write Short Stories that Sell, by Louise Boggess (paper) $7.95
One Way to Write Your Novel, by Dick Perry (paper) $6.95
Storycrafting, by Paul Darcy Boles $14.95
Writing Romance Fiction—For Love And Money, by Helene Schellenberg Barnhart $14.95
Writing the Novel: From Plot to Print, by Lawrence Block (paper) $8.95

Special Interest Writing Books

Complete Book of Scriptwriting, by J. Michael Straczynski $14.95
The Complete Guide to Writing Software User Manuals, by Brad M. McGehee (paper) $14.95
The Craft of Comedy Writing, by Sol Saks $14.95
The Craft of Lyric Writing, by Sheila Davis $18.95
Guide to Greeting Card Writing, edited by Larry Sandman (paper) $8.95
How to Make Money Writing About Fitness & Health, by Celia & Thomas Scully $16.95
How to Make Money Writing Fillers, by Connie Emerson (paper) $8.95
How to Write a Cookbook and Get It Published, by Sara Pitzer $15.95
How to Write a Play, by Raymond Hull $13.95
How to Write and Sell Your Personal Experiences, by Lois Duncan (paper) $9.95
How to Write and Sell (Your Sense of) Humor, by Gene Perret (paper) $9.95
How to Write "How-To" Books and Articles, by Raymond Hull (paper) $8.95
How to Write the Story of Your Life, by Frank P. Thomas $12.95
How You Can Make $50,000 a Year as a Nature Photojournalist, by Bill Thomas (paper) $17.95
Mystery Writer's Handbook, by The Mystery Writers of America (paper) $8.95
On Being a Poet, by Judson Jerome $14.95
The Poet's Handbook, by Judson Jerome (paper) $8.95
Poet's Market, by Judson Jerome $16.95
Sell Copy, by Webster Kuswa $11.95

Successful Outdoor Writing, by Jack Samson $11.95
Travel Writer's Handbook, by Louise Zobel (paper) $9.95
TV Scriptwriter's Handbook, by Alfred Brenner (paper) $9.95
Writing After 50, by Leonard L. Knott $12.95
Writing and Selling Science Fiction, by Science Fiction Writers of America (paper) $7.95
Writing for Children & Teenagers, by Lee Wyndham (paper) $9.95
Writing for the Soaps, by Jean Rouverol $14.95
Writing the Modern Mystery, by Barbara Norville $15.95
Writing to Inspire, by Gentz, Roddy, et al $14.95

The Writing Business
Complete Guide to Self-Publishing, by Tom & Marilyn Ross $19.95
Complete Handbook for Freelance Writers, by Kay Cassill $14.95
Editing for Print, by Geoffrey Rogers $14.95
Freelance Jobs for Writers, edited by Kirk Polking (paper) $8.95
How to Bulletproof Your Manuscript, by Bruce Henderson $9.95
How to Get Your Book Published, by Herbert W. Bell $15.95
How to Understand and Negotiate a Book Contract or Magazine Agreement, by Richard Balkin $11.95
How You Can Make $20,000 a Year Writing, by Nancy Hanson (paper) $6.95
Literary Agents: How to Get & Work with the Right One for You, by Michael Larsen $9.95
Professional Etiquette for Writers, by William Brohaugh $9.95

To order directly from the publisher, include $2.00 postage and handling for 1 book and 50¢ for each additional book. Allow 30 days for delivery.

Writer's Digest Books, Department B
9933 Alliance Road, Cincinnati OH 45242
Prices subject to change without notice.